Peter Carey

MANCHESTER
UNIVERSITY PRESS

Contemporary World Writers

SERIES EDITOR JOHN THIEME

Peter Carey

BRUCE WOODCOCK

Second edition

Manchester University Press

Manchester and New York

distributed exclusively in the USA by Palgrave

The right of Bruce Woodcock to be identified as the author of this work has been asserted by him in accordance with the Copyright, Designs and Patents Act 1988.

First edition published 1996 by Manchester University Press

This edition published 2003 by
Manchester University Press
Oxford Road, Manchester M13 9NR, UK
and Room 400, 175 Fifth Avenue, New York, NY 10010, USA
http://www.manchesteruniversitypress.co.uk

Distributed exclusively in the USA by
Palgrave, 175 Fifth Avenue, New York, NY 10010, USA

Distributed exclusively in Canada by
UBC Press, University of British Columbia, 2029 West Mall,
Vancouver, BC, Canada V6T 1Z2

British Library Cataloguing-in-Publication Data
A catalogue record for this book is available from the British Library

Library of Congress Cataloging-in-Publication Data applied for

ISBN 0 7190 6798 7 *paperback*

This edition first published 2003
10 09 08 07 06 05 04 03   10 9 8 7 6 5 4 3 2 1

Typeset in Aldus
by Koinonia, Manchester
Printed in Great Britain
by Bell and Bain Ltd, Glasgow

Contents

Acknowledgements

I would like to thank to the following for their help and advice: Peter Carey for reading and commenting on parts of the manuscript; the Department of English and the School of Arts at Hull University for supporting my study leave in Australia; Professor Elizabeth Webby and Professor Michael Wilding of the University of Sydney for their help with research resources; the staff of the Manuscript Collection at the National Library of Australia; Jennifer Sterland of Australian Broadcasting Corporation Radio Archives for help with the Carey interview tapes; Professor John Thieme for his careful editing; Jo Chipperfield for reading parts of the manuscript with customary vigour; Andy Butler and Roger Luckhurst for valuable suggestions at various stages; my Australian literature students of 1993–5 at Hull University for their enthusiasm and interest; Elaine, Rob, Jim and Carly for their friendship and hospitality; and, as always, Les Garry.

Series editor's foreword

Contemporary World Writers is an innovative new series of authoritative introductions to a range of culturally diverse contemporary writers from outside Britain and the United States or from 'minority' backgrounds within Britain or the United States. In addition to providing comprehensive general introductions, books in the series also argue stimulating original theses, often but not always related to contemporary debates in post-colonial studies.

The series locates individual writers within their specific cultural contexts, while recognising that such contexts are themselves invariably a complex mixture of hybridised influences. It aims to counter tendencies to appropriate the writers discussed into the canon of English or American literature or to regard them as 'other'.

Each volume includes a chronology of the writer's life, an introductory section on formative contexts and intertexts, discussion of all the writer's major works, a bibliography of primary and secondary works and an index. Issues of racial, national and cultural identity are explored, as are gender and sexuality. Books in the series also examine writers' use of genre, particularly ways in which Western genres are adapted or subverted and 'traditional' local forms are reworked in a contemporary context.

Contemporary World Writers aims to bring together the theoretical impulse which currently dominates post-colonial studies and closely argued readings of particular authors' works, and by so doing to avoid the danger of appropriating the specifics of particular texts into the hegemony of totalising theories.

Chronology

1976   Wrote 'War Crimes' and 'The Chance'.

1977   Joined alternative community at Yandina in Queensland, working part-time for Grey's and writing *War Crimes* stories and *Bliss*.

1979   *War Crimes* published by University of Queensland Press; worked with Ray Lawrence on screenplay based on 'Happy Story'.

1980   Left Grey's; formed joint advertising agency with Bani McSpedden; completed *Bliss*; returned to Sydney; selected stories published in London and New York as *The Fat Man in History*; awarded New South Wales Premier's Award for *War Crimes*.

1981   Moved to Gleniffer near Bellingen, NSW; *Bliss* published by University of Queensland Press and Faber; worked with Ray Lawrence on screenplay based on 'Life and Death in the South Side Pavilion'.

1982   Won New South Wales Premier's Award, Miles Franklin Award and National Book Council Award for *Bliss*.

1984   Met Alison Summers.

1985   Married Alison Summers; *Illywhacker* published by University of Queensland Press, Faber, and Harper and Row; won *Age* Book of the Year Award, NBC Award for Australian Literature, FAW Barbara Ramsden Award, and shortlisted for Booker Prize for *Illywhacker*; film of *Bliss* released, screenplay by Carey and Ray Lawrence – won best picture, director and screenplay awards from Australian Film Institute, and entered for Cannes Festival.

1986   Collaborative project with performance artist Mike Mullins, *Illusion*, an eco-political rock musical; began *Oscar and Lucinda*; son Sam born.

1988   *Oscar and Lucinda* published by University of Queensland Press, Faber and Harper and Row; won Booker Prize; elected FRSL.

1989   Awarded Miles Franklin Award, NBC Banjo Award and Foundation for Australian Literary Studies Award for *Oscar and Lucinda*; moved to Greenwich Village, New York; began teaching creative writing classes at New York University.

1990   Son Charley Summers born.

1991   *The Tax Inspector* published by University of Queensland Press, Faber and Alfred A. Knopf.

Contexts and intertexts

> People often live in nightmares without knowing it.
> The nightmare creeps up on them and even when
> it's at its most intense it feels quite normal to them.
> Not nice, but normal. (Peter Carey)[1]

IN Peter Carey's world, we are all creatures of the shadow lands. His fictions explore the experiences lurking in the cracks of normality, and are inhabited by hybrid characters living in in-between spaces or on the margins. His writing is strange and disturbing. It disrupts the reader's perceptions in ways which are simultaneously conceptual and imaginative: our ideas and views of the world are stretched and challenged. The effect is often that the supposed separations between normal and abnormal, the ordinary and the bizarre, the daydream and the nightmare, are undermined. This subversive and transgressive quality is similar to surrealism, effecting 'the prosecution of the real world'[2] through estrangement. It gives a political edge to Carey's work, not so much in the delivery of easily decodable messages, but in the sense of addressing issues to do with power and the disposition of power. As Carey has said, his fiction involves 'a form of political questioning: Do people want to, or have to, live the way they do now? What will happen to us if we keep on living like we do now?',[3] questions which take in individual and psychological experiences as well as the more generally social.

Where do Carey's strange speculative fictions come from? What factors from his life and context helped shape his writings? Carey himself is a hybrid, 'a *criollo*, born of European parents transplanted in the Southern Hemisphere'.[4] He was born in 1943 in the small town of Bacchus Marsh in Victoria. He has described it as 'the town of Frank Hardy and Captain Moonlight' (*Illywhacker*, 437),[5] a mixture of politics, history and legend suitably prefiguring the hybrid nature of his own work.[6] His father ran the local garage business, Carey Motors, and this background lends elements to a number of his works, from the portrait of the town in 'American Dreams' to the family history inlaid into *Illywhacker* or the inside knowledge of garage life in *The Tax Inspector*. But Carey finds 'reporting reality' rather boring and would much rather construct his own,[7] so while his life obviously informs his works, we should be wary of translating from one to the other.

Carey took a circuitous route into literature and writing. From the age of 10 he went to Geelong Grammar School, 'where the ruling class of Australia go to school',[8] a private school, equivalent to the British public school system – an ex-headmaster recently became the head at Eton.[9] The shift from a lower-middle-class family to a working-class primary school and then to this elitist context was 'a traumatic change'.[10] At this point in his life he had no particular interest in literature, failing his matriculation in English.[11] In various interviews he has insisted, with some bravado, that he did not read any literature until the age of 18 apart from Patrick White's *Voss* and Sinclair Lewis's *Babbitt*.[12] More recently he has qualified this as 'an exaggeration', revealing that he had also read the 'Biggles' and 'Just William' books, as well as *The Cruel Sea* [13] and war books such as *Stalag 17*, *I Flew for the Führer* and *Colditz*,[14] and adding 'basically I read crap'.[15] But this often-repeated piece of Carey-ology suggests that, to some extent, he relishes the cavalier image of literary insurgent afforded by his 'outsider' position: 'I'm used to saying something which is not quite true. I love saying to people that I'd never read a good book until I was eighteen. That's upset many people, including my old English teacher'[16] – the teacher persistently wrote to Carey pointing out that he had in fact covered Milton and Shakespeare at school.[17]

He studied chemistry and zoology at Monash University.

His attraction to these sciences was imaginative rather than rationalist: he saw science as 'a magic world' in which '[t]he modern alchemists were atomic physicists'.[18] A serious car accident, in which he 'virtually scalped' himself gave him a perfect 'excuse' for failing his first year exams and leaving the course.[19] So by the age of 19 Carey was working for National Advertising Services advertising agency in Melbourne, a 'very eccentric agency ... run by a [former] communist ... full of artists and writers'.[20] At this point he 'was a child of Menzies, and General Motors, and thought advertising might be interesting'[21] and 'probably was a political conservative'.[22] Ironically, it was through working in advertising that he received his education in literature and writing.

At the agency, he met the writers Barry Oakley and Morris Lurie who were already producing fiction. Carey used to drive Oakley in to work and, instead of contributing towards the petrol, Oakley, being 'a mean bastard',[23] would give Carey the latest novel he had reviewed. These included works by American and European masters such as Beckett, Bellow, Nabokov, Robbe-Grillet, Kerouac and Faulkner, experimental writers with interests in the bizarre or surreal. Carey has frequently recalled the impact of Faulkner's *As I Lay Dying* with its structural divisions so that the story is 'told from different points of view ... and people often contradict each other'.[24] It was the 'odd use of language' which attracted him to stories like Kerouac's 'The Railroad Earth', and which he found 'very liberating, exciting, wonderful'.[25] He would later absorb and transform such influences: Herbert Badgery in *Illywhacker* might recall the narrative voice of Beckett's *The Unnameable* as Tony Thwaites has suggested,[26] but he couldn't be mistaken for it.

Carey decided he too could produce stories and began writing with characteristic gusto. Oakley and Lurie, bemused by this audacity, offered a contradictory mixture of enthusiasm and discouragement. In 1964, Carey wrote a novel, *Contacts*, and was shortlisted in 1965 as an unsuccessful finalist for a Stanford writing scholarship. By 1966 an extract from *Contacts* appeared in an anthology called *Under 25*, which also included an early piece by contemporary experimentalist Murray Bail. Carey's contribution describes an embarrassingly inexplicit sexual encounter between two students, but is notable for its inter-weaving of the two prose voices as an enactment of sexual congress. His second attempt at a novel, *The Futility Machine*, was a reworked version of *Contacts* and was accepted for publication by Sun Books in 1967,[27] but did not appear owing to 'a disagreement between the directors'.[28] A manuscript of short stories under the title *Slides From a Magic Lantern Show* was also being compiled around this time: one of these, 'She Wakes', later found its way into *The Fat Man in History*.[29]

According to Carey, this period was 'a scary time' since in Melbourne in the 1960s, if you had long hair as he had, 'you'd walk into a pub and people would want to kill you'.[30] The repressive social mores and the conscription of friends for the war in Vietnam drove Carey to leave Australia in 1967, swearing never to return. He travelled to Europe and found himself in London during the decisive period of 1968–70, supporting himself with periods of advertising copywriting while absorbing the cultural fervour of the hippy ethos. The counter-cultural ethic had an ongoing impact on him through later experiences as a member of an alternative community. It appears in works as varied as 'War Crimes', *Bliss* and *The Tax Inspector*, often ironised or questioned. At the same time, he was working on 'this very maniacal and highly mandarin novel which out-Becketted Beckett and out-Robbe-Grilleted Robbe-Grillet'.[31] The novel, *Wog*, was again accepted, this time by a London publisher, before being rejected as too avant-garde.[32] Its manic experi-mentalism led Carey back to writing stories when he returned to Australia in 1970, eager for the sound of the Australian voice and freedom from 'the dead hand of history pressing [our] noses into the past'.[33]

He wrote 'Room No. 5 (Escribo)' and followed it with four other stories in quick succession: '[d]uring the late 1960s, early 1970s, I'd begin work every morning by playing *Blonde on Blonde* or *Highway 61* to get myself sort of wound up with vindictiveness and spite.'[34] It was around this time, after writing

'The Last Days of a Famous Mime', that he began to read the work of American writer Donald Barthelme and was 'particularly affected in terms of ways of talking about things' by his story 'The Balloon'.[35] At the same time, he was writing an unpublished realist novella, *Memories of Luke McClosky*,[36] and an episodic, utopian novel, *Adventures Aboard the Marie Celeste*,[37] which was contracted for publication, but which Carey withdrew in 1974 in favour of *The Fat Man in History*. Working in advertising for the Spasm and Mooney-Grey agency in Melbourne, he moved to work for Grey's in Sydney in 1974, and recalls going around with long hair and dirty jeans, drinking expensive wines and confusing everybody.[38]

He rented a flat in Wharf Road, Balmain, and by default became associated with the circle of avant-garde writers and intellectuals associated with this Bohemian suburb. The loose association of Balmain artists shared some common ground of intellectual, political and sexual radicalism, and had links to the Libertarian Society influences of John Anderson.[39] Frank Moorhouse has pointed out how disparate 'the Balmain Phenomenon' was,[40] while Carey himself was later 'horrified' by the suggestion that he might have been a member of 'the Balmain push'.[41]

One Balmain figure of importance for Carey was Michael Wilding, the English fiction-writer and academic, whose *risqué* satires like *Living Together* (1974) celebrated and exposed the freewheeling hypocrisy of the period. Wilding gave Carey valuable help in having his first book published: Carey has recalled how Wilding wanted to put together a collection of 'dirty, disgusting stories' for Open Leaves Press 'who I believe were normally publishers of porn',[42] and Carey obliged with the story 'Withdrawal'.[43] When this project fell through, Wilding passed examples of Carey's work to the University of Queensland Press, who invited him to submit the stories that became *The Fat Man in History*.[44]

It was an opportune moment to be writing the kind of fiction Carey was interested in. Novelist Kate Grenville has suggested 'there were several hot-house factors at work', which coincided to create a new climate for writers.[45] Patrick White's mythic modernism had been followed by the emergence of writers like C.J. Koch and Randolph Stow as a late Modernist 'spiritual' tradition, what John Docker, in relation to the emergence of this phenomenon in universities, has described as 'the metaphysical ascendancy'.[46] Nevertheless, despite this and despite diversely experimental work from writers like Hal Porter or Dal Stivens, the dominant perception of Australian writing during the 1960s was of a literature devoted principally to a nationalistic tradition stemming back to the 'barren anecdotal realism of local literature' found in the tradition of Henry Lawson's bush stories.[47] Kate Grenville recalls starting to read adult fiction in the 1960s and finding 'only a fairly narrow band of Australian experience was reflected in Australian writing. There was any mount [sic] of dust-and-drovers stuff full of men swinging themselves lazily up onto horses',[48] what White called 'the dreary dun-coloured offspring of journalistic realism'.[49] In the face of this, many younger writers turned to international models such as those to which Oakley had introduced Carey in Melbourne.

At the same time, wider political and economic factors were at work to change the cultural climate. The government commitment of Australia as America's ally in the Vietnam war created a disruption to Australian insularity, drawing it 'out of a comfortable, non-political ease'[50] into an international arena and the counter-cultural protests which characterised 1968 in America and Europe. The election of a new Labor government in 1972 led to renewed funding for writing through the formation of the Literature Board of the Arts Council of Australia, which allocated some $2,200,000 in grants and subsidies within the first two years of its life,[51] and became 'the major force behind the sudden increase in literary fictional publishing'.[52] This funding coincided opportunely with the policy of experimentation being pursued by Frank Thompson, the American manager of Queensland University Press, who established the Paperback Prose fiction list.[53] Craig Munro was commissioned to launch it, backed by a Literature Board subsidy, and his first three titles were books by David Malouf, Rodney Hall and Peter Carey.[54] Carey thus became one of the first of a growing number of Australian writers to reverse the dominant trend and 'publish with success in Australia before being published in the other major centres of English language publishing'.[55]

In addition, a new kind of fiction was evolving which dealt with a liberalised subject matter. 1972 saw the lifting of censorship restrictions[56] after challenges to restrictions by the student newspaper *Tharunka* which had invited Frank Moorhouse to write for them.[57] That same year also saw the launch of *Tabloid Story* magazine, edited by Michael Wilding, Frank Moorhouse and Carmel Kelly. Michael Wilding has recalled how in the late 1960s, writers wanting to deal with sexual material had previously been marginalised into the ghetto of 'girlie' magazines. *Tabloid Story* championed a new sort of writing: 'no more formula bush tales, no more restrictions to the beginning, middle and end story, no more preconceptions about a well rounded tale'.[58] Instead, *Tabloid* stories were 'often urban, inner city – dealing with things that in the 60s had been taboo: sex, then drugs'. *Tabloid* also expressed an interest in the fabulatory tendencies of non-Australian writers like Borges, Calvino and Barthelme, and in 'the literature of process' as epitomised by Kerouac.[59] Moorhouse suggested that the late 1960s created a climate in which a new fiction, 'the "narrative artefact", the story of artifice' which was deliberately 'gameful', might replace the 'event and observation centred' magazine story in Australia.[60] It was about this time that Carey read Gabriel García Márquez's novel *One Hundred Years of Solitude* (1967, trans. 1970), 'which just knock[ed] me right off my bloody head – such a beautiful, fantastic, perfect book'.[61] Carey described García Márquez as '[t]he writer I probably most liked in retrospect' for 'his ability to blend elements of fantasy and reality on a big scale',[62] and García Márquez's novel had a seminal influence on Carey's later writing.

In 1977 Carey moved to an alternative community at Yandina in the rain forest to the north of Brisbane, journeying to Sydney to work and back north to write and live like a hippy. In a 1979 radio interview he described this as 'real 1968 stuff, but

I've just discovered it … ten years too late as usual': the hippy ethic had 'lots of very good things to offer' and the cliché of '"being in touch with the earth" has an enormous amount in it'.[63] Again this experience coincided with a wider phenomenon. In 1973 the same area witnessed a now-legendary Aquarius festival, promoted by the National Students Union, who asked the existing inhabitants of the village of Nimbin whether they would mind hosting the event. Not knowing what was about to hit them, they agreed. Before the festival there were 250 people living in Nimbin; during the festival there were 10,000; and afterwards, there were 750. Hippy Nimbin had arrived and the area is now famous for its communes such as The Holy Goat, its New Age/Old Hippy lifestyle, and for evolving its own peculiar kind of alternative capitalism. The strange amalgam of mysticism and filthy lucre is summed up by the man who changed his name to 'Fast Bucks' and opened a local hippy real estate agency, a character not dissimilar to some of Carey's. In this fascinating time-warp experience, the Yandina community was pioneering, having been established in 1970 and consisting of some thirteen households with fifty people.[64] Carey later described it as 'really all rather bourgeois',[65] but the schizophrenia between business and hippy lifestyles nevertheless contributed creatively to his ambivalent experience as a writer. *Bliss* and many of the stories in *War Crimes* date from this period. In 1980, the year of his first major fictional award, he helped establish the successful small advertising agency, McSpedding-Carey, servicing clients such as John West. Trade papers put the agency as having reached an annual turnover of $5–6 million, although that figure is deceptively generous: Carey was the sole copywriter, working two afternoons a week only.[66] The fact of having a successful career elsewhere than in writing no doubt helped Carey in a number of ways. It meant he was freer than most writers to maintain his ongoing commitment to take risks and experiment in his work, without having 'to worry if something sells or not'.[67] He sold his share in the advertising agency in 1988. In 1989 Carey moved to Greenwich Village in New York with his wife, the theatre director Alison Summers, and has taught classes in creative writing at New York University, as well as the Universities of Princeton and Columbia.

If Carey can be seen as something of a hybrid, with his mixture of lifestyles and the transitions he has made from science to advertising and literature, this is equally true of his writing. He transgresses the conventional codes of what a fiction should be. His work refuses to establish a smooth narrative effect in the 'classic' traditions of European narrative art. Instead, he exploits cross-mixtures which create dislocations, disrupting any supposed norms of fictional practice. As we have seen, his arrival coincided with the emergence of other writers and literary trends with which his work seems to have analogies, but he somehow escapes categorisation with any single group of them. Nevertheless, we can see connections thematically and technically. His early published work was often virtually science fiction or fantasy, and was initially linked with a new generation of Australian fantasy and science fiction which emerged following the 33rd Annual World SF Convention in Melbourne in 1975. In 1977, one of his earliest interviewers and analysts was the science fiction writer and critic Van Ikin, editor of the Sydney-based magazine *Science Fiction*. He suggested that Carey was best seen not as a science fiction writer since 'unlike the average science fiction writer, Carey does not strive to prove the scientific validity of his extrapolations', but as a writer of 'speculative fiction' with fantasy or science fiction settings.[68]

Other Carey stories like 'Peeling' and 'Withdrawal' shared territory with Michael Wilding's explorations of sexual activity and alternative lifestyles in his novel *Living Together* (1974), and in Vicki Viidikas's collection *Wrappings* (1974). Frank Moorhouse's brilliant short stories had established a model of economy and style in his early collection *Futility and Other Animals* (1969). An exploration of American culture's impact on Australia is something Carey has in common with Moorhouse and with his closer contemporary Murray Bail. Moorhouse's seminal *The Americans, Baby* (1972) coincided with the increasing impact of US culture and politics on Australia,[69] and helped initiate an exploration of the Americanisation of

Australian society continued by writers like Murray Bail in *Homesickness* (1980) and Gerald Murnane in *Inland* (1989). Bail's 'Portrait of Electricity' from *Contemporary Portraits and Other Stories* (1975) examines issues of tourism and cultural museums which Carey considers in his earlier story 'American Dreams' as well as in *Illywhacker*. With Bail, Carey also shares a bizarre imagination coupled with an investigation of the afflictions of contemporary culture. David Ireland, although of an older generation, did not publish his works until the 1960s, and his savage satires of contemporary society have some similarities with Carey, albeit with a more definably political bent and eclectic experimentalism.

The self-consciously fictive tendency of Carey's work was echoed in near contemporaries like Dal Stivens and Rudi Krausmann, as well as by Wilding and Bail. Stories like 'Report on the Shadow Industry' and '"Do You Love Me?"' coincided with the experiments in metafiction being undertaken by Bail in his volume *Contemporary Portraits and Other Stories* (1975)[70] and with the fantasy and science fiction of Wilding's 'See You Later' and 'The Man of Slow Feeling' in his collection *The West Midland Underground* (1975).[71] Carey also shares some of these thematic and metafictional qualities with writers in Britain, where his work first appeared slightly later in 1980, and where British reviewers linked him with new writers like Martin Amis (*The Rachel Papers*, 1974; *Dead Babies* 1975), Ian McEwan (*First Love, Last Rites*, 1976), and later Iain Banks (*The Wasp Factory*, 1984). *Oscar and Lucinda* is clearly analogous to works such as John Fowles's *The French Lieutenant's Woman* (1969) with its playful narrator figure, its alternative endings and its pastiche deployment of conventions from the Victorian novel. Pastiche, along with other metafictional strategies, has been seen as one element in the wider phenomenon of post-modernism.[72] Given the political aspects which will become apparent as we consider his work, the wider provenance of the term post-modernism as describing the condition of late capitalism,[73] or the collapse of grand historical narratives[74] might well be applied to Carey. One interesting element of the often frenzied debates about the term post-modernism is the overlap between aesthetics and the commercial market of capitalism which John Frow highlights as 'the key aspect of post-modernisation ... the increasing integration of the aesthetic (in the form especially of advertising ...) into the marketing of commodities'.[75] With his ambiguous position as writer of adverts and short stories, Carey is almost the definitive product and critic of the post-modern experience.[76]

Equally, Carey's acknowledgement of the impact of Gabriel García Márquez's *One Hundred Years of Solitude* has led him to be associated with magic realism. This term characterises works which present often fantastic or surreal events through the authenticating manner and sharp clarity of the realist tradition. The difficulties of the term are compounded by the problematisation of it by some of its leading exponents, including García Márquez, who has argued that '[e]veryday life in Latin America proves that reality is full of the most extraordinary things' and asserted that '[t]here's not a single line in my novels which is not based on reality'.[77] Carey has an understandably ambiguous attitude to the category: he has said in an interview that at first he found it 'a lovely way to describe the sort of writing one finds in *Illywhacker*' but gradually felt it becoming 'a sort of cheap cliché', which led him to become 'wary of being labelled a magic realist'. Nevertheless, he went on to insist, almost in the manner of García Márquez, 'if I am going to have something extraordinary happen [in a fiction], I want it to be real ... If a ghost comes into the room, then you believe it because everything else is so real.'[78]

What Carey shares more generally with all these contemporary writers is a love of the bizarre, a fascination for the nightmarish, a delight in the sordid, the surreal, the lurid. Although there has been some debate among Carey critics as to the appropriateness of the term 'surreal' to describe his fiction,[79] there was an existing context of surrealism in Australia which gives credibility to the link. Australian painting had a thriving surrealist tradition from the 1930s onwards. The name of the model-maker in the story 'American Dreams', Mr Gleason, coincidentally echoes Australian surrealist artist James Gleeson, who wrote the first Australian surrealist manifesto 'What is surrealism?' (1940), and whose bizarre painting 'We inhabit the corrosive littoral of habit' Carey might have seen in the National Gallery of Victoria in Melbourne.[80] Most of the early Carey stories mix ordinary and extraordinary experiences in a surreal manner, and the capacity to mix narrative modes becomes a characteristic feature of Carey's fictional practice. He is an eclectic writer with a taste for the transgressive in terms of forms, ideas and the supposed orthodoxies of genres. Like his life, his fictions are often hybrids, crossing and confusing genres, juggling in the borderlands between the popular and the serious, the high and low. They also juggle with supposedly fixed categories or polarities such as male and female, capitalist and hippy, colonial and post-colonial, showing up the contradictory spaces between experiences, blurring any clear-cut oppositions.

Along with other fabulist historians like Salman Rushdie, he might, then, seem ripe for a case study by a post-colonial theorist such as Homi Bhabha, whose view of post-colonialism rests on the transformational possibilities offered by the patchwork hybridity of the colonial experience. Bhabha counteracts the binary model of a dominant centre and resistant margins in the colonial legacy, replacing such polarities with a process which sees the colonial experience as an interstitial, 'in-between' experience, a matter of border-lands rather than fixed border-lines, 'a place of hybridity, figuratively speaking, where the construction of a political object that is new, *neither the one nor the other*, properly alienates our political expectations, and changes, as it must, the very form of our recognition of the moment of politics'.[81] For Bhabha, this allows for a more subtle sense of the latent possibilities for infiltration, subversion and transformation of the supposedly dominant culture.

Carey shares this disposition for exploring borderlands, though the effect of his work is rarely the consoling one of suggesting transformational possibilities. Instead, he is interested in disruption, disturbance, menace. To achieve this, he sometimes adopts methods more akin to the cartoonist than magic realist: 'I try to write like a cartoonist – I look at things that exist, and push them to their ludicrous or logical extension ...

When you push far enough, you can find yourself in some strange and original places.'[82] The fictions often take an idea or image and explore it past its logical conclusion. The point at which a realist storyteller would stop is the point at which for Carey a scenario becomes interesting – the moment when it becomes bizarre. He has the ability to transform the ordinary into the most insane idea and flesh it out until it achieves nightmarish conviction, 'to find odd and surreal metaphors for contemporary problems that are so apt they don't appear symbolic or documentary as much as an aspect of what they depict',[83] as Harrison-Ford puts it.

This is what gives Carey's fiction its distinctive flavour of political questioning and success has in no way allayed this quality, or his taste for taking risks. His position as a post-colonial writer lends added emphasis to these elements in his work.[84] Having been 'a child of Menzies' and then worked in advertising, he has seen the savagery and absurdities of multinational corporate capitalism from the inside. He also moved to the left politically, describing himself as 'a socialist' in the 1985 interview conducted with his wife, Alison Summers,[85] while his hybrid writing interests have manifested themselves in a surprising variety of projects including screenplays and even a rockmusical called *Illusion* (1981–4; performed 1986). This was a Brechtian collaboration with composer Martin Armiger and performance artist Mike Mullins, with an ecological-disaster scenario warning against the threat of nuclear power and the bomb, for which Carey wrote the dialogue and lyrics.[86] The critical reception was disastrous – it was described by the *Sydney Morning Herald* as the flop of the year. More recently he has written the screenplay for Wim Wenders' futuristic film *Until the End of the World* (1991), with music by rock band U2 among others, and has moved into writing children's fiction with *The Big Bazoohley* (1995).

His early interests as a speculative fantasist or science fiction writer have never been subsumed in the conventions of 'high' art or realism. A recent work, *The Unusal Life of Tristan Smith*, is a myth-making fantasy. It reveals that the fascination for the weird displayed so brilliantly in the stories, and seemingly hidden by the apparently more conventional fiction of *Illywhacker*, *Oscar and Lucinda* or *The Tax Inspector*, was never eclipsed, instead forming a consistent thread throughout. His transgressive imagination challenges the reader's notions of the normal in literature and in life: it subverts any apparent division of fiction into separate categories such as realism, fantasy, science fiction; and it reveals the surreal beneath the surface of actuality. He is a writer of speculative and satirical fables whose ideas are often so strange – the pleasure bird which shits the seeds of a planet-demolishing tree; a character who is described as having a 'slightly melted nose',[87] a glass church floating round the bend of a river on a barge – as to make the reader laugh out loud at their thought-provoking inventiveness. Such varied and entertaining images mark the continued adventurousness of Carey's career as a novelist. This is not easily achieved: his risk-taking involves a concurrent anxiety and struggle to attain a sense of his own conviction about a new fictional situation, often against his own sense of the uncertainty of the writing process. He consistently indicates his anxieties as a writer both while exploring a scenario for a book and when beginning the whole process again.[88] His expectations of failure are coupled with an obsessive drive to explore new areas: 'my only way to safety is to do something ridiculously unsafe'.[89] The way this emerges in his explorations for a new novel is well documented in interviews: '[t]he whole business of writing is to live with doubt: to do what you don't know how to do, to place yourself continually in a situation of ignorance and inelegance.'[90] And it is graphically demonstrated in his initial drafts. Carey freely admits the process of writing to be muddy and incoherent, a seemingly shapeless circling which 'isn't the surface of something else: this is it ... I just follow the river of the idea on the typewriter. Then the river dries up and I can't think of anything else, so maybe I go back and run with it again, to see if this time it goes any further.' This gradual and painfully extended process of manufacture and creation can be glimpsed briefly in the early notes for *Oscar and Lucinda*, as we see Carey talking to himself through the medium of the typewriter, almost chanting incantations to his imagination in order to get it fired up and into gear:

THE GRANDFATHER IS THE ONE WITH THE GLASS.

HE TAKES IT HIMSELF

AFTER THE SHIP SINKS.

HE DOES IT HIMSELF.

ON LAND. HE NEVER CARED FOR THE WATER ANYWAY. TOO
MANY BAD THINGS. THE WATER, AS IT TURNS OUT, IS WHAT
DESTROYS IT

HE WAS A GAMBLER. HE HAD GAMBLED ON THE GLASS AND
THEN NEW GLASS HAD TURNED UP.

HE WOULD NOT BE BEATEN.

THE GLASS HOUSE.

THE CHURCH.

THE QUESTION OF A GLASS CHURCH.

THE GLASS CHURCH WAS NOT HIS ONLY ODD INVENTION.

<u>HE WAS UNLUCKY ENOUGH TO MEET A CLERGYMAN WITH</u>
<u>WHOM HIS FANCY</u>
<u>RECEIVED REINFORCEMENT. HAD IT NOT BEEN FOR THIS HE</u>
<u>WOULD NOT HAVE DIED SO YOUNG AND I WOULD NOT HAVE</u>
<u>BEEN BORN.</u>

The glass.

My grandfather's position in business is cloudy. Gambling.
Gambling and religion.

READ PASCAL[91]

If faith was a gamble for Pascal, writing seems to be an incessant gamble for Peter Carey, which is perhaps why he is such a constantly exciting writer. It is this restlessness which helps account for the fascination of his work. The excitement comes from a weird, quirky imagination which adventurously takes on unexpected material virtually book by book, and evolves appropriate but unexpected narrative solutions, promising continual surprises.

The stories

Things are becoming less and less impossible.
(*Collected Stories*, 60)

CHARACTERISING Carey's stories takes us to the heart of his fictional practice. Most adopt a mixture of narrative modes, a central feature of his writing. They contain elements of science fiction, fantasy, fable and satire. Like much science fiction, many are explorations of ideas and possibilities, experiments in subversive thinking or 'cognitive estrangement'.[1] Carey has described them as 'a collection of "what if" stories',[2] which start with an idea and develop characters 'to act out some peculiar whim ... to illustrate some sort of a point or push some tendency in society to its ridiculous degree'.[3] They are akin to the speculative thought experiments designed by physicists to test a set of circumstances or a given scenario, expanding it to conclusions apparently beyond the laws of possibility but in a way which is somehow consistent with them. In Carey stories, terminal societies trap characters in drive-in movie car parks, or offer the bizarre possibility of exchanging bodies, or generate a counter-revolutionary resistance movement led by fat men. An extra-terrestrial pleasure bird provides sensory thrills and relaxation when stroked, but kills when threatened, and through its shit disseminates the seeds of the world-destroying Kennecott Rock Drill tree. A society with a passion for mapping and listing is beset by a condition in which, because they are being overlooked, regions of the country, and then the people themselves, become less and less real, until they dematerialise altogether. Unlike the shadows in the story 'Report on the Shadow Industry', these fictional shadows aim to disturb rather than console.

Rather than 'reporting reality', Carey is interested in constructing his own 'possible worlds'[4] in order to see the real world from odd angles, or make reality clearer by dislocating it.[5] He creates a hybrid satirical fiction, not tied down to the demands of social realism, but with a distinctively political edge. Once we accept the opening premise of a Carey story, we find ourselves inexorably drawn into an often bizarre yet convincing world with multiple possible resonances, no single one of which would satisfy as a final reading. As Graeme Turner has suggested, Carey exploits 'the sensation of "hesitation"' which Todorov recognised as crucial to the genre of the fantastic, in which 'the reader is caught between the explicable and the inexplicable' and 'possibilities multiply'.[6] By mixing the fabular with other realist and non-realist narrative modes, Carey generates suggestiveness through a hybridity of form. This is also a function of his prose style, modes of delivery, narrative voices and so on. Strange ideas are tossed into the middle of the commonplace as in the story 'Ultra-Violet Light' in which the narrator describes his mother as being 'amused by novelties: foaming soap pads, oriental games with indecipherable characters, bird baths with unusual characteristics, plans for tourism involving apples' (*War Crimes*, 156). Although the exploration of ideas tends to dominate, the stories are not lacking in characterisation. Indeed, Carey became 'more and more interested in the characters',[7] particularly the longer stories such as 'The Fat Man in History', 'War Crimes' or 'The Chance', where the presentation of the central characters invests the exploration of a bizarre idea with psychological conviction. Equally, the inclusion of factual details such as real place-names in a story like 'Crabs' lends the air of authenticity to a fantastic scenario.[8]

Grouping the stories around themes and issues, and considering an example of each in detail alongside other related stories allows for a fairly comprehensive insight into Carey's shorter works, and provides some key threads for later discussions of the longer fiction. Four of the most significant areas are: American imperialism and culture; capitalism; power and authority; and gender.

America has a spectral fascination for many Australian writers, as Don Anderson has pointed out. He usefully quotes Jean Baudrillard to help explain this: 'whatever one thinks of the arrogance of the dollar or the multinationals, it is this culture which, the world over, fascinates those very people who suffer most at its hands, and it does so through the deep, insane conviction that it has made all their dreams come true.'[9] In 'American Dreams' Carey creates a powerful emblem for the relationship of Australia to America, and the problems of cultural dependency. The story juggles a number of narrative modes. It begins as an apparently realist story in the Lawson tradition, but soon reveals fantastic qualities. The unnamed narrator describes his home town whose inhabitants are haunted by the 'American Dreams' generated by the films at the Roxy, and which are utterly inappropriate to their provincial reality (171–2). The narrator looks back at the town's ambivalent relationship to one inhabitant, a recluse called Mr Gleason who built a walled enclosure up on Bald Hill in which he constructed a precise miniature model of the town, a perfect replica of buildings, people, animals. The model is found after his death and gradually becomes the object of huge media interest. It proves to be such a tourist attraction that the real town's inhabitants are paid to adopt the poses which they were given in the model by Mr Gleason while American tourists look down at them through telescopes and compare them with their miniaturised selves.

'American Dreams' takes the orthodox realist story of outback communities and injects a dislocating strangeness into it. The town itself is a peculiar mixture of the everyday and odd obsessions. In small-town provincial life eccentricities are, perhaps, normal, but these are bizarre. The narrator's father runs a gas station, but is also an inventor with 'plans for a giant gravel crusher' (172) which he is continually being distracted from completing. Mr Gleason himself spends five years producing the extraordinary model. No one in the town seems too surprised

when Gleason is caught up with building the walls up on Bald
Hill: they simply accept that he has 'gone mad' and pity his wife.
It takes the arrival of the occasional outsider asking about the
walls for the narrator to 'see, once more, the strangeness of it ...
this inexplicable thing' (174).

The model is a logical extension into illogicality, an eccen-
tricity whose strangeness is both believable and outlandish. As
the video 'The Most Beautiful Lies' suggests by intercutting
between Carey looking at the real town of Bacchus Marsh and at
a model of it,[10] a model-maker is like the fiction-writer, creating
a substitute version of reality. From this point of view, Gleason's
model offers a contradictory metaphor of art itself, an idea
explored through the ambiguous reactions of the townsfolk
when they first see it. At first, it provokes 'simple joy' (177): the
narrator thinks the model is 'the most incredibly beautiful thing
I had ever seen in my life' (177). The townspeople take delight in
admiring this simulacrum of a place they had always despised in
actuality: they tiptoe round 'lifting off each other's roofs, admiring
each other's gardens' and 'suddenly found ourselves' (178).

Superficially, Gleason epitomises the artist revealing the
ordinary as magical, seeing the significance of the commonplace,
showing, as Canadian writer Alice Munro has put it, how people's
lives are 'dull, simple, amazing, and unfathomable – deep caves
paved with kitchen linoleum'.[11] He might also embody the post-
colonial artist writing back against the colonial legacy, creating a
new hybrid out of the suppressions of the past, validating
otherwise marginalised experience. But rather than simply
endorsing such roles, Carey's story interrogates the contradictions involved in these projects. Art can be dangerous, and
when the narrator lifts off the roof from one of the model houses
to find the representation of Mrs Cavanagh in bed with young
Craigie Evans, he and the rest of the town react with 'fear' (178).
This image is a jokey version of the artist 'taking the lid off' a
reality we ignore or miss. The subsequent use of the model and
the disagreements over whether Gleason planned for the effect it
has on the town (177) wryly parody theories of artistic intention
and the death of the author. The narrator argues with his father

over the true meaning of Mr Gleason's legacy: his father believes Gleason's model was designed 'to let us see the beauty of our town, to make us proud of ourselves and to stop the American Dreams we were so prone to', and that the subsequent tourist exploitation was not in his plan, and certainly not a revenge for any offence the town might have caused him. The narrator feels 'this view of my father's is a little sentimental and also, perhaps, insulting to Gleason', and mysteriously suggests that '[o]ne day the proof of my theory may be discovered. Certainly there are in existence some personal papers, and I firmly believe that these papers will show that Gleason knew exactly what would happen' (177). This mixes a degree of vagueness with a sense of conviction or precision in a manner akin to Jorge Luis Borges, creating a fictional world which juxtaposes the familiar and the unexpected with the maximum suggestive effect.

Munro's 'super-realism', as she calls it,[12] displays the hidden richness of otherwise apparently ordinary lives. Carey's fiction reveals altogether more disturbing situations. The narrative metaphor of the model town suggests issues of cultural dependency and consumer capitalism. As the model becomes a focus for American visitors eager to compare the representation with the real thing, the town which had been subjected to dreams of America itself becomes an American dream, an object constructed for consumption by tourists. The inhabitants are grudgingly forced to play out the increasingly inappropriate roles they were given in the model to fit in with the expectations of the visitors. The model is sanitised for the tourists by having 'certain controversial items' (179) removed, like Mrs Cavanagh's adulterous liaison with Craigie Evans. In the frame of the story, the narrator is now 21 years old, but finds himself caught in a Baudrillardian shadow land between art and reality, having to pretend to be his own younger adolescent self only to be accused of not being the real thing. The tourists are suspicious and disappointed; they 'prefer the model' (181).

This suggests some of the ambiguities of post-colonial situations and their reliance on the investments of international capital through tourism. The town is caught in a dependency culture, trapped by the role of marginal provincialism, resent-fully but inescapably feeding on the hand-outs of American dollars from economic necessity, unable to achieve autonomy even through its own cultural representation of itself. Ironically, Don Anderson records presenting American experimental author William H. Gass with a copy of Carey's stories, only to receive the culturally imperialist response, 'Barthelme'.[13] Equally ironically, Carey recalls his mother saying that Bacchus Marsh was 'really upset' by the story when it came out, suggesting an ambivalent function in Carey's own fictional model-making.[14]

The critique of the obsessive consumer culture of tourism has become a significant concern for Australian writers and cultural commentators. They have witnessed the rebuilding of Sydney as a tourist theme park with the endless proliferation of shopping malls and the historically unreal 'reconstruction' of the Rocks, a convict frontier town now turned over to bistros, boutiques and outlets for Aboriginal art; and they have seen stretches of the North Coast bought up by Japanese businessmen from Tokyo eager for somewhere to play golf with prospective clients. Discussing the media presentation of tourist oppor-tunities in their guide to the 'myths of Oz', John Fiske, Bob Hodge and Graeme Turner argue that 'the media do not merely give us the global village, telling us that the rest of the world is our backyard; they construct for us a position of power in that village. Their Western-centred discourses, their white-eyed cameras, construct the rest of the world as there for *us* ... colonisation by looking, possession by the gaze, is continuing unabated, and tourism is an individualised extension of the symbolic colonisation by the media ... The photograph is the symbolic enactment of this: each print or slide is a piece of our world that we are taking home with us. The camera may be the final agent of colonisation'.[15]

Comparable fictional examples occur in Murray Bail's short story 'Portrait of Electricity' with its absurdist museum,[16] and its extension in his hilarious novel *Homesickness*. Bail's characters are Australian tourists who visit a series of increasingly surreal museums of culture, such as the museum of corrugated iron in

East Yorkshire.[17] A series of exhibitions marking the invention of photography illustrates how '[n]othing is real anymore'[18] as a result of the commercial gaze of tourism: the National Gallery replaces all the Renaissance masterpieces with X-ray photographs to show up the 'real' paintings beneath the paintings; the National Portrait Gallery displays a special exhibition of oil painting portraits of pioneering photographers; the Hayward Gallery puts on a series of boxing matches between painters and photographers; while the Tate Gallery takes down all its original paintings and replaces them with colour slides of the actual scenes of haystacks or lily ponds which inspired Constable or Monet.[19] As Don Anderson suggests, perhaps 'as an act of cultural revenge' for Carey's earlier story,[20] Bail has telescopes placed in Manhattan hotel rooms for the Australian tourists, from which they can observes the natives of America.

'American Dreams' is among the earliest of these writings, and is notable for its distinct and suggestive political implications. It questions whether autonomy can ever be found through cultural activities which are tied to a multinational global economy dominated by one or two superpowers. It reminds us of the complex but continuing effects of unequal power, a political and economic reality which it displays disturbingly and effectively. On the furthest margins of the story are the Chinese labourers who built the walls for Gleason in the first place and, after constructing a large brick chimney up at a mine at A.1 (174), return to knock them down. This party of marginalised migrant labourers, going around the country under orders from other people, building and destroying inexplicable monuments, is emblematic of the post-colonial market-place, and also of an unrecuperable strangeness which Carey's stories generate, and which cannot be easily corralled into demarcated meanings.

Other powerful metaphors of imperial and cultural domination appear in 'Crabs' and 'A Windmill in the West'. Both stories create anonymous futuristic scenarios which have their own fictional logic, conviction and multiple suggestivity. 'Crabs' presents a collapsing society in which the central character and his girlfriend are trapped in their 1956 Dodge in the Americanised environment of the Star Drive-in, living off hamburgers and banana fritters from the Ezy-Eatin diner. Crabs's attempt to abscond, by physically transforming himself into a Ford V8 truck, leads him inexorably back full circle to the movie theatre's parking lot, implying the inescapability of American cultural domination. The soldier in 'A Windmill in the West' performs an unexplained mission guarding a borderline along which 'the area to the west could be considered the United States, although, in fact, it was not' and 'the area to the east of the line could be considered to be Australia, which it was' (94). When the soldier realises that the sun is setting in the 'east' rather than the 'west', he becomes confused about which side of the line belongs to which designation. 'East' and 'west' have long been politically loaded terms, and the story presents a brilliant emblem of the arbitrariness of military imperialism, partly through this awareness of the arbitrariness of language and signs. The soldier's increasingly demented behaviour shows him as both the victim and the agent of a faceless authoritarianism. The terminal landscape of the desert acts simultaneously as a reflection of the psychology of the character and as a reminder of the actual military appropriation of the Australian desert at Maralinga for atomic tests during the 1950s.[21] This examination of the impact of American culture on Australia is carried on in *Bliss* and *Illywhacker*, while the wide issues of colonialism are central to *Oscar and Lucinda* and *The Unusual Life of Tristan Smith*.

The bleak pessimism of these stories also relates to others grouped around Carey's exposé of capitalism and embodied most powerfully in 'War Crimes'. This investigates the links between capitalism and the violent exploitation of power suggested in the title. In an interview before the book *War Crimes* came out, Carey acknowledged his work in advertising might be fostering myths of affluence 'in ways that are against the best interests of society', his own 'war crimes'.[22] Written in the late 1970s, this prophetic story envisaged capitalism entering 'its most pictures-que phase', and anticipated the savage market-forces world of the 1980s in a fantastic yet unnervingly accurate way. Carey invents two seemingly bizarre hippy/punk capitalists, but has stressed that the story is just like working in an advertising agency, Barto being based on someone he worked with, while the other main character is 'a total psychopathic distortion' of something he recognises in himself.[23] Although the story 'pushes things to extremes a bit', it captures 'the logic of business ... my view of late capitalism'.[24]

Bart and his partner are sent in as troubleshooters to revive a failing business. They do so by enforcing a reign of terror in which they literally shoot recalcitrant employees and act like horsemen of the Apocalypse as they cleanse the surrounding area of marauding bands of vagabonds and the unemployed, meanwhile listening to reggae music and becoming the toast of the middle-class intelligentsia who find them fascinating case material for their cultural studies modules. The story explores these contradictions with a powerful and blatant crudity which adds depth rather than lacking it. Its exaggerations are both absurdist and acidically true. The decadent extravagance of Barto's hippy/punk capitalist persona seems fantastic and exactly right (310–11, 316–17). Like Kurtz's 'unsound' methods in Conrad's *Heart of Darkness*,[25] the 'unconventional methods' (311) deployed by the two protagonists in their mission to rescue the ailing frozen food plant are merely the overt form of what the narrator sees as '"normal" market conditions' (322). Behind his decadent imagery, Bart has 'a business brain the like of which is rarely seen, as cool and clean as stainless steel and totally without compassion' (317). Business usually masks its violence behind images of conventional orthodoxy and acceptability, the decency of the pin-striped suit, the respectability of the briefcase. What 'War Crimes' suggests is that the briefcase may well be carrying a Baretta machine gun either for sale or for use.

The narrator speaks from a curiously double-edged position. He is appalled by his own activities and those of his elegantly horrific partner, and is sharply self-critical. At the same time he understands and even relishes the origins of his violence in a sense of inadequacy, and is driven to desire power as a compensation.[26] Raised among the poor, with a father who lost a hand in a factory, the narrator's terror of factories epitomises a fear of exploitation which drives him to want to be 'top dog'. His fear is the fuel for his 'craziness' (329): 'I began to understand why men raze villages and annihilate whole populations. The .22 under my arm nagged at me, producing feelings that were intense, unnameable, and not totally unpleasurable' (314). He throws this self-knowledge at the reader in a vitriolic indictment of the middle-class culture which flourishes in the savageries of business enterprise. This contradictory awareness suggests the uncomfortable overlap of individualistic 'go-getting' capitalism with a 'total psychopathic distortion' whose irrationality, as Carey has recognised, fuels the power of business and fascism.[27] Such contradictions help account for the otherwise apparently throwaway ending of the story. The narrator watches the apocalyptic destruction of the unemployed massing around the perimeter of the factory as Bart and the factory workers turn flame-throwers on them in a scenario echoing images of the Vietnam war. He wishes he had been a great painter so he might have 'worn fine clothes and celebrated the glories of man' and been able to stand above life and judge it. In fact, this is exactly his position as he parallels the sublime response to napalm in the morning of his contemporary, Colonel Kilgore in Coppola's *Apocalypse Now*, as he stands on the factory roof, looking down on the destruction and marvelling at the aesthetic beauty of his own arm. The suggestion is that the middle-class culture, which has all along fired the narrator's hatred of his weakness and his working-class background, forms the flowers on the chains of subjection and exploitation.

What is particularly disturbing here is the exposé of the complicity of the reader, specifically the academic reader. The story's first paragraph anticipates commentators as 'vermin, may they feast on this and cover it with their idiot footnotes' (310). The middle-class intellectuals who find Bart and his partner so fascinating for their style are unable to understand 'that we were no different from Henry Ford or any of the other punks' (328).

Alongside the brutal exposé, the story generates a laconic humour which adds depth. The narrator's comment that, with

Bart, 'capitalism had surely entered its most picturesque phase' (314), has an amused savagery, particularly when we recall the way an American hippy like Jerry Rubin went on to become a successful venture capitalist on Wall Street and market executive for a New Age nutritional drink, making some $600,000 in 1992, before his absurdist death jaywalking.[28] At the beginning of the story Bart pulls out his Colt .45 and says 'If it doesn't scare the cunts to death we can always shoot them' (311). On first reading this is funny and by the end of the story, shocking. Initially, he receives an unruly response from the office staff in the canteen and produces his Colt only to be laughed at: '[h]e stood there aghast, no longer feeling as cool as he would have liked'. The narrator comments wryly '[i]t was a particularly bad start' (314) and, invoking the language register of business he uses elsewhere (312), he invites the staff to 'discuss their futures'. This laconic tone has what the story calls 'the comic appearance of truly lethal things' (323) and, with the self-loathing and savagery, creates an utterly convincing narrative voice anticipating the psychopathic/psychotic character of Benny in *The Tax Inspector*. The terminal scenario of this story is shared by others such as 'Exotic Pleasures', 'The Chance' or '"Do You Love Me?"', while the treatment of business culture anticipates elements of *Bliss* and the ending of *Illywhacker*.

In the next group of stories, issues of power, control and paranoia often focus on a confrontation between individuals and an abstract or anonymous authority, with Kafkaesque overtones. In 'Life & Death in the South Side Pavilion', the nameless narrator is trapped in the pavilion guarding a group of horses from falling into a deep swimming pool of water and drowning. Like 'War Crimes', the story takes the form of a confession or self-justification, journal-like in manner with broken numbered sections. There is no explanation of the situation, adding to the effect of menace and the reader's sense of estrangement. The uncertainty infects the narrator's mental state: he has the revelation that his role is to stop the horses falling into the pool and assumes increasing responsibility for their fate to the extent that, as his involvement with his girlfriend Marie develops, he feels 'EVERY TIME I FUCK MARIE I KILL A HORSE' (54). The effect is to make him impotent so that Marie leaves him. In frustration he drives the remaining horses into the pool only to find a delivery truck brings replacements. The drivers ignore his pleas not to be left in charge of the horses, and his offer of a bribe of the television is rebuked with the comment that it is 'company property' (55).

Like many of the stories, the power of this derives from the mystery surrounding the situation: it generates a nightmarish logic and suggestibility, with the central character locked into a seemingly inescapable but utterly futile activity apparently created simply to occupy his time. The idea of the horses falling into the swimming pool creates a Magritte-like defamiliarisation which is not exhausted by possible interpretations. The link between the deaths of the horses and the narrator's sexual relationship invites a psychoanalytical exploration, as expressions of the narrator's paranoia and self-assumed guilt. The nameless company seems all-powerful, the narrator seems powerless. Yet there is no suggestion that he is being forced into the position he is in. He seems instead to back himself willingly into the shadowy corner he inhabits. Questions rather than answers are raised as a result of such ambiguities, particularly over the relationship of victim to victimiser and the uncomfortable possibility of complicity in subjection.

Similar issues of power and authority are explored in the stories 'Kristu-Du' and 'Room No. 5 (Escribo)'. In the first, an architect finds himself building his masterpiece for a vicious dictator. The location is unspecified, though the names of the tribal characters suggests Africa. The narrator's creative drive to complete the building, a great copper-domed meeting house for the tribes, leads him into complicity in the dictator's tyrannical practices, and his construction is used as a mass prison and a means for exterminating the dictator's enemies. The power of this story derives from the mixture of the ordinary and the terrible, generating a shock effect, as with the opening sentence: 'While the architect's wife carefully folded a pair of white slacks, five men were hanged' (15). The convincing settings along with the Russian and American tensions in the country all delineate familiar post-colonial parameters. At the same time, the title and the idea of the building itself, a great copper dome, recall Xanadu and the pleasure dome in Coleridge's 'Kubla Khan', as well as echoing the ideas of Hitler's architect Albert Speer. In his memoir *Inside the Third Reich* (first published 1970), Speer described his plans to embody Hitler's fantastic conception of a great domed hall as a place of worship and mass congregation. For Carey, Speer embodied the contradictory figure of a 'decent chap who ended up running the Nazi war machine' and an artist who was given creative freedom by a fascist dictator, ambiguities which also surface in the Borges-like story 'Fragrance of Roses' where an ex-concentration camp commandant spends his retirement under cover cultivating beautiful hybrid flowers.[29] As well as these analogies with other literature and with history, this is also a world in which three-dimensional holograms of the dictator are possible, so that Carey is evidently mixing fictional modes and resources to present a hybrid of realism and fantasy with a resultant metaphoric power which invokes disturbing suggestions.

'Room No. 5 (Escribo)' embodies many of the other characteristic narrative strategies in Carey's fiction. It opens with a bizarre image: 'I scratch my armpit and listen to the sound, like breakfast cereal' (56). The central character is trapped in an unspecified country waiting for a possible coup while the territory's leader is dying. Again, the story is saturated with uncertainty and menace. The narrator, and the woman who shares hotel-room five with him, is hemmed in by secret police, soldiers, borders and language. Language is particularly highlighted through the name given to the room, 'Escribo', the Spanish for 'I write'. The narrator does not know the language of the territory and therefore has to rely on translation by his companion, but even she finds the language confusing: 'You say there was a difficulty with the grammar, a doubt about the meaning of a certain verb and one or two words that are phonetically confusing' (61). The effect is of being caught in a limbo of unreliable information and uncertain outcomes. The narrator also has doubts about his companion, as she has about him: 'You said, you don't look as if you work in insurance. And I wasn't sure what you meant' (63). The atmosphere of uncertainty is generated by particular effects. In this example, the reader is partially unsure of the referent of the second 'you': if this is directly reported speech then the female companion is referring to the narrator; but if it is indirectly reported, she might be referring to herself.

This slippage between signifiers and signifieds is echoed in the narrative more generally. The story is told in the present tense, giving a sense of unease and possible, though as yet unspecified, disruption. The matter-of-fact reportage of the narrator's voice heightens a peculiar dislocation between events and his response. Details and events are given magnified importance, yet lead to inconclusive results. The narrator and his companion have regular yoghurt-eating sessions in the local café where they are watched intently by an audience of soldiers. During one of them 'you ask me to ask for the water. I have forgotten the word and remember it incorrectly. The waiter appears to understand but brings coffee and you say that coffee will do. Later, when I pay, I notice that he does not include the price of the coffee. Has he forgotten it? Or is it an elaborate joke, to bring coffee, pretending all the time that it is water. After eight days in this town it is not impossible' (61–2). These narrative and stylistic subtleties, effecting disturbing perceptual dislocations such as these, are characteristic of Carey's best shorter fiction.

Our final area is a group of stories dealing with gender identities and issues. 'Peeling' first appeared in *Meanjin* magazine in 1972, making it one of the earliest of Carey's fictions to appear in print. It reappeared through Frank Moorhouse's editorship of the resurrected short story anthology *Coast to Coast* in 1973. A number of other contemporary male writers were exploring gender and sexuality in disturbing or subversive ways. Colin Talbot's *Massive Road Trauma* (1975) explored the sexual obsessions of a man who has killed a woman,[30] while Ken Gelder describes Michael Wilding's *Scenic Drive* (1976) as being 'self-consciously about the "pornography of representation"'.[31] Gelder and Salzman argue that 'obsessional desire, specifically male desire, lies at the basis of much of the experimental or speculative fiction produced in the 1970s and 1980s',[32] a suggestion which would coincide with evidence from British and American writers such as John Fowles or Philip Roth. Some women writers were also producing sexually explicit work such as Vicki Viidikas's *Wrappings* or Amy Witting's 'A Piece of this Puzzle in Missing' which appeared in the eighth issue of Wilding and Moorhouse's *Tabloid Story*.[33]

Carey's 'Peeling' explores the borders of gender delineation, exposing the shadow lands of male fantasies about women as compensations for the culturally imposed distortions of male experience. The central character is a seedy, retired, elderly male. Using the present tense, he tells of his oddly anonymous relationship with a woman called Nile, who lives in a room above him and visits to clear up. Nile is notable for her obsession with collecting dolls, which she deprives of hair, eyes and teeth, and then paints white. In what is apparently their first sexual encounter, the narrator's story develops into a description of his gradual undressing of her as he is driven by the increasing urgency of his desire. When Nile is naked apart from an earring which she wishes him not to remove, the narrator is horrified to find on forcibly pulling at the earring that she peels in two, revealing a twenty-year-old male with the same face and another earring. Pulling this reveals a smaller woman dressed in stockings and suspender belt. As he removes the stockings, her legs disappear. Gradually 'with each touch she is dismembered' (93) and falls to pieces in his hands, finally shattering to reveal a small doll, hairless, eyeless and completely white.

The suggestiveness of this story-line results partly from the different possible views of the central character's activity of stripping the woman, linked with the deliberate uncertainties of the narrative. One possibility is to take the story as a 'stripping down' of male fantasies surrounding the feminine, a deconstruction of male mythologies about women. Even within the narrative's own frame, the figure called 'Nile' is obviously not 'a real woman'.[34] She is a fantasy, a pawn in the male narrator's

imagination, to be stripped and used for his own sexual gratifi-
cation like a sex doll or pornographic fantasy. The encounter is
couched in terms suggesting a liaison with a prostitute, with
controlling 'rules' imposed by the customer. But Nile breaks the
rules as the narrator's desire runs away with him against his will.
The fantasy of Nile offers him no final satisfaction and is actually
beyond his control, just as his desire seems always to be beyond
control – to be, indeed, a matter *of* control. Throughout the encounter, the narrator is obsessed with ideas of delaying,
deferring, with holding things back to make them last: '[t]he
prospect of so slow an exploration excites me and I am in no
hurry, no hurry at all' (85–6). At the same time, the language of
his narrative is saturated with a self-conscious suggestiveness
and self-titillation. Ideas of getting under Nile's skin, of moving
into intimacy layer by layer, of her throat as milky like the inside
of a thigh, of revealing things about her like her name, of picking at
threads that might unravel her clothing – all present themselves
with increasing insistence until the narrator's hands take on a life
of their own, as he says 'independent of my will' (90), and start
undressing her, only to confront the loathed white of the doll.

This exposes some of the contradictions within masculinity.
The male desire for the feminine harbours narcissism, a displaced
desire for a hidden male body, an awareness that rather than
being biologically determined, gender identity is a culturally
imposed demarcation which splits men off from their polymor-
phous potentialities.[35] The narrative hints at such ambiguities
early on when the narrator mentions that his friend Bernard,
who is himself an incessant masturbator, has suggested that the
narrator's relationship with Nile has 'a Boy Scout flavour about
it' (84). They are also enacted through the pronoun confusions
when the naked young man is revealed within the peeled
woman: 'She (for I must, from habit, continue to refer to her as
"she") seems as surprised as I am. She takes her penis in her
hand, curious, kneading it, watching it grow. I watch fascinated'
(92–3). The story invokes the contradictions of pornography, in
which the male makes love to himself by masturbation but can
generally do so only through a displacement on to fantasy

imagery of women as part of the ambivalent armoury of patriarchal ideology. The initial obsessive concern with stripping off clothing to reveal the hidden female body contains a concurrent but displaced homo-erotic desire for the taboo male body. This parallels the intriguing contradictions revealed in Marjorie Garber's book about cross-dressing,[36] a practice enjoyed by a remarkable variety of men (particularly truck-drivers apparently), through which the male explores a temporary reconnection with the taboos of 'being feminine' by adopting the fetishised patriarchal signs of 'the feminine' in clothing, make-up and lingerie. So within the narrator's new 'she/he' is another female garbed in the classic fetish objects of stockings and suspenders. What is being peeled away in this speculative fantasy is the male projection of desire and the hybrid nature of that desire which the conventional badges of gender identity cannot accommodate.

The white doll revealed at the heart of the peeling process suggests the dissatisfactions of this male character's sexuality. The dolls are introduced early into the story as Nile's obsession. It is she who plucks them bald, takes out their eyes and teeth, and then paints them white with plastic paint. The narrator admits he loathes white: 'I would prefer a nice blue, a pretty blue, like a blue sky. A powder blue, I think it is called ... Something a little more feminine' (85). Nile's final cardigan is suitably a powder blue (91). The doll's whiteness recalls the narrator's own white hair, the stale smell of milk in the unwashed bottles, the 'million gallons of milk' the narrator feels he may drown in when Nile smiles (92), and inevitably the semen produced through this masturbation fantasy, accompanied by a culturally-conditioned self-disgust which overlaps with the awareness of Nile's supposed work helping perform abortions. This suggests a number of possibilities – the urgent temporality of male sexual activity; a Lacanian insistence that there is no sexual relation, no place for the satisfaction of the desire which is continually being projected by men on to women as the desirable objects which should satisfy that desire; and the relocation of that aberrant, unrelatable desire, back to its place of origin.

'Peeling' allows for all these possibilities. It also invites a metafictional approach through the notion of 'peeling back layers of meaning'.[37] Such displacement effects are given body by the stylistic manner of the story – the use of the present tense, the uncertainties between the character voices, the strange awkwardness in the prose: 'Outside the fog is thick, the way it is always meant to be in London, but seldom is, unless you live by the river, which I don't' (84). This quality to the writing again creates a distinctive psychological terrain for the character voice, and is characteristic of Carey's short fiction more generally.

Gender issues arise in less direct ways in other stories. In 'A Schoolboy Prank', Turk Kershaw, a retired boarding-school teacher renowned for a tough masculine attitude, meets up with his successful ex-pupils on the day when his beloved dog has died. His visible grief undermines their view of him and, in response to their uncaring attitude which he instilled into them to make them men, Turk confronts them with their, and his, homosexual predilections. Their past threatens their carefully cultivated, conventionally masculine facades, contradicting the roles they have restricted themselves into: '[t]hey did not wish to know that they had sucked the cocks of boys who had grown up to be married men …' (245), while Turk himself seems to have betrayed the tough role he modelled for them. Their response is to take a bizarre revenge on Turk: they break into his garden, exhume the dog's body and nail it to his front door. The outcome is that this moment becomes part of a recurrent nightmare: 'For the people they continued to make love to in their dreams did not always have vaginas and the dog looked on, its tongue lewdly lolling out, observing it all' (249). For Turk, the dog had clearly been an object of displaced affection for a lost lover, 'a man who had died five years before and left his bed cold and empty' as well as for 'lost classrooms full of young faces' (239). For the ex-pupils, the dead dog is the emblem of their own repressed homosexual desires, repressed in the process of being constructed as 'men', an experience through which their sexual potentialities were restricted and curtailed to fit the appropriate behaviour of the orthodox male.

Similar issues can be found in the story 'The Puzzling Nature of Blue', which relates the issues of colonial capitalism and masculinity in an intriguing fantasy scenario. Its central male character, Vincent, is a hippy capitalist like the two characters in 'War Crimes'. Involved with the anti-war movement where he wears faded jeans and attacks American imperialism in Vietnam, he is also a first-rate economist and a newly appointed director of a UK chemical company, Farrow (Australia), with a fawn gabardine suit for the board meetings. The contradictions of dress, badges for seemingly opposing life-styles, embody the inner contradictions of his character. He is apparently a sincere supporter of anti-imperialism and suffers a continual conflict between his principles and his desire to succeed. He is a successful businessman and a failed poet. Business he sees 'as a creative act'. 'Cool and professional in his new suit', he has a leap of creative imagination to solve the seemingly unrelated problems of how to stop pilfering in a subsidiary works on Upward Island and deal with an unwanted supply of a company product, the now-banned drug Eupholon which has the peculiar side-effect of turning people blue. Vincent's solution is to store the drug in the Upward Island warehouse so that any pilferers will turn blue and be 'a living demonstration of the powers of the company to mark those who transgress its laws' (151). But the outcome of this commercial genius is guilt and remorse at his 'terrible brilliance. He had helped a colonial power (Farrow) wreak havoc and injury on an innocent people' (151). Yet his plan leads to unexpected results: after some pilfering and shootings, a revolution breaks out on the island reportedly led by people with blue hands, while Vincent is sacked from both the board and the anti-war committee when they each learn of his duplicitous involvement with the other, and he undergoes a collapse into drunken self-pity as a result.

This raises issues of colonial exploitation and the contradictions of individual complicity in that process. But the description of the story so far has left out a crucial narrative strategy. Vincent's story of the Upward Island revolution is contained within a narrative frame: the narrator of the story is a woman called Anita (158), who has taken pity on Vincent's self-destructive drunkenness but at the same time resents his dependency on her. Her attitude to Vincent in the first section of the story is itself contradictory: she feels exploited by him but cannot bring herself to assert herself and get rid of him. She welcomes his contributions such as building her a wall and is furious that Vincent seems to expect her to accept his sexual advances as a result. She plans revenge on him, part of which is to get him to tell the story of his involvement in the Upward Island situation so that she can use it in her work as a journalist. But when towards the end of the first section she reveals that Vincent has assaulted her, she declares 'warfare' on him and unrelentingly demands that he leave.

There are a number of repercussions from this narrative structure. The female narrator speaks in the first person and in the present tense, and retells Vincent's story of the Upward Islands within that frame. The account of the assault is grafted directly on to this so we have the sense of the narrative being written in the present at different times, with an ensuing sense of uncertainty about the possible outcome. When beginning to recount Vincent's story, the narrator warns 'I can't guarantee the minor details of what follows' (147), adding to the unreliability of the narrative. In addition, the issues of colonial exploitation in the Upward Islands are echoed in the relationship between the narrator and Vincent: he exploits her manipulatively, colonising her space, creating a reciprocal emotional dependency in her and inflicting violence which finally provokes her mini-revolution of telling him to leave. Although the story creates this parallel subtly, it is clear from the peculiar second half that the overlap of sexual exploitation with commercial and colonial exploitation is central to its concerns, but with surprising results.

The second part of the story reveals the narrator's capitulation to Vincent, but also the inversion of Vincent's own role as a man. Again in the present tense, the narrator tells Vincent's story, this time his remorseful involvement with the Upward

Island revolutionaries in an attempt to rid himself of his guilt at their exploitation, signalled in the blue stain of the drug, Eupholon. The islanders use his labour, his legal and economic expertise and elect him to the council. Finally the island president, Solly, who has befriended Vincent, suggests Vincent should adopt the common colour of the councillors, blue, by taking some of the Eupholon pills. Vincent realises that Solly had known of his complicity in their predicament all along and, moreover, that the revolutionaries 'are fucking delighted' that he sent the pills (158). But there is a catch: in order to get the pills and join the collective blueness, Vincent must get past the crack-shot guard he himself had posted outside the warehouse: he faces his own invention, in a test which has echoes of classical fables such as Theseus facing the Minotaur in the labyrinth.

This explores the ambiguous effects of the colonial process, disempowering but potentially capable of empowering trans-formation: the badge of exploitation, the blue colour intended as a policing device, is expropriated into a badge of pride, independence and freedom, a new identity. The story presents a fable of possible recuperation for post-colonial cultures, whose capacity to create a new hybrid culture from the impact of an exploitative history has been indicated by many post-colonial critics.[38] It also offers an emblem of the reciprocal effects of such transformations on the exploiter, akin to those found by George Lamming in his famous rereading of *The Tempest*.[39] In detailing Vincent's acts of penance towards the islanders, his acceptance by them and of them, as well as the gradual understanding between Vincent and the narrator, the story seems to offer a parable of redemption, sexual and political. Opening, as it does, with an image of masculine fragility, Vincent's crying, the story closes with Anita confessing her love and desire for Vincent as a result of his having changed. But it also offers a series of disturbing questions about the validity of that change and indicates how wary we should be of reading Carey's fictions as easily decoded fables. Vincent seems like a 'new man', although the story pre-dates the media invention of that concept, and anticipates many of the problems involved in it through the strange uncertainty of the ending. Vincent may have conned Anita; she may be reacting subserviently to his newly increased status; and Vincent's renewal seems predicated on 'applauding male acts of bravado'. Crucially, the story ends with Anita willingly performing oral sex on Vincent's resplendently blue penis, kneeling before him and sinking into 'a shimmering searing electric blue' as she deliberately disregards any further questions from the reader.

The barrage of questions we are presented with, the overtly stated refusal by Anita to solve them and the final absurdity of the blue penis disrupt any easy reading of the story as a naive parable, leaving us instead with an awareness of the problematics of change and the complex interrelationships between masculinity and colonial power. This subtle concern for gender issues and for the contradictions of masculinity continues in Carey's later works, particularly *Oscar and Lucinda* and *The Tax Inspector*.

These 'stories of the nether regions' (2) offer some of Carey's most experimental and disturbing work. They have the bizarre extravagance of J.G. Ballard or Kurt Vonnegut, but with Carey's distinctive imagination displayed at its quirky best. Their writing is sometimes patchy, awkward, almost deliberately raw or clumsy, sometimes with little sense of characterisation or plot; yet this sketchy and unfinished quality generates a sparky electricity. Despite his apparent move into a more realist narrative practice, his longer fictions share a surprising amount with his stories in ways which have become increasingly clear as his work has developed.

Bliss (1981)

Here on the outposts of the American Empire ... (*Bliss*, 9)

CAREY's first published novel capitalised on the success of his stories to exhilarating effect. Its anarchic narratology puzzled many reviewers,[1] but as Carey's *œuvre* grows, its mix of satiric realism, fable, fantasy and manic cartoon quality seem entirely characteristic. After *War Crimes* was awarded the New South Wales Premier Award in 1980, *Bliss* received the same prize in 1982, as well as the Miles Franklin and the National Book Council awards. It became a well-received film in 1985, the year of *Mad Max III*, winning best picture, director and screenplay awards from the Australian Film Institute, as well as being shown as the official Australian entry at the Cannes Film festival.

In *Bliss*, the hippy capitalists of 'War Crimes' are replaced by the more conventional scenario of hippies versus capitalists, but with a complex sense of the contradictions which cross these seemingly opposed cultures as Harry Joy is caught between the two worlds. Harry is an innocent, a 'Good Bloke' (9), blissfully unaware of the corruption of the world and his own complicity in it. His near-death experience leads to his being reborn, waking to the realities around him but unable to escape them until the last section of the book when he finally joins Honey Barbara's hippy community on Bog Onion Road.

This story-line displays the opposing poles which Carey's cautionary tale investigates. The Joy's advertising business provokes an exposé of the effects of capitalism, embodied in the 'decadent utopias' (246) and American dreams of the world of business and in the novel's futuristic cancer epidemic. The interrogation also takes in the related cultures of paranoia, power and institutional violence, as well as the construction and enforcement of 'normality'. This exploitative social order is opposed to Bog Onion Road and the post-1968 dreams of natural living in the hippy commune with its alternative lifestyles; but the novel reveals the interrelationships between the two worlds, the way in which the hippy ideal was dependent on the capitalist world it rejected. These ambiguities and contradictions are foregrounded through the novel's hybrid narrative strategies. The mixture of satirical realism, fantasy, and political-moral fable, in a narrative which is also a story about storytelling, creates a peculiar double vision, playfully post-modern and satirically post-colonial at the same time. We can see some of the ambiguities involved by considering first the stylistic and formal aspects of the novel.

Although Carey felt at the time that his writing was moving away from the experimental,[2] *Bliss* is characteristically eclectic. The sudden crossover from satirical realism into fantasy with the revelation of the futuristic cancer epidemic indicates the extent to which Carey presents an uneven narrative mixture in which he deliberately refuses to smooth over the narrative cracks in order to achieve the mythical status of a 'classic' fictional artwork. Instead he exploits the narrative jumps, from the futuristic to an almost eighteenth-century 'dear reader' address (33). Anthony Hassall calls this an 'unsettling combination of post-modern form and traditional satiric indignation ... that transgresses both the ordinary boundaries of the text, and the self-referentiality of much post modern writing.'[3] The effect is to dislodge the fiction in ways which, as Karen Lamb suggests, 'unyoked it from the conventional expectations of longer narratives' in a manner that most of the novel's reviewers could not recognise.[4] Elements of speculative fantasy are signalled immediately with Harry's 'out of body' experience, a speculation about multiple coexistent universes, not unlike the theories of contemporary physicists,[5] or the mind-bending quantum 'smearing' entertained more recently by Australian science fiction writer Greg Egan in his novel

Quarantine (1992). The end of the book reveals the novel to be a futuristic narrative by Harry and Honey's children post-dating the cancer epidemic (282).

There are also elements of allegory and satirical comic fantasy. The allegorical strand is signalled by the emblematic names: Joy, Honey, Krappe Chemicals, Detectives Macdonald and Herpes. The comedy is equally overt. Harry's confrontation with the police after his Fiat has been squashed by an elephant is both farcical and a notable satirical moment in the novel's treatment of state institutional violence: the police are less interested in the true story about how Harry's car was flattened by an elephant than in being entertained, and let Harry go once he has told them an engaging story, despite the fact that it had nothing to do with his arrest (65–73). Equally acute is the absurdly funny episode depicting the visit of the Sea Scouts to the mental hospital in the belief that it is the ginger toffee factory (137–40). Carey's comic style allows for sarcastic points to be scored through a bleak comic mode, as with Harry's sojourn up the fig tree in his back garden which reveals Bettina's affair with Joel and the incestuous antics of his son and daughter; or when Harry is visited in hospital by the Reverend Desmond Pearce with his personal creed of the 4Ps, 'Prying, Preaching, Praying, and Pissing-off-when-you're-not-wanted' (38). The Rev. Des is a good example of Carey's comic caricatures with his bluntly consoling theological arguments: 'Well, you've got a bugger of a problem ... Look old mate ... do you really think God is such a bastard he wants to punish you for all eternity?' (40–1).

Also important for the comic impact at the stylistic level is the distinctive mixture of the clipped prose style and idiosyncratic imagery, which can be simultaneously funny and keenly observed: 'When, sitting by the window, he dropped his nose into the brandy balloon it was like the proboscis of some creature whose evolutionary success had been based on its ability to live on the fumes of volatile fluids' (62). Such off-beat ideas and vivid expression are characteristic of Carey's imagination and style, exploiting the application of a common idea to an unexpected experience with surreal results. In line with Carey's own perception of the cartoon-like elements in his work, the comic effects come close to the manic style of a Garry Larson, while the action of the novel can get frenziedly Tom and Jerry-ish.

This eclectic mixture is held together by a narrative which has elements of magic realism alongside social satire. Notably, there is the García Márquez-like manner of anticipating future action through changes of tense and the use of the future in the past.[6] As in Rushdie's *Midnight's Children*, this fluid treatment of time, with its suggestion of the plurality and simultaneity of multiple histories, allows a usefully disorientating flexibility. The opening anticipates the future: 'Harry Joy was to die three time ...', and then jumps to the present: 'There is Harry Joy ...', and then back to the past: 'Harry Joy saw all of this ...' (7). Such tense shifting creates a narrative drift which allows the mixture of different periods of the characters' lives, past and future, imminent or distant. In part one, Joel does not yet know of Harry's near death, and '[i]t would be another minute before he would know ...' (11). As in Márquez, the effect is also to give a fatalistic sense of the destiny of the characters as almost pre-determined in an existing script.

The most obviously Márquezian of these is the early antici-pation of David's death in part five: 'When he was about to die in a foreign country, years later, Harry's son would tell his captors that he had been born in an electrical storm' (26), which overtly echoes the opening of Márquez's masterpiece: 'Many years later, as he faced the firing squad, Colonel Aureliano Buendía was to remember that distant afternoon when his father took him to discover ice'[7] with its magical mixture of the terminal, the marvellous and the conditional. David's future death, when he becomes mythologised as The Man with the White Suit, after abandoning his business principles to run guns for the liber-ationists, is told later in fragmented parts in the future perfect (189–91, 231–6), creating the sense of there being a multiplicity of possible stories about these characters alongside the ones we are hearing, rather like the layers of different worlds Harry briefly inhabits in his out-of-body experience.

This sense of narrative plurality in the story-line gives the novel a metafictional quality, foregrounded through Vance's stories to Harry and Harry's later role as a storyteller. The word 'story' and the notion of telling stories recurs throughout the novel[8] as part of an examination of how the characters develop the dreams they have and how they delude themselves about the lives they lead, 'how stories can trap people or lead them astray, or take them, once in a while, to blissful conclusions'.[9] This allows Carey to explore fictionality as an issue, playing self-conscious post-modern games, and at the same time use this as a satirical strategy to expose the fiction of normality.

This analysis of normality is central to the satire in the book. Harry's 'death' shocks him out of his complacency into an awareness of the true nature of the life he leads, albeit in the absurdist form of his belief that he is a 'Captive' in hell and surrounded by 'Actors' who are substitutes for the people he knew. Harry's paranoia about his life in 'hell' suggests that normality is an illusion or construction encouraging complicity in a state of affairs we might otherwise reject or question. Through Harry's bleakly comic attempts to break with the given fictions and scripts of normality, Carey deals with the existential experience of achieving authentic behaviour, what Sartre called the possible 'self-recovery of being which was previously corrupted' that might lead to existential authenticity and freedom.[10]

Harry's relationship with his son David is an example. After the night when Harry took him out into the lightning (26), David lives a double life, agreeing to be a doctor, pretending to a fiction of conventional self – to 'be like his father, that was what they all wanted' (27) – but in actuality evolving a successful business empire as a drug dealer and having an incestuous relationship with his sister, Lucy, in which she gives him blow-jobs in return for deals of marijuana. The misunderstandings between father and son are captured when David visits Harry in hospital: David feels 'an almost overwhelming desire to tell his father what he was really like' and Harry wants to tell David about his death experience, yet 'neither of them quite knew what to do' (35). When Harry returns home, David reveals part of the truth (53–5), and Harry accepts it just as he does Lucy's revelation that she is a Communist (56). Harry's acceptance is merely an ambiguously authentic act, since he mistakes David's truthfulness as part of the elaborate pretence he imagines himself trapped in, and sees these events as confirmation that the people surrounding him are actors pretending to be his family (54–6), acting to a script of normality which he has seen through.

In the case of David, his dreams of 'Other Places' (27) take their shape from the stories Harry inherited from his father, Vance, and which he passes on to David. The tale of the Beggar-King, in Harry's 'directionless' and depoliticised version (28), inculcates an avaricious element in David's character through fantasies of conquistadors in South America (29). His fate is fragmentarily linked to another of these tales, Vance's story of the butterfly in Bogotá, an anecdote of anticipation, romance and disappointment, emblematised by a butterfly flying away in the sunlight (29). This enigmatic image recurs for Harry when he is trying to write his note of farewell (45), and in the narrative future at the moment of David's execution. He determines to die for a futile cause, and although '[f]or an instant panic fluttered its wings in his ears', in doing so becomes himself the centre of a mythic story told as an embodiment of heroism after his death by the commandant in charge of his execution: 'The story of the man with the white suit ends formally, always the same, with the sun coming out as he falls, and they say *Pero era sólo una mariposa* (but it was only a butterfly) *que se volaba* (flying away). The wrapper of a sweet confection delivered fifty-five years through time' (236).

David lives out a script arbitrarily handed down to him through his father, which is then equally arbitrarily handed on. Carey's image picks up on the classic statement of chaos theory – a butterfly which flaps its wings in Tokyo may cause a hurricane in South America. In doing so, it suggests how the hidden effects of handed-down scripts and stories on a character's destiny might embody this peculiarly post-modern aspect of organic physics. Within the apparently contingent and random nature of life, chaos theory argues that there is nevertheless pattern, but the pattern is to be found in natural irregularity rather than regularity, disorder rather than order. Carey explores this further in *Oscar and Lucinda*, as he does the experience of father-son relationships.

Normality is investigated as a social as well as an individual phenomenon. As Gramsci argued, normality is a political state manufactured and maintained through agencies of coercion and consent, and effectively covers up the truth with soothing delusions of the dominant cultural hegemony.[11] Prior to his first 'death', Harry's existence was structured around his own self-satisfaction and complacency. His lifestyle, his illusions about his family, his ability to make other people think of him as simultaneously knowing and a Good Bloke while in fact being an ingénue (9, 23–4), are symptoms of his normality, complicity and his role as an archetypally successful middle-class business-man, and are reinforced by cultural mechanisms which help manufacture consent. Harry believes what he reads in the papers (9, 10, 61); he is ignorant about the true nature of his success in advertising and naively unconscious of the inequalities and injustices around him, in which he later realises he was involved. Indeed, 'his very blindness reassured those around him and made them feel that their fears and nightmares were nothing but the products of their own overwrought imaginations' (10).

This investigation of the illusion of normality and the related issues of personal responsibility widens to encompass the detrimental effects of Western capitalism and of the institutions which support it. The focus on the media world of advertising invokes the post-modern condition of what Douglas Kellner calls 'techo-capitalism', in which the fusion of advertising and art into a 'commodity aesthetics' constitutes 'new forms of culture which colonise everyday life and transform politics, economics and social relations'. In this social configuration, advertising has become 'the aphrodisiac by which a submission to corporate advances could be achieved'.[12] Bettina's obsession with her designs allows Carey some digs at the advertising business world. We are instructed about 'comps' (179), and are given a sense of advertising as a new art (205) like 'wonderful flowers which grew amongst the rubble' (182), as well as discovering the corrupt side of the business through Adrian Clunes of the bluntly named Krappe Chemicals (115).

On a wider level, the advertising business is the embodiment of the imperialist forces of Western capital. As in the stories, Carey shows Australia as one of the 'outposts of the American Empire' (9) with its city inhabitants subject to American dreams. Harry developed his ambitions for the trembling 'glass towers' of New York (15, 18) from his father, Vance. These are also the seed of David's 'vision of New York' (31) and his business drive as a dope dealer. Bettina's dreams of New York (20–1, 90–1) are the badge of her lust to succeed in business, to become 'an advertising hot-shot' (91), in the service of which she 'became more American than the Americans' (94). As Lucy says, '[s]he believes the whole American myth' (214).

The element which reveals the nature of capitalist delusions most explosively is the cancer theme. The linkage between capitalism and cancer is part of the satirically apocalyptic side to the novel. Aldo, the owner of Milano's who himself has cancer, has a theory about 'this cancer business': 'it is being sent to punish us for how we live, all this shit we breathe, all this rubbish we eat … cancer is going to save us from ourselves. It is going to stop us eating and breathing shit', to which Harry responds naively 'What shit?' (61).

What finally shocks Harry into realising his own complicity in environmental exploitation are Alex Duvall's revelations about the businesses represented by the advertising agency. Alex is 'a man of principle', a Communist Party voter (77), but also utterly compromised by his role in advertising and its unprincipled acceptance of clients known to be producing carcinogenic products. His solution to this state of affairs is to live an inauthentic double life, manufacturing undisclosed critical reports expressing his true views and then filing them in a private cabinet as a future justification to 'the revolutionary investigators he imagined would one day sit in judgement on him' (77). The reborn Harry cannot accept such double-think and starts attempting to clean up the business by jettisoning the Krappe Chemicals account, and obsessively cleaning the house to the frustration of his wife and son (86–9); but Alex confronts his new found contrition with blunt honesty: '[a]ll your life you walk around and never see anything bad … Now you bloody wake up. God knows why' (131). When Harry reveals to Adrian Clunes of Krappe Chemicals that he has evidence that their products cause cancer, Adrian Clunes tells him he is 'a child', 'the newest, most impossible idealist in the world' since '[t]he whole of the western world is built on things that cause cancer. They can't afford to stop making them' (116). Rather than be a dangerously naive idealist, Harry should learn that we 'are all in Hell … It's a question of making yourself comfortable' (145).

Other characters present different views of the cancer theme which explore these social and ethical contradictions further. Lucy and her ex-communist boy friend Ken are millenarially aware of being 'the first people to come to the end of time' and Ken is compiling a 'Catalogue of good things about the end of the world' (202). From this terminal state not even Honey Barbara with her demineralised water is safe: '"You'll still get cancer," Lucy grinned, "just like the rest of us"' (206). As we might expect, this link between capitalism and cancer is challenged as political and subversive by characters representing capitalism's supporting institutional forces. The police interrogating Joel after Bettina's act of 'terrorism' find a book called *The Politics of Cancer* and ask Joel whether he thinks 'cancer is political' (243). When Harry asserts that saccharine causes cancer, Alice Dalton, director of the mental hospital, accuses him of being a communist. She argues with partisan institutional acumen that cancer is produced by emotional repression,[13] thus accounting for the number of cancer patients imprisoned in her hospital's 'growth industry', while the communists and liberals who see cancer as a product of corrupt business practices are simply jealous of power and success (159–61). Alice Dalton's hospital is a model enterprise run by someone who has uncompromisingly clear market priorities: 'this is a business and I am doing it to make money, just like everybody else' (138). The institutional control of identity is exposed as Harry finds his name has been reallocated to Alex, so that he must effectively become someone else (144). The hospital section exposes violence in the psychiatric industry with a satirical comedy akin to Ken Kesey's *One Flew Over the Cuckoo's Nest* (1962).[14]

From Aldo's introduction of it, the word cancer repeats itself with increasing emphasis until the sudden revelation of an apocalyptic epidemic which brings about the chaotic disruption of Western civilisation, as 'the angry cancer victims could no longer be contained by devices as simple as Alice Dalton's Ward L, and took to the streets in what began as demonstrations and ended in half-organised bands, looting for heroin first, and then everything else' (249). The unexpectedness of this futuristic glimpse complements the increasing anarchy of Harry's life and the fragmenting society in which he is implicated. The terminal quality is well caught in Carey's view of how the film version of the book should have been: 'Visually, there should have been a poisoned paradise. There should have been crap pouring into the sky. Visually, the viewer should have seen what Harry Joy didn't see'.[15] The film, in fact, is perhaps even more hybrid and eclectic than the novel itself, though with less successful results, as indicated by Carey's unhappiness with the way the film 'trivialises the book', when it should have 'been informed by a very strong political sense, a broader sense of what hell might mean'.[16]

Bettina's fate as a victim of the epidemic illustrates how *Bliss* might be seen as an ecological cautionary tale. She is an utterly selfish character who 'didn't want to be good, she wanted to be successful' (14). As she admits to Harry, 'I was never a sweet little wifey. I was a hard ambitious bitch' (173). Bettina believes in 'her glittering visions of capitalism' (177) and 'accepted fumes in the air' (206) without realising that the two were intimately connected and would kill her. She also believes 'that the whole cancer theory was a Communist conspiracy' (215). The irony of Bettina's role in the novel is that at the moment of her potential success, she 'wakes up' to find she has contracted a terminal cancer and '[h]er whole life had been built on bullshit' (240). Her cancer and suicidal revenge on the petrol company executives (241–2) can be seen as moral retribution for her unredeemed egoism, while Harry's escape to the homely role of storyteller and tree-planter in the commune illustrates the possibility of positive transformation and redemption.

For some critics this ecological moralism is too simplistic. Graham Burns sees the book as repeating 'the false notion that the vast majority of cancers are environmentally caused', a 'paranoid view of cancer as the evil retributive force lurking at the heart of industrial capitalism'.[17] In support of his critique, Burns quotes Susan Sontag's influential text *Illness as Metaphor* (1978). Sontag argues that such views of cancer are dangerously metaphorical distortions and, effectively, mystifications. As such she finds them morally impermissible, an insufficient response either to the actual problems of illness or to the problems of society, 'an encouragement to simplify what is complex'. According to Sontag, to see cancer as retribution for capitalism's, or for that matter communism's, environmental sins is 'a cliché' and 'as unsound scientifically' as to say it is caused by 'mismanaged emotions'.[18]

Yet *Bliss* is not a political tract, or even simply an ecological fable. It complicates its potential messages so that even the apparent positives are to some degree ironised, while the supposed negative elements display a contradictory energy and dynamism. For example, Harry's redemption is by no means clear-cut. He finds it difficult to abandon his involvement in the hell of business civilisation. He agrees to promote Bettina's advertisements, well aware that the cancer map 'glowed malignantly in his mind's eye' (195). It is Bettina who displays the creative energy, however cynical or misguided, and justifies Carey's assertion that it is the women in the book who 'have the drive and the ideas'.[19] The first of a number of powerful women characters in Carey's work, Bettina is an advertising genius, an artist (176, 180–1), capturing for Carey the genuine 'passion' people in advertising felt about their craft.[20] Captivated by her creative inspiration, Harry temporarily abandons the redemption offered by Honey Barbara and relapses into his former trust of the *status quo* and 'the protection of Those in Charge ... It was they who trafficked in poisons, controlled the distribution of safety, the purity of water and air, or, more probably, the lack of it' (225). It is only through Bettina's suicide and Honey Barbara's disappearance that Harry is able to escape; but what he escapes into is itself subject to satirical scrutiny.

The hippy commune of Bog Onion Road is hardly presented as a plausible alternative to the corruptions of the business world. Honey Barbara may be the agency for Harry's change but she herself is critical of the commune she lives in and a contradictory character in her own right. She sees much of what goes on in the commune as 'Hippy mumbo-jumbo' (274). While she has a belief in healthy eating and practices T'ai Chi, she is nevertheless a practical person with her bee-keeping skills (164) and has a 'Victorian' moral puritanism in her attitude to drugs and hedonism (201, 214). She is also 'Honey Barbara, pantheist, healer, whore' (169), fascinated by the attractions of city life (126–7) as her father Paul is fascinated by Harry's stories of city life (270), helping support the commune and herself by a yearly period of 'turning tricks'. She epitomises the contradictory way in which the 1968 message of 'tune in and drop out' was both a valuable counter ethic and proposed a false dichotomy, since in a sense there is no 'outside' of the system to escape to. Although her father leaves the Peugeot rusting in the forest, they are nevertheless dependent on her Commer van using multinational petrol (264–5), while 'Clive and the other paranoids', with their specially contrived maze of forest roads, pretend to a delusory self-sufficiency and autonomy: as she realises, '[i]f the cops wanted anything important, they'd do a helicopter bust. They didn't need roads' (267).

The commune is viewed as a 'peculiar hotch-potch of religion and belief and superstition' (163), including Krishnas, Buddhists, the Horse people, the Ananda Marga, and others with any number of beliefs about the nature of reality (256, 123). As with Damian, Honey's companion who selfishly fails in his responsibilities to sell the dope crop (125–6), or the rather manic Clive who threatens Harry with his bush hook and owes work to other commune members (258), New Age religions are no guarantee of socially responsible behaviour. Carey's own experience of community living seems to have left him sceptically enthusiastic for its ideals and healthily sarcastic about its deficiencies: even in the commune, 'there are evil fuckers around the place. There're guns and there is witchcraft going on …'[21] Two years after writing the novel in Yandina, while still arguing 'I believe all that stuff', he was also stressing that Harry's salvation in *Bliss* was not 'a blue print of salvation for the rest of society', adding wryly 'I mean, I think trees are wonderful …'[22]

His simultaneous scepticism and regard come through in the hilarious portrayal of the terminally stoned and appropriately named Daze, meditating about wedges and trying on Harry's silk shirts as if they might be dangerous. The portrait is absurd, humorous and affectionate all at the same time: 'He did not think anything very profound, but he enjoyed his thoughts and he discovered and rediscovered things for himself all day in this manner. If he had had company he would have talked about the wedges, punctuating his meditations with "Mmms" and "Ahs" and his companion would sometimes be amused, sometimes bored, sometimes even enlightened' (253).

Yet, despite the satirical critique of the commune, the ending of the novel endorses Harry's escape from capitalism, while Harry himself is elevated from Good Bloke to tribal storyteller and tree-keeper (276–7). Harry's role as communal soothsayer at Bog Onion Road is based on the stories he learned from his father, a package of dreams which at first corrupted him, but finally help regenerate him through his new role, and which he retells to these 'refugees from a broken culture who had only the flotsam of belief and ceremony to cling to' and 'were hungry for ceremony and story' (277). The truth of Vance's stories about Native American Hopi customs, or of the Vision Splendid (16–17), is less important than their role as conduits for some kind of ancestral memory. Carey's text seems to suggests that stories are consoling delusions and also, perversely, the carriers of human truths through the exploratory power of the imagination.

Bliss is a dystopia which ends by wearing its hidden utopian heart on its sleeve a little too overtly for some critics.[23] A more charitable reading might suggest that the novel's shifting narrative tones or manners add complexity, depth and ambiguity to what might otherwise seem a straight moral fable. Carey himself has indicated that he intended the ending as an unalloyed celebration, commenting that 'the whole book stands or falls' on the pastoral lyricism of the ending: if he had titled the book as he had wished, *Waiting for the Barbarians*, 'that would have placed the ending in the right context' which might have avoided the accusations of its being escapist since it would have suggested merely a temporary escape from a terminal future.[24] Nevertheless, the play of tones throughout the book does not necessarily fulfil his own prescriptions by privileging the final note of benevolent celebration adopted through the voice of Harry's children. The ironising of the commune is as satirically significant as the critique of the more life-threatening absurdities of the advertising business. If we take the moral fable as part rather than all of the novel, then 'the final Happy Ending is pure fairy story', as Jill Neville has suggested,[25] and fits into the mixture of narrative genres through which Carey creates his satirical form. Rather than being a weakness, the shifts from satire to farcical comedy to bleak apocalyptic warning dislodges too simple a view of the pastoral panegyric of the ending in fruitful ways. Carey's imagination engages with the conventions of realist fiction without necessarily becoming trapped by them. He is able to transgress realist norms in ways which are conceptually exploratory as well as fictionally convincing.

Perhaps this is a reflection of the final status of the narrative as a series of stories about Harry Joy told by his children (281–2). The extent to which this finally revealed narrational source actually works throughout the book is questionable. The narrative voice generally adopts a conventionally omniscient and knowing third-person point of view.[26] The jumps in tense, for example, are also dependent upon a use of the narrator voice which is at times deliberately up-front, as in the ironic address to 'you, dear reader' after we have seen aspects of Harry's family he has no suspicion of (33), or in the instructional tone of the imperative address: 'But, look …' (36); 'Look at him …' (49). Meanwhile, other sections, such as Honey Barbara's view of her relationship with Harry (217), adopt a different narrative position, while the section devoted to Daze evokes an intimacy with the foibles of life in Bog Onion Road commune which does suggests an insider's viewpoint. The 'community of narrative' achieved by the pluralistic ending[27] is more rightly viewed as a heteroglossia, a Bakhtinian polyphony of narrative viewpoints, tones and angles characteristic of this eclectic and adventurous fiction.[28]

Illywhacker (1985)

You people don't realise what it is you have to sell.
(*Illywhacker*, 348)

WITH *Illywhacker*, Carey's success achieved international dimensions. It was published first in the UK and USA, something of an irony for a novel exposing cultural imperialism.[1] The University of Queensland Press acquired the Australian rights and implemented a wide advertising campaign using international responses as promotion. The effect was to increase Carey's profile and sales dramatically in Australia and abroad.[2] The novel won three of the major Australian literary prizes and was shortlisted for the British Booker Prize.

Illywhacker examines twentieth-century Australian history with the savage humour and fantasy of the earlier fiction now placed within an epic framework. The result is a novel with energy, panache and sardonic vision, which mixes family history with satirical fable and fantasy in an abundance of play and arraignment. Like *Bliss*, *Illywhacker* transgresses and undermines presumptions of formal continuity and genre coherence: it both entertains and indicts as it investigates the construction of fundamental Australian mythologies, the visions, dreams and lies of the national psyche. In the process, it deconstructs the contemporary state of the nation. Through this picaresque treatment of the Badgeries' family history Carey felt as if he were 'at last trying to come to grips with what it means to be an Australian and what Australia is'.[3]

The novel opens with an epigram from Mark Twain:

'Australian history is almost always picturesque; indeed, it is so curious and strange, that it is itself the chiefest novelty the country has to offer … It does not read like history, but like the most beautiful lies'.[4] The epigram also formed the basis for the title of Brian Kiernan's anthology of contemporary Australian fiction, *The Most Beautiful Lies* (1977), a title Carey suggested to Kiernan after discovering the Twain quote at 'the end of the late 70s', having 'kept it for years' and feeling he was never going to be able to use it himself;[5] and it became the title for the 1986–7 film on Carey by Joanne Penglase and Don Featherstone.

Lies and lying are significant in *Illywhacker* in two related ways – as characteristic of the narrator, Herbert Badgery, and as part of the analysis of Australia's self-construction. While in gaol, Herbert studies history and comes across the fictional M. V. Anderson's history of Australia with its biting exposé of national origins.[6] The invented extract (456) acts as a programme for the lying theme, achieving increased significance in the more recent context of the Mabo land rights decision with its challenge to the notion of *terra nullius*.[7] By linking its central narrator's fabulatory capacities with white Australia's misrepresentation to itself of its past and present, Carey's novel creates an exposé of the colonial process through a post-modern extravagance and the way various narrative elements adopt emblematic qualities. These include the narrative metaphor of the pet shop, the treatment of histories, and the presentation of Herbert himself, all as part of an investigation of the state of the nation.

Herbert tells his rambling autobiography in a wry manner which creates a distinctively risqué tone: 'now I feel no more ashamed of my lies than my farts (I rip forth a beauty to underline the point) … I think I'm growing tits' (11). Even when dealing with the diverse stories about other characters, his voice in many ways *is* the novel. Having started the early draft in the third person, Carey reconceived Herbert as a liar and as first-person narrator while sitting in a doctor's office.[8] This gave him the vehicle to carry the anarchic mixture of narratives, stories and forms which the book spawns, as Herbert's children are '[s]pawned by lies, suckled on dreams, infested with dragons' (359).

Herbert proclaims himself a liar at the outset and occasions the novel's first joke: 'I have always been a liar. I say that early to set things straight' (11). With the audacity of a master salesman, he disclaims any responsibility for our irritation or disappointment as purchasers of his memoirs: '*Caveat emptor*' (literally 'let the buyer see to it'). Herbert tries our credulity to the full by revealing that he is 139 years old – which, since he also tells us that he was born in 1886, would place his present narrative in the year 2025. It is a deception whose full significance is only gradually revealed.

This novelist-as-liar device has analogies with the 'jumble of incident, dialogue, reflection, etc.' which forms Joseph Furphy's anarchically experimental Australian anti-novel *Such is Life* (1903),[9] but Carey's immediate context is the post-modern unreliability of the storyteller. Herbert's unreliability is comparable with that of Rushdie's narrator in *Midnight's Children* (1981). There, Saleem reveals his own mistakes, getting the date of Gandhi's assassination wrong, for example, and then telling us so later in the novel.[10] This reinforces a sense that history is a construction from particular subjective points of view: like the perforated sheet through which Saleem's grandfather viewed his future wife, there is no whole picture available to anyone. Instead, individuals construct history from whatever materials are at their disposal and the reader is made aware of that partiality.

Carey incorporates something of this into *Illywhacker*. The book displays itself as a yarn spun 'on the hoof' by an incorrigible 'yacker' with an obsessive inclination to tell tall stories. Herbert tells us how he spent a summer in Mallee living in a hole in the ground (33), how an Australian Chinaman taught him to disappear and generate dragons (220–1), and how his Blériot monoplane was eaten by cattle in Darley in 1917 (163). This last detail, along with many others, was based on actuality: it happened to Carey's grandfather and the remains of the plane hang in the Sydney Powerhouse Museum.[11] Herbert also plays tricks on us as readers, such as promising us 'hanky-panky' at the outset (12), only to castigate us later for expecting any (227), and then admit he was lying as he delivers some (303).

Yet, despite his role as an 'illywhacker', a professional trickster or con-man, Herbert is primarily a digressive narrator rather than a game-playing one. As with any shaggy dog story, *Illywhacker* is full of sub-narratives branching off from the main one. Within Herbert's there are any number of other stories, being told by Herbert or by other characters through him. His storytelling backtracks on itself and assumes an audience *within* the novel as well as the audience of the readers *of* the novel, as when he tells Jack McGrath of his early life (38), or Leah of his year-long relationship with Phoebe's mother, Molly (328, referring back to 205–6). Herbert tells us the history of Leah Goldstein up to her arrival in his makeshift camp in 1931 (233–90), cutting suddenly back to the present in the camp (245–6), and later to an episode of his own life earlier that year when he tried to sell an A Model Ford to Miss Adamson of Morrisons (265–71). Herbert's son, Charles, has his story told in Book Three, and himself digresses into telling his earlier life story to the Chaffreys, only to be interrupted by Herbert telling us of his life in prison (391, 409, 415).

As in Sterne's *The Life and Opinions of Tristram Shandy* (1759–67), Carey's novel leads the reader in extravagant and fantastical circles as we follow the fortunes of the Badgeries. Like Joseph Furphy,[12] Carey acknowledges Sterne as a precursor, although he believes his novel is 'better structured'.[13] In *Tristram Shandy*, the hero purports to tell us his history and is side-tracked by digressions to the extent of not actually being born until the third volume of the novel. In *Illywhacker*, despite his digressions, Herbert dominates the proceedings and is unquestionably the centre of his own story, so much so as to explode all the conventions of probability associated with traditional first-person narrative.[14] He quite simply knows too much about the other characters. Like *Tristram Shandy*, the book is the narrator: its formal coherence derives from the centrality of Herbert, and from thematic shaping of the three books around the generational expansion of the Badgery family.

As in many other post-modern novels, Herbert also becomes an author as well as a storyteller. This allows Carey to investigate storytelling and fiction-making, raising issues similar to those found in *Bliss*. Herbert's double role as surrogate author and dealer in lies presents him in the process of constructing his own identity and destiny, foregrounding the theme of personal and national representation. With Leah, he writes a version of his prison experiences called *Gaol Bird* which, he admits, was 'a pack of lies' (409). The status of the novel itself shifts when we read chapter 54 of Book Three, a letter written as if interjected into one of Herbert's 'little hoard of notebooks' (549), in which Leah accuses him of distortion and lying in his account of their lives. As Elizabeth Webby and Martin Duwell have noticed,[15] lying and fiction-making are also analogous to Herbert's other great fabricatory activity, building, as he moves from improvised shacks to the more ambitious dreams of his house for Phoebe or his 'opening out' of the emporium.

Illywhacker is a less obsessively self-conscious and self-exposing fiction than we find in John Fowles's *The French Lieutenant's Woman*, Elizabeth Jolley's *Miss Peabody's Inheritance* or even Margaret Atwood's *Lady Oracle*. The surprises Carey pulls out of his fictional hat are incongruous and incredible enough to satisfy Twain's view of Australian history, rather than being the kind of narrative deceptions practised by Fowles, and this book's project is not so much to play tricks with the history of the novel as to do so with the history of Australia. But like these other works, the exposure of fictionality is also used to reveal how social roles can become restrictive scripts which might be changed if we took existential responsibility for our lives. Carey has said he found 'the idea of lies becoming truths was an interesting thing to deal with in writing fiction' and allowed him to 'make Herbert Badgery the author and these people in the cage creatures of his imagination',[16] a theme which leads directly to the novel's post-colonial exposé of national mythologies.

Illywhacker depicts a particular phase of Australian culture and nationalism, a search for identity which went wrong. Carey conceived the novel as a survey through three generations, from the confidence man, through 'a kind of degeneration from entrepreneurial capitalism', to 'the pet shop people'.[17] Herbert's 'salesman's sense of history' (343), which gives such priority to salesmanship and putting on a show, reveals Australia itself as a 'show', a product constructed from illusion and deception; and his life parodies his country's. Rejecting the colonial dependency which led him to sell American-made Ford motor cars, his early vision is of an independent Australian aeroplane business making an autonomous product, yet by the end of the book the Badgery entourage has become a 'menagerie' (594), exhibits trapped in the American-funded Best Pet Shop in the World.

Initially Herbert embodies what Carey has called 'a kind of entrepreneurial optimistic nationalism'.[18] Herbert's combative nationalism displays itself in a number of ways, although not as parochial chauvinism. Instead, he celebrates the diversity and detail of Australia, its landscape, localities, societies, people and characters. Despite the fact that Carey had not read him,[19] there is a Dickensian feel to the characterisation in the novel, with vivid miniature portraits of minor figures – Jack McGrath with his obsessive talk about transportation (29), the tragic O'Hagen family, or the eccentric Dr Grigson with his faded sweets, his anxious walk (147), and his hair-raising enthusiasm for the Hispano Suiza (149). This range helps account for the epic texture of the novel: it is a *One Hundred Years of Solitude* of the outback, with small-town lives and incidents woven together into a panoramic account of national history.

Herbert's life is presented as that history in the making. His narrative blends the local with the national, indicating that in Australia the two are synonymous and overlap with a proximity difficult to envisage in many other national contexts. So Herbert's revenge against his father's ill-treatment occurs in June 1895 just after a historic defeat of striking shearers by the squatters (40–1); the wake for Molly's mother takes place in the Crystal Palace Hotel, Ballarat, during which 'everybody became very Irish and very stirred and chose to remember that the dead woman's father had had his leg broken by policemen at the Eureka Stockade' (95); when Izzie Kaletsky is expelled from the Communist Party, he and Lenny are forced to sell balloons for a living at the moment of the opening of Sydney Harbour Bridge (290); and when Herbert is 'opening out' Charles's emporium he discovers bricks signed with the thumb-prints of the convicts who made them (542). The chronological structuring of the novel reinforces this proximity of the local and national: significant dates in Herbert's progress coincide with periods of Australian history as in the section covering the 1930s and the Depression.

The impetus of *Illywhacker* is both satire and commemoration. As Carey has said, the book comprises 'an extraordinarily bleak view of Australia ... and yet it is celebratory'.[20] Out-of-the-way places like Ballarat, Geelong and Carey's own Bacchus Marsh occur alongside cosmopolitan centres like Sydney, with the implication that such localities matter as part of the fabric of national life. At Herbert's bigamous marriage to Phoebe in Melbourne, 'city of dreams' (160), Dr Grigson, champion of the electric belt, feels so overcome that, he says, 'I could fancy ... that I was sitting, this very moment, in Paris', to which Herbert's unspoken response is 'I was so happy I could not find it in my heart to ask the old gentleman what was wrong with sitting in Melbourne' (161). The impulse behind Charles's pet shop is a desire to be 'lyrical about the uniqueness and beauty of Australian birds and animals' (485). But this transformation of the local into the epic is achieved with knowing irony. The celebration of the ordinary which Herbert undertakes, with his odes to obscure places and to hessian bags (48, 64), is done with a wry awareness that this is also all there is. The ambivalence is caught in Herbert's own contradictory response to Charles: Herbert wants to applaud him as 'brave and optimistic', mock him and Emma, and at the same time transform them and their drearily melancholic landscape into 'a very superior and spiteful kind of beauty' (436–7). Carey follows Herbert's comments here with a comic and affectionately sarcastic passage devoted to his home town, Bacchus Marsh, into which he squeezes a mention of his own family among names which, while they resonate perhaps in Bacchus Marsh local history, hardly make it to the world stage (437–8).

Alongside the honouring of the local, then, is an ironic sense of the provincialism of Australian society, the limits set on the dreams and visions of individuals by the lack of opportunity, resources, or connections with the international arena. It is this which frustrates Phoebe and her lover, the history teacher Annette Davidson. Phoebe's outrage against small-town attitudes is epitomised by her reaction to Mrs Kentwell and her Geelong ladies (57–9). Her rebellion against petty-mindedness is partly what undermines her relationship with Herbert. She wants adventure in other places, poetry; she wants talk of Paris, but what she hears is talk which 'was really a celebration of towns as plain (and plainer than) Geelong' (37), while all Herbert ever wants, as he admits later in the novel, is a fire and slippers (538). It leads Phoebe to Sydney and the delusory achievement of her literary efforts and soirées, captured in the title given to her magazine, *Malley's Urn* (513), a joke referring to the hoax modernist poems of Ern Malley which caused such a furore in 1944.[21]

As the title of the novel indicates, Australian language, too, receives some attention. Carey recalls the relish with which he came across the word 'illywhacker': 'I used to sit at night and I'd flick through Geoff Wilkes's *Dictionary of Australian Colloquialisms*, and other books – you know, all at random. You look through and you think "isn't that interesting", "I'd forgotten we used to say that". And I came across illywhacker. And I thought, "Oh, fantastic – exactly right". But it took me three years of looking to find it.'[22] As a 'yacker', Herbert displays many of the distinctive characteristics of Australian English, and Carey has acknowledged his efforts to recapture accurately the language of his grandfather's era, the 1930s and 1940s.[23] Herbert introduces one of the O'Hagen boys as 'Goog, which, until we started to forget our language, was the common name for a hen's egg' (63). The book is itself saturated with the flavour of Australian English and imagery: there are debates about Australian speech and language comparing it with English usage (54, 126) or American (518); there are overtly signalled usages of Australian English as when Leah and Charles debate the term illywhacker (245–6), listing its associated terms as spieler, quandong, ripperty man, and con-man; there is distinctively Australian imagery, as in the descriptions of gum trees (318), goannas (462), and the activities of swaggies, bagmen, johns and rattlers (338); and, as Paul Sharrad has mentioned, there are many other 'recondite Australianisms', such as snaffle every staver (35), cackleberry (273), and bullswack (291).[24] Adrian Mitchell for one has queried whether anyone actually used or had even heard the expression illywhacker prior to Carey's creative intervention,[25] but the success of the novel and consequent renewal of currency for the word emphasises the potential for a subversive reshaping of the English language which post-colonial writing can achieve.

Herbert can get combative in his assertion of Australia's strengths and potential. During the meeting Jack McGrath sets up to discuss the possible aeroplane manufacturing industry, the offensive 'Imaginary Englishmen' Oswald-Smith and Cocky Abbot the younger, representatives of what John Pilger calls the 'colonial mentality disciplined to serve overseas interests',[26] are confronted by Herbert with his captive king brown snake, which he claims as the emblem of the true untameable Australian: 'This snake ... has been in gaol. It is a mean bastard of an animal and it cannot be bought' (140). The tragic outcome of Herbert's arrogance on that occasion is Jack's suicide using that very snake as his instrument of death; and throughout the book Herbert's strident assertions of Australian identity are similarly qualified by implied or overt criticism. It is Leah who teaches Herbert that his vision, enthusiasm, dreams and arrogance on behalf of Australia should be tempered by kindness. In the opening pages Herbert admits that with all the other changes occurring to his aged body 'I may even, at last, have become almost kind' (12). Leah's philosophy of 'kindness' (259, 323) resonates like a chorus (12, 141, 151, 195, 444, 455), but like other obsessive visions in the book, it becomes a dangerous and enslaving idealism. Despite her bodily revulsion from Izzie (271, 316–17), Leah submerges herself in an idealisation of him (303) and sacrifices herself to him once he has had his accident as a way of fulfilling her desire to do 'one really fine thing' (257). As she later recognises, 'I wanted to be good and kind and I made myself a slave instead' (473; also 359).

It is also Leah who teaches Herbert that Australia's history is itself lies, that 'the raw optimistic tracks' of its pioneers were made at the expense of another society, and 'cut the arteries of an ancient culture before a new one had been born' (553). Herbert believes in the potential of Australia as a place of self-trans-formation, like the Sydney Hissao sees, 'something imagined by men and women, and if it could be imagined into one form, it could be imagined into another' (561). Herbert embodies and parodies the classic Australian myth of the 'battler' to whom Australia is 'a veritable land of promise', a potential 'Utopia under the Southern Cross', the 'Workers' Paradise': as Pilger's *A Secret Country* points out, '[t]he truth was complex and very different from the distant idolatry'.[27] This is the myth which Leah disabuses Herbert of in her attempt 'to analyse the history of this country' (230). Once Leah and Herbert connect, he gets his recurrent urge to settle down and Leah exposes Herbert's impulse to 'make a place' for himself and his family: 'This is *not* your place and never can be ... The land is stolen. The whole country is stolen. The whole nation is based on a lie which is that it was not already occupied when the British came here. If it is anybody's place it is the blacks. Does it *look* like your place? Does it *feel* like your place? Can't you see, even the trees have nothing to do with you' (307). Herbert's defensive reaction is to argue 'This is my country ... even if it's not yours.' But he also acknowledges privately that the landscape had 'always seemed alien to me, that it made me, in many lights, melancholy and homesick for something else' (308). The contradiction in Herbert's response to Australia is fundamental to the way the novel pursues its two projects of celebration and exposé, working through the modes of comedy and savage satire.

Phoebe, for example, represents a failed vision and enthu-siasm, and there are many similar examples. Les Chaffrey's wife reveals to Charles that her husband is a technical genius whose talents are being dissipated by the lack of any nurturing circumstances to develop them (421, 428). Les characterises that double-edge to the novel which displays the unrepresented and unclaimed histories of lost individuals as both heroic and unheroic at the same time. Like an Australian *Middlemarch*, *Illywhacker* shows talent and aspiration draining away into the sands of ordinary life. As Herbert admits half-way through the novel, while the great events of history and culture were being enacted elsewhere, he himself is stuck with describing Badgery & Goldstein (Theatricals) 'wandering through the 1930s like flies on the face of a great painting' (326).

The newness of colonial Australia overlaps local and national histories, but the continent is also so ancient as to allow its newer settlers to *have* no real past. On a number of occasions Leah argues that for the colonists and their post-colonial condition there is 'no history' (229–30, 254, 257, 262): her argument about the corrupting effects of gold on working-class Australian perceptions is that it has led them to imagine that all they need to achieve freedom is luck, or land stolen from 'its real owners' (229).

The delusory nature of Australian dreams and visions of identity are also examined in the context of an international arena, in particular through Herbert's legacy to Charles and Hissao. Herbert's depiction of his own early life presents him as a man with an obsession – to make an Australian aeroplane and in doing so remake Australia independent of the colonialist legacy. 'You have invented yourself, Mr Badgery ... You are what they call a confidence man. You can be anything you want' (91), Phoebe tells him with unconscious irony in her use of the word 'confidence'. His grand idea and enthusiasm (80) are what capture Jack McGrath's imagination, and they represent a dream about Australia as a self-determining autonomous nation producing its own culture. During Jack's meeting, Herbert argues against a crawling dependency on the English, against continuing in the role of being 'a child serving a parent' (136, 141). But the novel also exposes this grand idea as a delusion, asking what is the difference between lies, dreams, visions; and at what point do they become dangerous? Herbert's plans for the Australian aeroplane originate in his true talent for spinning a yarn, and he is the first to express his surprise: 'I had never been in a situation where my lies looked so likely to become true' (60).

His ideas derive not from his own invention but from plagiarism: he tinkers with existing plans for a British plane and claims them for himself (119–20). This episode has an ambiguity to it. As in Zee Edgell's *Beka Lamb* where one of the girls changes the country of origin on the label inside her guitar from Spain to Belize,[28] this is potentially an image of creative appropriation. But it is also an image of continued dependency, and this is the contradiction Herbert wrestles with. He sees his nation going wrong: by 1931, 'the lies that once smoked like dreams have diminished' (228). But the lies are also the origin of the errors, and the most memorable exposé of this Australian dreaming is Charles's pet emporium.

Along with the three-generational structure, the metaphor of the pet shop was the genesis of Carey's conception of the novel: 'I began with the image of my country as a pet shop, people living in cages, being well-fed, thinking they are happy, but denying the nature of their prison',[29] 'culturally and economically a collection of pets who are going around thinking that they're all really wonderful, not really feeling that they're in cages or on leashes', since 'one of the great lies Australians tell themselves is how proud, free, independent and anti-authoritarian they are'.[30] He instanced as an example the British government's intervention through the Governor General of Australia to bring down the Whitlam Labour government in 1975, coincidentally the year Carey's first book appeared: 'We think of ourselves as a proud and free and anti-authoritarian people, and that's ludicrous. Why did everyone do nothing when Whitlam was fired. The Headmaster said he'd been a naughty boy, so he must have done something wrong. It wasn't the response of a freedom-loving, questioning people who hate authority. It seemed to me one of a people who really love authority.'[31]

The imagery of caging animals and birds is a powerful emblem of colonisation, particularly given Australia's penal past. As Elizabeth Webby points out,[32] it has its origins in the first lie Herbert tells Phoebe about the snake he captured on landing his Morris Farman in Ernie Vogelnest's front paddock: '"What's the snake for?" Phoebe said … "It's a pet," I said' (27), when in fact he was aiming to sell it for five bob to Mr Chin the Chinese herbalist (25). Keeping the snake prisoner Herbert later sees as his great mistake (231). Given the symbolic status Herbert later gives the snake as representing the true Australia and the part it plays in the money-making scam of the 'snake trick' which he undertakes with Leah and Charles (343–6), this overlap of the spurious with the mercenary forms a founding lie in Herbert's life comparable with that of the first colonial invaders' misappropriation of the land as a *terra nullius* (literally 'an empty place'), investing this opening incident with aesthetic pertinence for the central thread of the novel. It continues with Herbert's attempt to build a home for Phoebe. The house he builds for her she sees as a temporary camp but he sees as a home (161). Eventually it becomes a 'savage poem' (204) epitomising for her Herbert's desire to contain her through the role of wife and mother. The parrots he buys are emblems of Herbert's attempt to win back Phoebe and his desire to cage her (200–1, 205). With a structural shapeliness unexpected in such a digressive fiction, Book One ends with Herbert, and his howling son, trapped in a gaol of his own making.

The same aesthetic ordering is apparent in the rest of the novel. The dragon-making legacy of Goon Tse Ying shapes the opening and closing of Book Two, and as Goon explains to Herbert, a dragon was his mother's name for lies and liars (370). Book Three is ordered by the origins and outcomes of Charles's pet shop. Again, this has mixed intentions: partly it is a celebration of 'the uniqueness and beauty of Australian birds and animals' (485); and partly Leah suggests it to him to assuage her own guilt at not looking after him when he visits Sydney to track down his mother (408). His first pet is almost accidental when, incited by his teacher, he catches a cockatoo (304); but his enthusiasm soon becomes an obsessive version of Herbert's dream of an autonomous Australian venture: he too wants to be 'someone who would one day do great things not just for himself, but for his country' (386). He is, after all, a Badgery: 'He had grand visions ... He was an enthusiast, a fan' (480).

The true lineaments of his vision are significantly and

humorously revealed in the first encounter with the American entrepreneur, Nathan Schick, after the attempt at playing the snake trick in Craig's Hotel in Ballarat. Schick declares that what he wants is 'an Aussie act' for America: 'This is a great country, but it hasn't even started to be exploited. You people don't realise what it is you have to sell', to which Charles retorts: 'Wombats' (348). The comedy contains the issue that emerges to dominate the rest of the novel. Like Herbert with Phoebe, Charles becomes a collector who turns the things he loves 'into a product' (472). As is often the case, it is Leah's role to reveal the ideological issues behind the action: 'Look at what we've done. Look at all his cages ... We are all perverted. Everything good in us gets perverted' (473).

This perversion of Australian dreams has its political implications – the increasing commercial and economic subjection of the Best Pet Shop in the World to the neo-colonial power of America and Japan. Charles's emporium in the old Stratford Arcade in Pitt Street becomes 'an expression of the purest patriotism – pure Australiana', but 'Sydney was not big enough to support such poetry' and the Americans 'saved his arse' (481). The imagery of the emporium becomes memorably vivid, and appropriate for a city which sports the wonderful Queen Victoria building, in which the beautiful intricacy of the internal architecture and gallery walkways sits ambiguously alongside the economic dynamic of selling and shopping.[33] Sydney is seen later in the novel as a façade, a city 'full of trickery and deception', 'a trick', 'a veneer', a 'clever forgery' (547). Herbert's time in prison is spent living through the delusion generated by Leah's letters, and when he is released and visits his son's enterprise, Charles's grand vision seems like another delusory dream: 'I could not separate my son's industry from Goldstein's lies' (504). With significantly anticipatory imagery, he has 'the sense of stepping into a vision ... like a Barrier Reef tourist in a glass-bottomed boat, I could not have felt more entranced or more alien' (504).

Cumulatively, the novel exposes the delusoriness of national dreams. We have noted already how Leah has revealed the way 'Australians' don't belong to Australia: 'It is not a

country where you can rest. It is a black man's country ... We
can only move around it like tourists' (323). The original colonial
Australians may have appropriated the land but that did not
mean they belonged, any more than casual visitors: their dreams
were categorically not like the Aboriginal 'Dreaming', with its
mythic, non-materialist conception of a spiritual connectedness
between land and people. It is not for nothing that during his
study of history in prison, Herbert proclaims his speciality as
'[t]he role of lies in popular perceptions of the Australian
political fabric' (488).

Carey turns the experiences of the Badgeries into emblems
of the state of the nation in the same kind of way that Dickens
creates national metaphors out of fog and Chancery in *Bleak
House*. The pet shop is a diverse emblem. It is both poetry and a
slum (522); its human inhabitants are family pets (526, 536–7);
and like the car Charles promotes to his father as his dream of an
indigenous Australian motor industry come true, the whole
enterprise is a dream based on American money. Another
emblem is formed by the thread of images about prisons already
noticed. Herbert's period in prison is one of a number of gaol
images, including the house he builds for Phoebe and the cages in
the emporium for the pets and for the Badgery family members
(536–7). With the implicit link back to the convict past of
Australia, made explicit in episodes like the finding of convict
thumb-prints on the bricks of the emporium (542), the gaol
imagery becomes expressive of the state of contemporary
Australian society, trapped by its history, imprisoned in its self-
created present, caught by these legacies in the future.

The Vegemite jar containing Goon Tse Ying's finger is
another powerful emblem. Goon, the Chinaman who brought up
the self-orphaned Herbert and taught him to disappear, represents the increasingly important Asian axis within Australian
multicultural identity. His legacy to Herbert is double-edged.
His book of magic which Herbert steals proves to be a delusion
when it is revealed to be nothing more than crass business advice
to his sons (373–5). But it is also from Goon that Herbert learns
'the power of lies' (375), their power to make dragons. The finger

in the bottle is emblematic of the transformative vision of Australia Herbert champions: it is changed by the dreams and visions of its owner (519). As Carey points out, it 'has the ability to transmogrify' and epitomises 'the power of the imagination to invent the country'.[34] It becomes a symbol of the potentialities of the battler's Australia, since it can be '[a]lmost anything you're brave enough to make it into' (520). But it also encapsulates what Australia has actually become, its self-made reality. It becomes a dragon, an 'evil fucker ... a nasty piece of work' (579) and is a direct cause of Charles's suicide. It represents the 'fucked-up dreams' (578) whose perpetrators become their own victims. The Badgery family are trapped by their own aspirations and mythologies, embodying the direction of contemporary Australian society. Herbert's desire to make history, or Leah's sense of there being no history, represent phases in a search for an Australian identity, but 'the days of the pet shop were over ... It belongs to the Yanks' (580). In this indictment, Carey suggests that Australia has been overtaken by other histories or another phase of history, the neo-colonialism of the USA and Japan. Hissao embodies a more knowing and, after his tragic failure to save the last gold-shouldered parrot, more savagely cynical dedication to 'fierce nationalism' (560). He has the moral clarity to see the damage that his father's business was doing and that 'it was one of those great Australian enterprises that generate wealth while making nothing new' (561). If Herbert and Charles's dreams and visions were compromised by their dependency on American finance, Hissao represents a new phase of the neo-colonialism of Australia in the form of Japanese finance: he is an entrepreneurial whiz-kid of a kind that the 1980s became familiar with, 'decadent' and 'tough' (585).

The impact of this is revealed by contrasting the opening of the novel with its final scenes. The scenario of the ending has much in common with 'War Crimes' and 'American Dreams', and with Murray Bail's travelling menagerie of Australians in *Homesickness*. The Badgery emporium has become a museum of Australiana with exhibits made up of people displayed in cages – the Bondi Surf Lifesaving Club, shearers, inventors, manufacturers, bushmen, Aboriginals, and Herbert himself. We end where we began, with Herbert addressing us as readers. If at the outset we are captivated by Herbert's ironic manner and perhaps disturbed by his self-disgust at his ageing bodily functions, we are probably also misled by the comic expectations engendered through his yarning. We expect to be, and are, hugely entertained by his subsequent tales. The difference is that by the time we read the ending we realise the context for Herbert's yarn, his present situation in the pet shop, and this injects a mocking savagery into the mode of his address. We realise that the experts whom Herbert described as investigating and authenticating him in the opening (11) were doing so as curators of a valuable exhibit in the horrific theme park which Charles's emporium has become through Hissao's terrible revenge. And Herbert himself, as Tony Thwaites has pointed out, 'survives here because of his storytelling alone': the label on *his* cage is the novel's title.[35]

Hissao is Herbert's 'creature, my monster' (597), his dragon, the future he engendered for himself, the destiny we were forewarned that he was fated to live with (206). Even Leah, who has acted throughout as a touchstone of political insight, integrity and clear-sightedness, and whose dancing echoes anarchist Emma Goldman's famous saying 'if I can't dance, I don't want to be part of your revolution',[36] cannot escape the emporium (553): she becomes an exhibit, the 'Melbourne Jew' (599) whose function it is to explain that the exhibition is based on lies, the dissident contained by hegemonic dominance. One such lie is blatantly clear on the sign of Herbert's cage door which states that he is 139 years old: 'It also says I was born in 1886, but there are no complaints.' The implication of this is that the chronology does not add up: either the novel is set in 2025, which seems unlikely despite the futuristic elements of the last section, or the door sign is a blatant lie which the exhibition visitors nevertheless accept because 'visitors prefer to believe the printed information' (599).

The whole sequence is a brilliant and savage exposé of contemporary corporate capitalism, how its disinformation is willingly accepted by a subject population coerced through what

Noam Chomsky terms the manufacture of consent.[37] Despite his ardent vision and dreams, Herbert's life epitomises the self-production of Australia as a subject nation. In an undeveloped angle analogous with 'War Crimes' the ending suggests that 'the enemies of the emporium' are confronting the corporate multinational capitalism it represents in a latent civil war against the police. This suggests a hidden liberating positive in the novel, endorsed by Carey's comment in a radio interview on the book that 'if we have the power in our imaginations to imprison ourselves, we surely have the power to free ourselves'.[38] But the aim of *Illywhacker* is not to project into 'the interesting times ahead' in the future (600) so much as to expose a present and how Australia got there.

The narrative addressed to us as readers here takes on a new twist, again similar to that in 'War Crimes', since we are also placed as spectators in the emporium: 'Take my photograph any way you like', Herbert tells us (587). As visitors to the exhibit, we are on the inside, one of the 'customers' Herbert is supposed to be entertaining (154) and complicit in the 'blame' (587) we are supposedly interrogating. We are addressed as 'Professor', a person of 'fine scruples, sensitive to the vulgarity of the salesman type' (561).[39] From this point of view, Herbert's insistence in the opening that we put down our red pens and 'relax and enjoy the show' (11) takes on a menacingly sardonic quality. We are implicated in the 'show', the lies, the dangerous dreams. After all, haven't we just bought this salesman's history?

This ending is as odd and disturbing as anything in Carey's earlier stories and highlights the fact that Carey's imagination is essentially transgressive and not compromised by the demands of realism or orthodox narrative conventions. The postmodern entertainment and the post-colonial exposé collide with a jarring abruptness that, as Tony Thwaites puts it, 'disorders and discomforts its own realist and genre affinities by bringing them to sustained crisis'.[40] Indeed, the shifts in narrative position and address in the last twelve sections of the novel are quite bewildering. We chop from Herbert (section 53), to Leah's letter (section 54), through sections which locate themselves in the thoughts of Leah, Hissao, Charles and Emma (sections 55–8), to Herbert's present-tense confrontational style (section 63), and finally the fantastic and futuristic vision of the last section, a world with sonic curtains (598) and apocalyptic social collapse (599). These disconnections re-emphasise the way in which Carey is prepared to sacrifice a sense of linear narrative continuity and completion in his endings in order to achieve a stronger impact through the dislocations.

Carey demythologises contemporary Australia in a manner analogous with John Pilger's in *A Secret Country*. Both books reveal a hidden history beneath the surface 'show'. Pilger argues that Australia's brief and tenuous moment as 'an independent country' has been undermined and compromised by the neo-colonial effects of multinational capital, the ambitions of the superpowers and the continuing legacies of colonial history such as the marginalised oppression of the Aborigines and the astounding *coup* in 1975. As a result, contemporary Australia suffers from a 'regression'[41] which is masked by a veneer of pretence. Unmasking the 'beautiful lies' is the project of both writers.

Perhaps in doing so *Illywhacker* presents a somewhat hermetic image of Australian culture. The resistance to the international corporate domination of the pet shop by 'the enemies of the emporium' is located outside its jurisdiction and merely referred to on the penultimate page of the novel (599). All the groups represented *inside* are reduced to passive exhibits with no suggestions of possible points of resistance. Such a view is at odds with the actual heterogeneity of Australia's ethnic components whose positive contributions over the last two or more decades, contained as they may be, nevertheless suggest a challenging diversity which has more in common with Homi Babha's view of the post-colonial situation than Carey's symbolism perhaps allows. Nevertheless, with its hybrid mix of narrative forms, its post-modern playfulness and the savagery of its critique, *Illywhacker* is a remarkable and memorable work.

Oscar and Lucinda (1988)

elegant as civilisation itself. (*Oscar and Lucinda*, 490)

At first sight a book beginning with the life of a boy brought up among the Plymouth Brethren in the middle of the nineteenth century might sound unpromising as a good read. Yet that book has proved to be Carey's most popular novel so far. Published first in Australia, perhaps to remedy the charge of cultural imperialism suffered by *Illywhacker*,[1] it won its author the prestigious Booker Prize in 1988, along with three belated Australian prizes the following year, and has been made into a successful film by Gillian Armstrong, Australian director of *My Brilliant Career* and *Little Women*.

What engages most readers immediately is the self-conscious comedy of the book, coupled with its strangely magical quality – the extraordinary and fantastical elements, obsessive characters, eccentric situations, and bizarre wonders such as a church made of glass being carried across a desert. Like *A Hundred Years of Solitude* or *Midnight's Children*, or *The Tin Drum* by Günther Grass, *Oscar and Lucinda* uses a large-scale fabulatory form to interweave the fantastic and often painfully absurd adventures of extravagant fictional characters with the actual events of national or international history to create a gigantic teeming canvas. While not strictly speculative fiction, *Oscar and Lucinda* might be termed 'retro-speculative' fiction,[2] with its simultaneous historical realism, fantasy, an improbably knowledgeable narrator, and its hypothetical opening 'If ...' (1).

Nevertheless, this remarkable novel does have its roots in

actual history. The use of an historical narrative was a new element in Carey's repertoire as his hybrid post-modern and post-colonial approach addressed the nineteenth-century past directly for the first time. The book continues a number of areas of investigation from *Illywhacker*, including the dangers of obsessive dreams or idealisms and the hidden imperial history of white Australia's colonisation of Aboriginal land, a theme which may seem tangential in the finished novel but which was at the heart of Carey's original idea for the book. The video *The Most Beautiful Lies* caught him half-way through writing *Oscar and Lucinda*. His working title was 'Holy Ghosts' and the video shows him introducing the book with reference to a faded weatherboard church set on the flood plains of the Bellinger River. Carey used the haunting quality of this image to point out how deeply imbued with Christian culture his life and Australian history has been. He has also recalled his originating image envisaging the church coming 'along the Bellinger River on a barge gliding like a dream into the landscape'.[3] At the same time he recalled that the landscape around the little church was haunted by other ghosts and dreamings from another, obliterated culture, that of the Aborigines who were massacred in order that the land could be claimed for the church to stand on.[4] The peaceful pastoral image of the church thus hides and commemorates a holy war. *Oscar and Lucinda*, often misremembered after a first reading as an endearing period piece, reveals that brutal cultural expropriation with disturbing violence.

Perhaps crucially for its appeal, though, it does so through the love story indicated by its title, or rather anti-love story, since Carey's other major idea for the book was 'to prevent them consummating their relationship successfully, because I'd already decided way back there that they weren't going to be allowed to'.[5] This frustration of the romantic element of the novel has much to do with its post-modern playfulness, but it also signals an ongoing concern in Carey's work, human isolation, a theme we can introduce by looking back briefly to *Illywhacker*.

Failure of communication is a significant element in *Illywhacker*. Herbert and Phoebe, Herbert and Leah, Leah and Izzie,

Charles and Emma, all suffer from crossed wires and dramatise the isolation of individuals within relationships. In Herbert and Phoebe's case, their misunderstandings are rooted in a facet of Herbert's character which none of the other characters seem to see, a conservative desire to settle down to 'a fire and slippers' (538). Misunderstandings proliferate until the power balance between them is seriously misaligned and Herbert finds himself desperately pursuing his wife's affections (198–200). Herbert's relationship with Leah is not dissimilar in its misalignment: he desires to contain the relationship and stabilise it whilst she defies his impulse to settle, 'wanting to be an independent woman' (549).

Many other characters suffer from a similar blindness, losing their sense of the other in their own obsessions and schemes. Leah loses her true Kaletsky love relationship with the life-enhancing Rosa (255) in the surrogate relationship with Izzie. Charles and Emma also undergo a painful process of estrangement: the crisis over Charles's attempt to enlist establishes an emotional patterning to their relationship in which Emma uses her supposed fragility as a powerful weapon over Charles (466). In their case the crossed wires result in the tragic suicide of Charles 'because he had misunderstood' (576) the contents of the Vegemite bottle, which he took to be Emma's aborted foetus (567). Even Hissao's liaison with Rosa Carlobene on the plane to Japan suffers from the same kind of problems: he shows her the beginning of a smile which '[n]aturally she misunderstood' (592).

Relationships in Carey's fiction are generally fraught with gaps in understanding between people. The aloneness of the individual is alleviated by alliances which are often initially joyful or anarchically happy, as in the case of Herbert's with Phoebe and Leah, or Charles's with Emma. But almost inevitably a solip-sistic sense of personal isolation also generates an awareness that it is impossible for individuals truly to know each other or relate fully with each other, while emotional patterns and habits are established which become cages which are difficult to break out of, as in Emma's case: 'she did not guess that she was already clearing a path for her emotions to travel along, that the path would soon be a highway combered, sealed, with concrete guttering along its edges' (466). As this characteristically sharp imagery demonstrates, Carey is particularly perceptive at presenting this sense of the tensions and contradictions between people, and this is equally if not more the case with *Oscar and Lucinda*, exemplified by Oscar's relationships with his father and with Lucinda.

As in *Bliss* and *Illywhacker*, the father and son relationship is portrayed with an insight which reveals the ambivalence present in the filial bond. The tensions between father and son lead to one of the first comic incidents in the novel: having punished Oscar for eating a morsel of Christmas pudding pre-pared for him by a pitying cook and maid, Theophilus takes his son to help him collect specimens on the beach. Oscar, nursing a growing anger as he watches his father wading in the fearful ocean, prays fervently and with profound seriousness: 'Dear God … if it be Thy will that Thy people eat pudding, smite him' (20). And when he looks, he is horrified to find his father soaking wet from a fall in the sea. But this portrait of parental and filial alienation has its emotively tragic side. When Theophilus finds the divining stone in Oscar's pocket, he takes it 'so he might be close to the boy' (37), but his desire for intimacy merely serves to reveal the awkward embarrassment of uncommunicated feeling between the man and his son. Oscar realises that his father's 'soft and pleading' look 'did not belong in that hard, black-bearded face' and that he would never be able to hold on to the 'soft and lovely centre in his father's feelings' (38). This bitter-sweet sense of alienation characterises the rest of his relationship with his father, as when his father comes to visit him at the Strattons' and they meet subsequently as Theophilus is carrying his buckets (64–71), or when Theophilus sees Oscar off on the Levi-athan (212–19). With his girl-like frailty, so out of place in 'the world of men' (357), the contradictions of masculinity origin-ating in his relationship with his father are something Oscar continues to experience throughout the novel.

This theme of isolation within relationships dominates the short period of the novel in which Oscar and Lucinda are together, and for most of that time they totally misunderstand one another. This is partly due to Lucinda's self-isolation within her 'great clanking suit of ugly armour' (361), a defence and assertion against what her proto-feminist upbringing leads her to recognise as 'the power of men' (146). Despite Oscar's decidedly non-masculine character and her own desires, she finds it difficult to relinquish her armour (389, 446). Their visit to the glass factory, in which Oscar tries his best to be 'manly amongst her men' (368), merely serves to inflame Lucinda's anger over gender inequality and to reinforce the awareness that they were 'strangers to each other' (367). Carey's treatment of the sexual politics between the two characters is informed by a late twentieth-century sense of the impact of feminism on male-female relationships, perhaps shaped in part by Miriam Dickson's feminist history of Australia, *The Real Matilda*, which he has declared 'a wonderful book' and one which he thinks about frequently.[6]

Lucinda's realisation that 'I am in love. How extraordinary' (377) accompanies the changing ambivalence of their relationship, whose protean form echoes the ambiguities of Lucinda's visions of glass: 'They looked at each other and saw each other change from combative stranger to familiar friend and back again, not staying one thing long enough for certainty' (374). This uncertainty is also instrumental to the plot. At their closest in chapter 76 when setting up house together, their happiness is based on a timidity which perpetuates 'a considerable distance' (359) between them. Despite their awareness that they love each other, each of them fails to realise how the other is feeling or thinking. There is also one fundamental 'misunderstanding' (362). Fearing Oscar might think her eager to capture him as a husband, as Miriam Chadwick is to do later in the novel, Lucinda invents 'the romantic story of her passion for a clergyman whom Bishop Dancer had so cruelly exiled to Boat Harbour' (341). The effect is that Oscar sees Lucinda as in a mirror 'so he understood her back to front' (382). In combination with their shared obsession – gambling – and their individual visions, hers for glass, his for self-sacrifice to a cause, the romantic fiction about Hasset and the glass church expedition are all too effective in deferring the consummation of their love. The outcome is the tragic dislocation of their relationship through their absurd and perverse wager, as Oscar gambles for Lucinda and for their inheritances. This mad scheme to prove his love takes the form of a crazy expedition with the fascistic Mr Jeffris to deliver a glass church across the hinterland to the Reverend Hasset, the man Oscar wrongly believes Lucinda to be in love with. The idea of the church for Mr Hasset is 'a dreadful laceration' of Oscar's feelings (383), which he is nevertheless ready to entertain self-sacrificially as 'a prayer to God' because 'she would, therefore, because of it, love him' (384). The aim of giving the church to Hasset, Lucinda insists, 'would not be personal' (384), but each of them interprets that phrase in diametrically opposite ways. Her ironically pointed question 'Do we understand each other?' is echoed later when she finds the doggerel verse from Oscar revealing his assumption that the venture was to 'gain your trust' when in fact he already has it. Realising the confusion of motives between them, she cries out 'How could you misunder-stand me to such an extent' (445–6).

This exploration of the solipsism of relationships reveals them to be subject to apparently arbitrary and contingent laws, and this is a theme of wide significance in the novel, illustrating the convergence of Carey's metafictional capacities with his investigation of the imperialist exploitation of Australia. Like other post-modern fictions by authors such as Peter Ackroyd or John Barth, *Oscar and Lucinda* employs a deliberate and playfully displayed self-consciousness about the fictionality of the writing, and a knowing pastiche of existing styles and conventions, though the effects created are quite distinctive. Part of this effect emerges from the humour of the book. There are jokes galore. The prose is peppered with puns and wordplay, such as Oscar's being 'called' to the priesthood by calling 'heads' to the flip of a coin (189); or the Biblical echo when Oscar and the Reverend Stratton, representatives of two rival religions, meet each other for the first time, and Hugh Stratton had to edge 'around the boy who did not move from the path, although the path was narrow' (23). There are absurd episodes reminiscent of Henry Fielding, such as the Judds taking Oscar's invitation to enter his house literally and climbing through the window (315–19); or Oscar's boarding the boat Leviathan in a cage (204–5), or Bishop Dancer's remarkable trickery with the tablecloth (320–3).

Alongside the humorous parody are various playful strategies, such as the role allocated to the narrator. In *Illywhacker*, as in *Midnight's Children*, the narrator is an actor and the centre of the story he tells. Carey's narrator in *Oscar and Lucinda* is not like that, but he is nevertheless a definite character. He is our near contemporary, writing in 1986 – we know this because he tells us that it is 120 years since the arrival of the church in Bellingen in 1866 (508); and we know he is a 'he' because when Kumbaingiri Billy is telling the narrator about his great-grandfather's arrival, he calls the narrator 'Bob' (488). He is also a controlling voice like the modern-day narrator in *The French Lieutenant's Woman*, and, although Carey had not read Fowles's novel at the time,[7] he plays with our expectations in a similar way. The starting-point for the novel creates not only a setting but a narrative structure which is crucial to the overall effect. Like Herbert Badgery, by his own confession the narrator of *Oscar and Lucinda* is untrustworthy: at the very beginning of his book he advises us that he himself 'learned long ago to distrust local history' (2). Having said that, he goes on to tell us his own convoluted local history, playing games with our assumptions in the process.

One of those games is the convolutedness of the enterprise. The narrator begins by considering how his great-grandfather the Reverend Oscar Hopkins (1841–66) came to Australia and how the little church of St John's at Gleniffer came to be where it is, a church which so obsessed the narrator's mother that, when he was aged ten, she was prepared to sacrifice the household's supply of fuse wire to make Advent wreaths for it (4), causing a family upset. The story of Oscar takes us back to the early Victorian age in southern England and the complications of his life with Theophilus and the Strattons. It also takes us to Australia, where the other half of the book's title is undergoing not dissimilar tribulations in a parallel life. Both characters are the same age (92); they both become different kinds of orphan –

Lucinda's intellectual and unconventional mother, Elizabeth, dies leaving her daughter with a large inheritance – and they both become avid gamblers. While Lucinda sells up, moves to Sydney wearing her modern-woman bloomers and begins her brilliant careers as the owner of a glass factory with the help of the Reverend Hasset and as a gambler with the help of Mr d'Abbs, Oscar is busy at Oriel College, Oxford, learning the finer points of racing from his sarcastic friend Wardley-Fish, in the sincere belief that gambling is one of God's works. In a book with such a title of course, despite living in opposite corners of the Earth, their paths are fated to cross; and like a trick in one of their own games of chance, they find themselves on the same boat back to Australia after Lucinda's visit to England: as the narrator tells us half-way through the book on the occasion of their meeting, '[i]n order that I exist, two gamblers, one Obsessive, the other Compulsive, must meet' (225).

Hero and heroine do so in chapter 50, virtually half-way through the novel. Their relationship, however, suffers from a series of setbacks and it is not until chapter 70, when Lucinda finds Oscar down-and-out having been sacked from his post, that their 'relationship' truly begins. It lasts for a mere twenty chapters in a total number of 110 – or 111 in the American or later Faber editions[8] – and is immediately beset by separation through the expedition. After the nightmare journey, the expedition arrives at Bellingen. Oscar is suddenly overtaken by Miriam Chadwick, a young woman on the look out for a new husband. Miriam marries him and conceives a child by him, the child who is to become the narrator's grandfather. But Miriam is doomed yet again to wear her hated mourning weeds as Oscar dies, trapped in the sinking glass church; leaving her the beneficiary of his will and the inheritor of Lucinda's fortune and glass factory. And *that*, the narrator seems to say at the end of his bizarre, incredible and convoluted story, is how the little church of St John's came to established in Bellingen. It is also, we realise finally, how it comes to be that Oscar is the narrator's great-grandfather, but Lucinda is *not* the narrator's great-grandmother as the book's title has invited us to think.

So the plot of *Oscar and Lucinda* effects its narrative trickery through a manipulation of our assumptions. The title leads us to expect union, a love story, a communion, if only Romeo-and-Juliet-like in death. The playfulness of Carey's conception of a love story which is not consummated pinpoints his deliberate frustration of the fictional conventions of nineteenth-century realism. Once we are told on the opening page that Oscar was the narrator's great-grandfather, the book's title leads us to expect that Lucinda will be the narrator's great-grandmother; and that Oscar and Lucinda must, at some point therefore, have consummated their love. Instead, Miriam Chadwick is the great-grandmother, and like a shaggy dog story, the plot plays a great trick on us. Unless, that is, we have read carefully, since there are hints and warning signs that all is not as it appears to be. So on the opening page, we are given the pre-emptive information of Oscar's death (1), while the narrator mentions in passing that years later Lucinda would lose her fortune 'to my great-grandmother' (81) – as clear an indication as we might want, but given *before* we can see any implications and as a result easily overlooked on first reading.

As the novel plays with storytelling, so it also plays with history. While complete in its way, the history the narrator tells us of Oscar and Lucinda, is also full of multiple and diverse loose ends. At least one is a mistake in the chronology overlooked by Carey and his editors: in chapter 36, Lucinda's lost fortune is said to be two years away from 1859, yet by chapter 48 we are already up to 1865.[9] Other loose ends have a deliberately self-conscious effect. So we are told that, with the death of Oscar and the loss of her inheritance, Lucinda's 'real life' was about to begin: she would become 'known for more important things than her passion for a nervous clergyman. She was famous, or famous at least among students of the Australian labour movement' (506). But we are given no indication as to the nature or reality of this future life. The novel which has engaged our interest and affections for five hundred pages suddenly takes on the quality of a passing encounter, an arbitrary byway in Lucinda's real life, as if all lives contain within them tantalising potentialities whose true significance can only be seen after the event.

The book also confuses fiction with apparently real history. Oscar and his father are based on the historical figures of Edmund Gosse and his father, Philip Gosse. The account Edmund Gosse gave of their life together in his *Father and Son* (1907) is acknowledged as a source for the novel in Carey's prefatory note. The Christmas pudding episode is one much-elaborated link, although Carey has also acknowledged his fondness for Norman Lindsay's children's story *The Magic Pudding*.[10] Lucinda's mother, Elizabeth, is said to be a friend of Marian Evans, the real name of author George Eliot, with whom she corresponds, and who Lucinda herself meets while on her visit to London in chapter 46, becoming the subject of one of George Eliot's letters. Such trickery is again similar to episodes in *The French Lieutenant's Woman* in which the mysterious Sarah becomes involved with the Pre-Raphaelite poets and painters.

Also like *The French Lieutenant's Woman*, *Oscar and Lucinda* plays with history and fiction in ways which remind us that history too is a storytelling process and something we must be wary of.[11] To some extent, as in *Illywhacker*, through the display of self-conscious fictionality, it also makes us aware that the social roles we inhabit are like fictions which might have other possible endings than the ones already contained in the conventional social script of our existing society. But it achieves an individual quality which is quite distinct from Fowles's book. It creates a sense of an alternative history, almost a parallel universe; and so convincing is this illusion that it almost has the effect of virtual reality, making us wonder about looking Theophilus Hopkins up in the *Encyclopaedia Britannica*, or checking George Eliot's letters to see if Lucinda and her mother are there, or researching Lucinda's role in the Australian labour movement – before we realise with delight that we have been taken in and fallen for the narrative's sting.

The impact of this is comic, but for the post-colonial writer there is a serious side to this game-playing. It indicates the arbitrariness and the partiality of history. Like the narrator's mother with her mistaken belief in the function of Oscar's celluloid (190–1), we misconceive the legacy of history, misreading its remnants through the glass of our own distorting viewpoints. Like Oscar living in Notting Hill unaware of the ghostly past of a previous racecourse or the future significance for gamblers of the street-name Ladbroke (178), we live with the ghostly traces of past and future over- and under-laying our present. Not only is history made up of chance occasions and potentialities, it also contains many different points of view. Any history, the book suggests, is merely one view of the past, and may hide many other possible versions of the same events. For example, the narrator's distrust of local history is occasioned by the fact that 'Darkwood, for instance, they will tell you at the Historical Society, is called Darkwood because of the darkness of the foliage, but it was not so long ago you could hear people call it Darkies' Point, and not so long before that when Horace Clarke's grandfather went up there with his mates [and in his reading of this passage on the video, Carey pauses pregnantly on this ideologically loaded Australian word] … and pushed an entire family of aboriginal men and women and children off the edge' (2). As with Herbert Badgery, the story the narrator tells is a family history which is also a national history, presented predominantly from the point of view of the central white characters; but this dominant outlook is shadowed all the way through by a hidden history which emerges most powerfully when Kumbaingiri Billy tells his version of the arrival of Jeffris, Oscar and the expedition. This forms a damning indictment of the pretensions and hypocrisies of Jeffris's attempts to enter the annals of exploration, discovery and empire-building – which leads us to the glass church.

The theme of glass and images of glass haunt the novel throughout,[12] and it has a range of possible significances. In the form of the Prince Rupert's drop it is an image of the contradictory nature of life: it is both 'like a tear, but also like a seed' (132), 'a symbol of weakness and strength' (134), liquid and solid, whole and fragmentary. Seen like that, it is changeable, shifting, indicating that life too cannot be fixed: 'Glass. Blinding white. Glowing red. Elastic. Protean. Liquid. Vessel for light'

(370). For Lucinda, it is also an obsession, the material of her dreams, of her idealism. On falling in love with the contradictory nature of the Prince Rupert's drop, Lucinda believes glass to be 'a joyous and paradoxical thing, as good a material as any to build a life from' (135). But as Dennis Hasset tells Lucinda, idealisms or obsessions can be a 'dangerous thing' (148). Glass can easily shatter, break apart into 'scimitars, stilettos, daggers, pig stickers, a jigsaw armoury waiting to be released from its captive sheet' (315).

In the form of the church, glass becomes an emblem of the love and the misunderstanding between Oscar and Lucinda – a fantastic and beautiful conception, but one which takes the place of real communication between them. In a wider context the church becomes an emblem of the colonial process, an idealism whose obsessive reality is utterly destructive. The novel is set during a period of great intellectual ferment, when a crisis of faith was being felt as contemporary science challenged and undermined literal belief in the historical truth of the Bible. Theophilus Hopkins is a man living out such a crisis: as a member of the Plymouth Brethren he accepts the literal truth of the Bible; as a natural scientist he finds the evidence of evolution in every stone; but his reaction to this challenge to his faith is to enforce a sincere but tyrannical and repressive belief system on the fifteen-year-old Oscar. The critique of religion anticipates the later critique of the church as an agent of imperialism. Despite his antipathy to the church itself, Mr Jeffris realises that it will be the instrument through which he will carve his way into the pioneering exploration of Australia: 'Each pane of glass, he thought, would travel through country where glass had never existed before, not once, in all time. These sheets would cut a new path in history' (441). In doing so, an Aboriginal tribe is massacred to satisfy Jeffris's imperialist megalomania, and Jeffris himself is killed by the joint efforts of the docile Mr Smith and Oscar.

One of the most memorable images in the novel is the scene in chapter 104 in which Miriam sees the glass church being towed round a bend in the Bellinger River on a barge, with the black-suited Oscar caught within its beautiful transparency like a fly, recalling earlier passing uses of the imagery (310, 352). The surrealism of this episode calls to mind two other similarly bizarre and oddly appropriate images from films by German director Werner Herzog. At the end of *Aguirre, Wrath of God* (1972), the power-crazy Spanish conquistador Aguirre, played with great gusto by Klaus Kinski, is seen drifting down river in the middle of the Amazonian rain forest, alone on a raft which is overrun by monkeys. It is an extraordinary scene capturing the insanity and absurdity of the imperial enterprise. Aguirre's kingdom is a few yards of wood, his subjects the jabbering monkeys, both of them emblems of his own insanity, the lust for power which drove him over the edge; and against this is the backdrop of the implacably indifferent vastness of the forest and nature, which he tried to tame. Equally powerful is the film *Fitzcarraldo* (1982), in which Kinski again gives a *tour de force* performance as an obsessive, this time determined to carry an entire opera house into the heart of the South American jungle. Again it is an emblem of empire-building, but this time of cultural imperialism rather than the more blatant power of the conquistadors; and again we get the surreal image of a symbol of Western civilisation wrenched from its context and misplaced absurdly in an alien environment. The analogy with Carey's scene is particularly apt since one of his next projects after this novel was to work on the screenplay for the film *Until the End of the World* by another German director whose work contains surreal aspects, Wim Wenders.

The church on the barge in *Oscar and Lucinda* is as 'elegant as civilisation itself' we are told (490); but civilisation, empire, pioneering, the glorious myths of the Victorian age and of the Australian outback are exposed for their devastating effects and their true history. Like Fitzcarraldo's opera house or Aguirre's lust for gold, the glass church is a grand idea whose implementation becomes an *idée fixe*, a horrendous and destructive obsession. It costs Oscar his life as he goes down trapped in the church like one of the insects, and enacts his own worst nightmare of drowning. But it is more than personally destructive: it is emblematic of the whole imperial venture, the conquest of Australia itself, the land and the people, by a seemingly transparent but ultimately destructive material invasion of people and culture. Jeffris is a version of Conrad's Kurtz, a man with a savage vision undertaking the 'sound work' (472) of empire-building, or Patrick White's Voss who was modelled on the nineteenth-century explorer Ludwig Leichhardt. He is an egomaniac dedicated to writing himself on to the map and into history. As he tells Oscar, who is appalled by the savagery of the enterprise, '[c]hurches are not carried by choirboys ... Neither has the Empire been built by angels' (473).

For Oscar, the perverse outcome of Lucinda's dream transforms him into Jeffris's murderer, while the church becomes 'the devil's work' (500). For Kumbaingiri Billy and his tribe, the boxes containing the panes of glass are 'the whiteman's dreaming' (469), the sacred relics of the white race; and those relics are dangerous, since, as the title of chapter 99 indicates, 'Glass Cuts'. Behind the peaceful rural image of the quiet country church seen in 1986 lies the hidden history of a war between the holy ghosts of two totally antipathetic cultures. And as we saw in the opening of the book with the narrator's mother's own obsession, the lingering violence of those wars haunt the twentieth century.

Through its play with fictionality, then, the book creates a number of effects and investigates a number of issues – to do with history and to do with pattern within seemingly arbitrary experience. In this last sense, the narrative thread of the gambling is central. The book itself is a kind of elaborate gamble, toying with the reader's expectations. Carey's novel suggests that the post-colonial experience is a displaced, hybrid state in which inchoate and contradictory fragments are constantly re-forming themselves into new wholes. Like the Prince Rupert's drop, *Oscar and Lucinda* is both a series of shattered bits and a complete thing. If we consider the overall narrative, we can see that it is structured as a series of fragments and of patterns, with a definite shape to the short chapters achieved through the initial parallelism of Oscar with Lucinda, their overlap at the centre and then their divergence. The effect has similarities with the notions of chaos theory which we touched on when considering *Bliss*'s use of the butterfly image. According to chaos theory, the conventional laws of science are merely crude and reductive approximations of much more complex organic processes. Rather than having any simple recognisable order, nature works in far more random and irregular ways; but within the apparently irregular and random processes there is a pattern – patterned irregularity. Nature is, by nature, episodic, spasmodic, non-linear. What chaos theorists have proposed is that the accumulations of seemingly random events build up to patterns which are not discernible to any one individual or from any one viewpoint.

The novel embodies a similar outlook, for from its apparently random episodes and fragmentary circumstances, a strange pattern emerges in which life itself seems a designed gamble, a play of contingency and chance. Carey had what Pascal said about belief in God being a gamble in mind while writing the novel.[13] The chaos theory view of the novel also links with the post-colonial hybridity since gambling 'seemed to be the chief industry of the colony' (308). This is enacted in the image of 'the carelessness of Mr d'Abbs house' (158) where Lucinda finds gambling her *raison d'être*, a place which is 'so second rate, colonial' that she 'did not feel herself constrained by the corsets of convention' (227): 'It was a ball of string … the sort of place where you are always arriving where you do not expect' (157).

The novel also expresses a chaos-like pattern in its form. Despite the classical realist elements of the narrative, *Oscar and Lucinda* shares with Carey's other works a dislocating abrupt quality, most noticeable in the sudden turn-around of the ending and Oscar's death, which on first reading comes for many readers with the unexpectedness of catastrophe. Carey has described the short chapters which evolved during the writing of the novel as a series of narrative compartments or boxes within which were defined actions, places and characters 'but the meanings of the things that happened within those compartments continued to change completely'.[14] This Chinese-box quality to the book is part of its chaos-like perspective. It creates the experience of an unstable text in which quantum-like 'packets' of experience bounce against each other almost randomly, creating the simultaneous effect of pattern and chaos. As in quantum physics, we simultaneously see the wave, the wider picture – the story, the parallel lives, the linking motifs of glass, gambling – and the particle, the minutiae of individual events and actions – the arbitrary coincidences such as Wardley-Fish 'banging at the wrong address' and meeting Oscar (105), the tor and coin-tossing to decide Oscar's fate (33, 189, 347), the random meeting of hero and heroine on the boat where '[t]here were two doors. She chose the right-hand one' (231). Out of the diverse, multifaceted complexity of living experience at any particular moment any number of different permutations of existing elements might produce any number of different possible stories leading to unimaginable futures.

The book creates an effect not unlike the cosmological theory envisaging an infinite number of parallel universes coexisting with each other in which every conceivable permutation of possibilities is being explored simultaneously.[15] When we reach the end of the narrator's story and realise how the church got to be where it is, the effect is of a sudden backflip to the beginning of the whole book[16] – 'Oh – *that* church!' – even to the recall of particular events at the beginning of the book. This effect is enacted linguistically. Faced with the horrendous crimes of Jeffris, Oscar prays '[o]h God, give me the means to smite Thy enemy' (478; also 475). In confronting and killing Jeffris, Oscar reverts to the language of his confrontation with his father on the sea-shore (20), and the imperialist patriarchal authority of colonial ideology in general. The overall sense is that this is the possible universe in which these events might happen.[17]

In Thomas Hardy, chance can often be seen as a deterministic mechanism of retribution, part of a hostile universe programmed by a malevolent fate revenging itself on the characters through circumstantial coincidence. In *Oscar and Lucinda* chance is a matter of risk, but also of opportunity. At the end of the novel, Miriam's chance encounter with Oscar is her opportunity to escape the loathsome bereavement weeds she has been trapped in on and off since the age of seventeen. It is also the fulfilment of

Lucinda's gamble of losing her inheritance in her bet with Oscar over the delivery of the church. The birth of the narrator himself is also a matter of chance (225), so that the very existence and recital of the story is a chance affair; and throughout the book there is a sense of the haphazard coincidences and circumstantial opportunities of life as it is lived moment by moment. The novel simultaneously exposes and celebrates the risky business of living, the responsibility people have continually to make new choices, to live authentically and freshly in the moment, to reinvent their universe rather than re-enact well-tried scripts and roles from the past. This awareness of the freedom and the anxiety of choice gives the book an existentialist feel. For Lucinda, whether through gambling or through the absurd pact over the expedition, chancing her future is an experience which makes her feel alive (435). During her argument with Mr d'Abbs in chapter 86, and in the face of his unimaginative and conventional attitudes, Lucinda asserts '[w]e are wagering everything. We place ourselves at risk ... We are alive on the very brink of eternity' (419). It is this, in fact, which makes the link of 'recognition' between herself and Oscar on the boat: '"Our whole faith is a wager, Miss Leplastrier ... Every *instant*," he said. She felt she knew him' (261–2).

Above all for us as the novel's readers, there is the gamble of the story itself – the unexpected twists and turns which keep us avidly reading simply because we want to know what happens. This compulsive narrative drive is generated by a number of strategies – the generally short chapters, often with surprising twists within them or at the end; the clever parallelism of Oscar's story with Lucinda's to create a narrative interweaving; and most especially perhaps the extravagant imagination that could conceive of these two eccentric characters and their beautiful, doomed glass church.

The Tax Inspector (1991)

> in proportion as capital accumulates
> ... [i]t makes an accumulation of misery a necessary
> condition, corresponding to the accumulation of wealth.
> Accumulation of wealth at one pole is, therefore, at the same
> time accumulation of misery, the torment of labour, slavery,
> ignorance, brutalization and moral degradation
> at the opposite pole. (Karl Marx)[1]

*T*HE *Tax Inspector* is Carey's most savage novel to date, and it captures Marx's vision of the ravening effects of capital. The book takes us full circle back to the power-crazed psychopathic business world of 'War Crimes', but with the unsettling awareness that this is no longer fantasy. Carey paints a vitriolic portrait of social decay and disintegration, the collapse of communal ethics and the sheer rapacity of the business world consequent upon the global market economy of the late 1980s. As in *Bliss*, he links together two areas of urgent concern, rampant capitalism and child sexual abuse. Abuse in the family is seen in relation to wider failures of social responsibility manifest in the corrupt abuses of power and wealth in the business and criminal worlds of Sydney. Gran Catchprice's dream of a flower garden and her charitable attitude to the family business are poisoned by secrets and the corrosive effects of a disintegrating social system. The product of her attempt at benevolent capitalism is her psychopathic grandson, Benny. The brutal story-line is matched by an urgent narrative, almost filmic in intensity, which, along with the urgency of the social issues, marks a dramatic and adventurous shift of direction for Carey's fictional practice.

The framework for this investigation of the state of the Australian nation at the beginning of the 1990s is simple. The novel depicts four days in the life of the Catchprice family, during which the family motor-dealing business is under investigation by government tax inspector Maria Takis. There are three main strands to the story, the Catchprices, Maria, and a young Armenian called Sarkis. The story opens with the youngest Catchprice, sixteen-year-old Benny, being sacked from his job in the Spare Parts Department and undergoing a crisis which his brother Vish is called in to help overcome. Vish himself has escaped the family home and business to become a follower of Hare Krishna. Benny undergoes a miraculous transformation from a slob in Doc Marten boots and Judas Priest tee-shirts to an elegantly manicured and silk-suited salesman ready to rescue the family business from debt and the tax inspector. Worryingly, we learn that beneath his silk suit he has shaved off all his bodily hair, as if he 'had been peeled of history' (132).

Meanwhile their father, Mort, his sister Cathy and their mother, Gran Catchprice, are struggling together over the future of the family firm. Cathy is in the process of deciding to abandon the business for her life as a moderately successful country and western singer with a record in the charts. With her husband Howie egging her on to make the break finally at the age of forty-five, Cathy is also trying to get her mother put in an old folks home. Gran and Mort form a temporary alliance to try and prevent Cathy's projects. Into these machinations steps the tax inspector, the eight-months pregnant Maria, a lingering social idealist who believes that in the past her job might have helped redistribute the inequalities of wealth, but who has been overtaken by a new ethic which forces her to investigate tinpot firms like the Catchprices'. Dissatisfaction leads her to try and stop the investigation by breaking into the tax office computer with her friend Gia. The ploy does not work, but Maria's later friendship with Jack Catchprice, Gran's other son, leads Jack to 'fix' it so that Maria is pulled off the job. Gia has her life threatened by Sydney mafioso Wally Fischer for some indiscreet remarks in a restaurant, and Jack manages to help 'fix' that too.

In the meantime, the family histories of sexual abuse emerge to explain Benny's increasingly psychotic sense of his life's mission. He befriends and then tortures Sarkis, an unemployed Armenian hairdresser and the subject of Gran Catchprice's latest charitable enterprise. Benny's experiment with Sarkis forms a trial run for his later abduction and capture of Maria. The final scenes of the novel work to a terrifying climax as Maria gives birth to her child in Benny's horrendous cellar, while Gran Catchprice attempts to blow up the garage with gelignite. Gran succeeds in blowing herself up as well, while Maria finally manages to get the child back from Benny only by cracking open his skull.

Within this nightmarish framework, Carey digs back into Catchprice history, interlinking it with a wider social history. He uses a number of fictional strategies to effect this, some familiar from earlier work. One device is a form of flashback, what Jen Craig calls Carey's manner of 'telescoping time with an incident or object at either end of it'.[2] He gives us some surprising or urgent moment in the present action and then goes back to explain how the reader got there. This injects adrenalin and momentum into the narrative and, along with the insistent reminders of the time of day, keeps it very much in the present moment. For example, section 1 ends with Vish at home on Sunday evening peering 'right into the darkness of Benny's open mouth' (9). Section 2 then backtracks to explain how he came to be there, and section 3 returns to eleven o'clock on Sunday night and Vish looking into Benny's mouth for a second time (18). This method is also used to give us the histories of the characters and action along with a wider sense of the context of their lives. So section 10 opens with Gran in her apartment above the car yard, feeling angry about what happened in her past sixty-five years before (52). We then learn the history of Gran, Cacka and her gelignite before section 12 returns us to 'six o'clock exactly' on Monday, the day her family tried to put her in a nursing home (60).

This narrative intercutting gives the book an almost cinematic quality, as a number of reviewers noticed.[3] While undertaking the ninth of twelve revisions of the novel, Carey was also working intensively on the filmscript of *Until the End of the World*, producing dialogue to order as urgent faxes arrived from director Wim Wenders.[4] Perhaps the overlap helped drive the momentum of the novel into what is often virtually a screen-play form, with vividly visualised action and clipped dialogic sequences as in section 54. The effect is to intensify the portrayal in ways which mark a new departure for Carey, although overall the novel remains within the genre frame of realist, almost naturalist, narrative practice, in this case perhaps a necessary if unusual domain for Carey and one which seems to obviate his introducing any other fictionally innovative elements to the book. This curbed quality to the novel's artistry is possibly revealed through signs of strain in the text, whether authorial or editorial. For example, what little historical detail there is seems confusing. We are told that Cacka had a complete set of the HMV recording of *Die Zauberflöte* conducted by Sir Thomas Beecham (59); but this historic recording was not issued until 1938. If, as seems likely, Frieda McCluskey is twenty-one years old when she meets Cacka Catchprice – having escaped from home at the age of eighteen, she had spent three more years 'being "strong", we are told (59) – this would mean that the present action of the novel was taking place in the year 2003. Yet, although reviewer Diana Giese did suggest that the novel is 'set slightly in the future',[5] there is no real sense in the book of it being located anywhere other than in or around 1990, its date of writing. Equally, we find on pages 159 and 230 a virtual repeat of a paragraph of Gran Catchprice's reminiscences about Cathy as a child, presumably an editorial oversight rather than necessary repetition.

Nevertheless, Michael Heyward for one saw the book as possibly 'a quantum leap in the development of Carey's art': whereas in earlier Carey fiction the Catchprices might have provided an 'exotic sideshow', in the novel '[t]ry as you might, you can't get round them ... they won't reduce to comic irony or Gothic wit, and keep coming at you, in white cowboy boots or glistening grey suits or loaded with gelignite, like visions from a nightmare as real as they are strange'.[6] Through their narrative scenario, questions of family and social responsibility are articulated representing the decay of a paternalistic society and its replacement by a vicious and uncaring ethic of competition, power and money-making. In doing so Carey reveals a range of ethical and social issues, generated through the collisions between the different world views of Benny, Maria, Jack and Gran Catchprice.

Frieda 'Gran' Catchprice is a good example of the way Carey's vivid portraiture gives physical solidity to the characters, while simultaneously investigating the issues of which they are embodiments. Gran is a caricature grotesque: 'She liked to smoke Salem cigarettes. When she put one in her mouth, her lower lip stretched out towards it like a horse will put out its lip towards a lump of sugar' (7). But she is also given psychological substance through a history which enacts many of the novel's central concerns. Like Harry Joy, Gran is not innocent. She has colluded in the production of the family business in two decisive ways. Firstly, she gave her husband Cacka the business, raising questions of female responsibility in nurturing and supporting male power. Through her deluded love of Cacka, Gran supplied the energy to develop the corrupting Catchprice empire – the 'chook' farm, which was the first battery farm west of Sydney (90–1), the property development with its asbestos sheet houses (87), and the poisonous garage. Gran viewed this as a caring capitalism, a paternalistic and benevolent business enterprise: she employed homeless or institutionalised kids (87–8), giving them a chance (96), and encouraging them to remake their lives, to 'invent themselves' (228) as she had invented herself. But what she in fact creates is a competitive enterprise culture based on exploitative practices and the self-destructive family she presides over. What she wanted, she tells Vish, was babies and a flower farm (52); what she got was the 'poison' of the garage which covers the earth with concrete 'like a smothered baby' (163–4).

This is the second element in her collusion, since it becomes increasingly clear that she knew and was silent about Cacka's sexual abuse of their children: 'she had let Cacka poison her children while she pretended it was not happening' (167). The overlap echoes the use of the cancer theme in *Bliss*, and the environmental and family poisoning are related through imagery and structure. First Cathy (232–3) and then Mort (244–7) reveal the ongoing cycle of sexual abuse behind the facade of the family. After Cathy's accusations that she knew what was happening, Gran's response is that she *did* know, but refused to admit it to herself since 'I couldn't have loved a man who was doing that to my children' (246). This scenario unveils the problematic contradictions of the love, support and nurturing of patriarchal attitudes, behaviour and power within the family.

Mort's painful defence of his father's character speaks volumes in this respect, and takes Carey's exploration of the father-son theme from *Bliss* and *Oscar and Lucinda* much further. Mort cannot accept the idea that his mother did not love his father and defends his father as 'a good man' who '[w]hatever he was ... loved us'(244–5). His defence is a contradictory one. It is a plea for understanding of his father rather than outright condem-nation. It is also a plea for his mother to take care of his own bruised feelings and psyche as a victim of Cacka's abuse. And at the same time it is a compromised self-defence of his own position as an abuser of his own son, Benny. Mort is manipu-lating his mother's feelings *and* asking for genuine under-standing and support. These contradictions help make the presen-tation of the issue of sexual abuse more complex.

Mort epitomises the cycle of abuse through which victim becomes victimiser, a legacy of patriarchal oppression handed down from father to son. Through him, the book poses subversive questions about social attitudes to, and legislation over, abuse. In section 32, Benny confronts Mort with his now hairless naked body, inviting him to resume their 'dirty habits' (153). Mort's response is to defend himself by saying '[l]ook ... My father did it to me. His father did it to him. You think I like being like this?' (155) and he declares their sexual involvement finished. But he later realises that like himself, Benny will go on to become an abuser:

> I am the one trying to stop this stuff and he is crawling into
> bed and rubbing my dick and he will have a kid and do it to

his kid, and he will be the monster and they'll want to kill him. Today he is the victim, tomorrow he is the monster. They do not let you be the two at once. They do not see: it is common because it is natural. No, I am not saying it is natural, but if it is so common how come it is not natural? (158)

Mort's perverse self-justification opens up a social and ethical can of worms, whose repercussions social, welfare and counselling agencies are currently attempting to deal with. But it also raises the problem of categorisation: the 'victim' becomes the 'monster' and '[t]hey do not let you be the two at once'. In other words, social fear of sexual abuse as an issue can lead to a schizophrenic reaction which condemns abusers but fails to understand their own experience as victims. Mort's view of abuse as 'common because it is natural' does two paradoxical things: it states the often denied fact that abuse is common and at the same time raises the wider question of what is 'natural' – who defines 'natural' sexual practices and for whom? This is not to suggest that this passage invites us to condone abuse; but it does problematise easy condemnation or legislation. It questions the relationships between social ethics, social policing and definitions of sexual behaviour. As in the work of Michel Foucault, we are led to examine the social definitions of sexual practices as forms of control.[7] Carey derived much of his information about sexual abuse from his wife Alison Summers's work for a play she was directing on the issue.[8] The complexity which he draws from this material belies the response of reviewers and critics who, like Peter Pierce, thought his treatment 'reductive', or who, like Robert Dixon, challenged the representation of sexual abuse.[9]

In his review, Dixon called the treatment of sexual abuse 'one of the great achievements of the novel' and established an interesting angle of debate in seeing a relationship between the novel's material and recent media treatment of serial killings and sexual violence. But for Dixon this was also a source of weakness. Carey had mistakenly made sexual violence a metaphor for public corruption: 'By bringing the problems of political and business corruption into relation with child abuse, Carey's text creates the impression that the sexually abused teenager can be regarded as a symbol – *the* symbol – of corruption in Sydney.'[10] This is an interesting and significant criticism which Dixon fleshed out in an article, arguing that the effect of this displacement from 'systemic to symbolic explanation' of corruption leads to a failure to 'address coherently the problems of contem-porary Sydney', leading to a 'mystified explanation of social decline'.[11]

However, it is Dixon rather than Carey, who is conflating the narrative of sexual abuse with that of political corruption. The Catchprice family generally, and Benny in particular, are not seen as the cause of corruption, but rather as its perpetrators and victims. It is true that the novel offers ample scope for criticising Gran's complicity in family violence, whether it be sexual abuse or business, or for indicting Cacka and Mort as abusers, but this by no means implies some simple equation between them and political corruption generally. Maria's investigation of them is presented by her throughout as a misguided deflection from the true mission of the tax office to nail the big dirty money. The different levels of corruption portrayed are related, interlinked, juxtaposed, but are not neces-sarily equated with each other. The novel does not offer the simple paradigm that because Mort is a child abuser he will necessarily be involved in corrupt business and produce a monster who is synonymous with Wally Fisher. It offers the possibility of seeing links between these different levels of experience, but in ways which suggest a complexity in those links rather than a straightforward equivalence.

With this material in mind, the phrase 'family business' takes on deeper overtones, different from but related to the cycles of exploitation and corruption revealed elsewhere in the Catchprice empire. The world Gran and her family business are responsible for is made up of diverse displaced people living on the margins. In section 18, Sarkis chaperones her home because he fears for her safety at the hands of the 'ferals' and 'Nasties' (93–4) who inhabit the derelict wastelands of Franklin; but Gran seems oblivious to the creatures on her estate. They might be emblematic of the fractured and disintegrating society, but the novel also shows what Carey has called 'a newer Australia that we still haven't mapped'.[12] In contradiction to the anglophone Catchprices, it gives a significant presence to the non-Anglo/ Celtic Australia of the various immigrant communities such as those represented by Sarkis and his mother, or Maria and her father, characters who epitomise Homi Bhabha's 'in-between' people, the 'unhomely lives' of the post-colonial present.[13]

Sarkis's mother has rejected her Armenian background in an attempt at 'reinventing herself as Australian' (84), but all this has meant is her continued exploitation at the hands of another immigrant character, the taxi driver Pavlovic. Maria's mother was exploited in piece-work sweat shops which cost her her hearing in one ear and provoked the cancer she died of (34–6). And nostalgia for home on the Greek island of Letkos proves no solace for Maria during their visit to the island (32–3). The displacements of these characters' lives are integrally connected with a debate about the kind of society Australia might become. 'The future' which Maria sees in Australia (34) is one of possibility but also one compromised by the ongoing effects of the poisons of the past, the 'convict beginnings' which Carey has said 'have their effect on the Australian culture – I think our easy tolerance of corruption might spring from that'.[14]

This is captured brilliantly, if implicitly, by one piece of dialogue between Benny and Sarkis in section 39, where we a reminded of the colonial origins of the continuing exploitation of immigrant communities in Australia. Benny tells Sarkis 'I am in control of you', to which Sarkis retorts 'Hey, come on – what sort of talk is that?', only to receive the reply 'English' (175). As in *Oscar and Lucinda*, the mapping of territories becomes an emblem of imperial and historical control over individual destinies. After his torture by Benny, Sarkis feels a 'prisoner' (92) of the Catchprice estate, trapped in the grid of history embodied in streets named after members of the Catchprice family: 'Sarkis could not know that he was limping back and forth across the Catchprice family history' (217). He passes through places of decisive importance – like the spot 'where Cacka, following doctor's orders, first began to stretch the skin of his son's foreskin' (217). Sarkis is the victim of a victim who has become a victimiser.

Benny is the main outcome of this poisoned environment. When, naked and hairless, he asks his father 'Who was it made me like this?' (154), he poses a question of responsibility which takes in the family and society. The characterisation of Benny is a disturbing portrayal of a psychopathic mental state. The term 'psychopath' is often applied to young adolescent males displaying abnormally anti-social behaviour, but there are disagreements among experts as to whether psychopathic behaviour is a form of mental disorder or illness analogous to psychosis. The 'psychotic' suffers from an illness such that their competence as a person is called into question, epitomised in delusions of perception or thought for example.[15]

Benny's case seems to share elements of both definitions, since he is psychopathically anti-social and undergoes psychotic misapprehensions about the nature of reality. But Carey's text suggests that Benny's behaviour is not so much the product of an illness as consequent upon his abuse by his father Mort. This represents an anti-psychiatric explanation of pathology as the result not so much of illness as of the politics of the family and society, along the lines suggested by the work of anti-psychiatrists R.D. Laing and David Cooper. The distinction is important since it indicates the political nature of this novel's explanation of individual behaviour as socially produced and therefore capable of being changed.

The presentation of Benny is managed through brilliantly vivid characterisation. It gives us a dramatised view into Benny's mental state through the increasingly bizarre and disturbing things he says and does. Initially we sympathise with Benny's predicament in being sacked by his aunt. But our first view of Benny has him sitting catatonically with his mouth hanging open to provoke his brother Vish's sympathy and then coming out with the refrain from his father's favourite Beach Boys song, 'Bah-bah-bah … Bah-Barbara-ann' (15). In context this nonsense has the same menace as the ending to Carol Ann Duffy's dramatic monologue 'Psychopath', in which, after revelations of the rapes and murders he has committed, the title character addresses the reader: 'Drink up son,/the world's your fucking oyster. Awopbopaloobop alopbimbam', quoting Little Richard's rock classic 'Tutti Frutti'.[16]

From this point onwards, Benny's words and actions appear more and more erratic as they reveal and embody his psychological state. After his transformation in the cellar, he takes up his place as potential salesman in the front office with a psychotic awareness of power, at once assured and inconstant (47). To complement that power, he looks at an image in a bondage magazine of a woman strapped to an n-shaped board being 'fucked up the arse' (48). As he examines the detail of the image, it seems to validate his inner transformation and new sense of control, so that he thinks 'this is not nothing'. It is the beginning of a series of disturbing statements indicative of a deranged psychosis. When he sees Maria Takis leaving, he says to himself '"She's mine." He meant it too. He committed himself to it as he said it', and he goes on to determine that he will 'rise up from the cellar and stand in the fucking sky' (51). Or there are his pathological assertions of power and control over other characters in the book, such as with Vish: 'You are inside my fucking head and I have got the key' (114), a statement which has the frightening authority of Dennis Hopper's recitation of Roy Orbison's 'In Dreams' to Kyle MacLachlan in David Lynch's film *Blue Velvet* (1986). Among other things, Benny is a brilliantly realised creation linguistically.

Equally disturbing is the vision of the future Benny promotes, his business 'ethic' with which he intends to save Catchprice Motors, by 'making it possible' (150), the vague menace of that 'it' incorporating all the disturbing overtones of his language so far. Like the characters in 'War Crimes', Benny represents a rampant enterprise culture which, as his family name suggests, merges catching customers or 'prospects' with 'cut price' and 'cut throat'. Ironically in view of his personal responsibility for Benny, Mort upholds the integrity of Cacka's business principles, while Cathy reminds him that the world has changed (68–9). Benny embodies that change. For him, Mort, Cathy, Howie and Gran are 'creatures at the end of an epoch' (70), a redundant or outmoded business practice, whereas he is 'going to run this business effectively ... By various methods' (103). He gives vivid demonstrations of his 'methods' in the shadow lands of his cellar: 'Down here I make the future, our future' (102).

The novel's structure links Benny's view of business with that of the Sydney crime underworld represented by Willy Fischer. The swindle which Benny tries to manipulate Gino Massaro into when Gino attempts a trade-in on his Commodore (171–5), is scuppered by Sarkis, and in retaliation Benny takes Sarkis into the cellar and straps him down (175–83). He leaves Sarkis in no doubt that '[t]his is a serious business you have got yourself involved with', as he straps him on to his own version of the n-shaped bondage contraption for eight hours (180). Equally, when Vish tries to stop Benny, he leaves Vish in no doubt that part of the motivation behind his actions is revenge for his own past: in accusing Vish of abandoning him to follow his own redemption as a Krishna, Benny says '[i]t's because of you I'm here. You put me here, Vish ... Where else could I come except down here? You think I was going to stay with Old Kissy Lips alone? Is that how you were looking after me?' (104) It is at this point that the novel enacts a strategic intercut: we learn in section 41 of Jack Catchprice's intervention in Gia's difficulties with Sydney gangster Wally Fischer, who has threatened her life in retaliation for her insulting him in the restaurant (sections 15 and 35). The narrative thus juxtaposes organised crime and the mafia-like power of Wally Fischer with Benny's manipulations and ambitions for his family business.

Benny is also structurally and thematically juxtaposed with Maria Takis and her residual social idealism. This contrast brings out how the characters foreground problems as *ethical*, while the novel itself shows a wider context in which they are seen as undeniably *political*. Maria, as Karen Lamb puts it, uncovers 'secrets far more obscene than anything to be found in a balance book' as an investigator of society's deceits.[17] Maria's view of the world coincides in a certain way with Carey's initial impulse for the novel. Carey has described how he attended a dinner party when the infamously corrupt Queensland Prime Minister, Joh

Bjelke-Petersen, was making his bid for Premiership on a 'flat tax' ticket. To Carey's horror the supposedly intelligent middle-class diners were selfishly welcoming this for the financial benefits it would give them: 'I came away so *angry*'.[18]

The incident is transformed in sections 53 and 55 of the novel into Maria's encounter with the artists, suburbanites and the Attorney General at Corky Missenden's dinner party in a rich Sydney suburb. Maria's anger is generated by her disgust at hearing rich people complaining about taxes, and derives from her belief that her work in the tax office has some potential social effect in redistributing 'all this criminal wealth' (216) to counter-act poverty and homelessness. As she tells Jack Catchprice when stating what is in effect her *credo* in section 46 of the novel, 'You don't need socialism to fix that, you just need a good Taxation Office and a Treasury with guts' (216).[19]

As with the hippy commune in *Bliss*, Maria's idealism is questioned. For one thing, her place, and by implication her position in terms of what she represents in the tax office, is increasingly a marginal one. She is now sent out on insignificant investigations such as the one into the Catchprice business, rather than crusading against the big business corruption she knows exists, as she had in the past. This is partly the result of the demotion of her previous boss and ex-lover, Alistair, the father of her child. Alistair had had a vision of the tax office as an agency for 'equity and care' (31), as a force for 'public good' (124); but he has lost his hold on the office, to be replaced by public servants with a diminished sense of their wider possible social responsibility (123–5). Alistair himself is a compromised character, a man with a sense of social mission whose personal life in his affair with Maria and treatment of her and his wife shows him to be 'a shit' (31), 'the great man of principle' whom Gia sees as 'a coward and a creep' (125). The novel tarnishes both Alistair and Maria as possible emblems of social good, thereby suggesting that the moral mission Maria envisages for herself as a tax crusader is in no way a panacea for the social and political ills the rest of the novel depicts. The contradictions in Maria's position come out clearly in her dealings with Jack Catchprice.

Her anger at the dinner party leads her to leave abruptly and afterwards to have an indignant confrontation with Jack. Her relationship with him has already been presented as something of a test for her integrity and vision. Jack's initial view of her is as someone with a moral imperative (170), whereas she is suspicious of him and only gradually comes partially to trust him. The uncertainties between them have ironic effects. In Maria's case, we see her integrity tested by the plush life Jack launches her into. She is attracted by his car, despite her puritan reaction to rich things, and Jack explains this as an understandable reaction to 'addictive things' which make you feel wonderful, like crack cocaine (195). The ambiguity of this is compounded at the dinner party where her usual condemnation of wealth as 'a form of theft' is compromised in the beautiful setting of Corky Missenden's house by her response 'as if she were allowing herself to be sexually excited by a criminal' (239). Maria's escape from the house seems to redeem her, as does her condemnation of what she has seen. But the situation is complicated by Jack himself. He is undoubtedly caught up in the corruption of the business world he works in, and this comes across in their conflicting usage of the verb 'to fix'. Whereas Maria's notion of 'fixing' society's ills involves having a good tax office, Jack is a 'fixer' in a different sense – a manipulator and a dealer in shady opportunities. He 'fixes' Gia's problem with Willy Fischer; he fixes it so that the Catchprice investigation is curtailed, thinking this is what Maria wants, although only at the cost of involving himself in some dangerous connections (236). He even tries to manipulate the dinner party so that he and Maria might sit together. Ironically he doesn't manage this minor rearrangement, with the result that Maria hears about Jack Catchprice as a representative of 'dirty money' (243). Jack's *credo* rewrites Gran Catchprice's. Her philanthropic, if deluded, view of her work has been expressed earlier in relation to her helping Sarkis: 'This is what I always liked best about having a business. I liked giving young people a chance' (96). In her son Jack this charitable ethic has been reformed: 'What else are you worried by? Let me fix it for you. It's what I like most about business … there's almost nothing you can't fix' (215).

Maria sees Jack as belonging to 'an alien culture' (251); yet whereas Jack's effect on Maria is potentially a corrupting one, her effect on him is potentially a transformative one. Although Maria expresses her belief in the potential for society to change for the good, it is Jack who apparently embodies the living reality. Faced with Maria's moral integrity, Jack declares himself a Catchprice 'damaged, compromised, expedient' (250); but he does so in the hope and belief that through her influence he might change. Ironically, it is Jack and his nephew Benny, who express the need for people to understand and empathise with each other. Benny's insistent refrain is that he wants to 'show' his life or the lives of his family to other people (134, 155, 227), and although he goes about this in bizarre and reprehensible ways, his point is the significant one: 'We're people, not numbers' (135). Jack is more orthodoxly articulate and respectable, but his point is not dissimilar: '[i]f no one can change ... what point is there in anything? If we cannot affect each other's lives, we might as well call it a day. The world is just going to slide further and further into the sewer' (251–2).

This touches on an element which Carey has suggested is central in the novel. In the interview with Robert Dessaix for ABC radio in 1991, Carey said that his notion of the characters in the book was 'as plants in poor soil, or even poisoned soil ... struggling in some way towards where they can see some light ... struggling to reinvent themselves ... the problem with the characters is the nature of the soil ... a repressive, abusive environment ... without, I don't know if you can say "spiritual food"'.[20] For Carey, the horrific scenarios dealing with Benny in his cellar, an emblem of the inferno that the family 'business' has become (163, 234), are counterpoised by the moment of Benny rising up from hell towards the light, transformed into a hairless angel. Benny is ironically surrounded with and invaded by ideas and images of light and the angelic, from the perverse angel wings tattooed on his back to the names of angels scrawled on the walls of the cellar. This imagery of angels is possibly linked to Carey's work with Wim Wenders, whose previous film was *Wings of Desire* in which a beautiful angel falls in love with a trapeze artist and decides to be transformed back into a human being. The idea of angelic transformation contradicts the brutality of Benny's experience in ways which are provokingly ambiguous.

The opening image of Vish peering into the darkness of Benny's open mouth (8) captures the ambiguity: 'Whatever it was he was meant to see in there, he couldn't see it' (18). It is only later that the image is explained in Benny's terms and we realise that it epitomises both his own sense of identity and the impossibility of his communicating that to another person. In the cellar he is trying to explain himself to Vish, to 'show' his life to his brother: 'he opened his mouth for his brother to look in. What he meant was: light. I have light pouring out of me' (114). It is a tragic emblem of Benny's entrapment within himself and his circumstances, and his desire to escape, to be transformed, to become an angel. Another example is Benny's repeated mantra 'I cannot be what I am' (21). As Chris Floyd has pointed out,[21] this catchphrase – perhaps another echo in 'Catchprice' – is a paradox. It implies 'things are preventing me from being myself'; but the tone could also be read as horrified disbelief: 'I *cannot* be what I am'. The first reading suggests Benny's desire to be transformed into a megalomaniacal individualist; the second emphasises his status as victim.

Both Benny and Jack are calling for affective relationships between individuals. The novel thus ironically structures its potentially positive ethical centres through two of the most problematic characters, whilst at the same time compromising the supposedly positive character of Maria, as she expresses her rejection of the baby she is bearing. When Jack offers to look after Maria and the baby too, her angry response is articulated with ironic glances at Benny's light imagery: '"I wish you could have it, Jack. I really do." She looked like a Francis Bacon smeared with neon light. "I don't want the fucking thing. I don't want to give birth to anything"' (251).

As a culmination of all these themes, Benny 's capture of Maria in the latter part of the novel is central in terms of plot and thematic development. At one level, it is the confrontation between two world-views, two alien cultures – progressive social

change and rapacious social exploitation. But such an interpretation is too simplistic. Just as both these characters have been
seen to be compromised or contradictory, so the denouement of
the novel is deeply ambiguous.

When Maria enters Benny's cellar she discovers 'the innards
of Catchprice Motors' (259), an emblem of the corruption hidden
at the heart of the family and business. Benny abducts Maria
with the intention of raping her as part of his affirmation for his
actualization course, and Maria realises ironically that both she
and Benny have been following the same course on identical
cassette tapes, so that she knows exactly what this means. Benny
has become an angel of fire and lust, and at this level Maria's
struggle against him might represent the triumph of her compromised idealism and principles over the corruption embodied
in Benny and the Catchprice empire. But this view is subverted
by other elements in this final scene.

Benny is an apocalyptic figure of retribution: his shooting of
Vish and Maria echoes his own shooting by his mother Sophie
after she has found Mort 'sucking her younger son's penis' one
Saturday afternoon (105). Yet Benny is also peculiarly a possible
figure of redemption. His sexual terrorism of Maria is
undeniable as is his terrifying appropriation of the baby, whom
he christens little Benny (276) and whispers over like 'a sorcerer
laying spells' (277) as if he were passing on his poisoned legacy.
Yet, under the pressure of the circumstances of Maria's labour,
Benny also breaks out of his psychopathic mental prison to aid
Maria give birth, and then undeniably if ambiguously seems to
care for the baby, asserting 'Why would I kill a baby? I am an
angel ... I changed myself ... It's possible' (274).

It is *this* figure, along with Benny the potential rapist, whom
Maria hits on the skull with the tyre lever in order to retrieve her
new-born infant. Benny's probable death in the dregs of
'puddled seepage' on the cellar floor (279) is simultaneously the
destruction of an embodiment of social evil and a tragic end for a
by now genuinely tragic figure, victim as well as victimiser, a
demise which generates empathy as much as revulsion. The
effect is hardly alleviated by the additional sentence Carey added

to the paperback edition of the novel's ending: 'They would have to wait for the emergency rescue squad to free them.'[22]

Equally ambiguous is the very notion of the child born in the cellar. It is an emblem of potential redemption, a new Benny salvaged from the corruption, a kind of bizarre Nativity. But if it is such, then is Carey indulging a male fantasy of hope for the future embodied in a female figure nurturing a new-born infant in the manner of, say, Achebe in *Anthills of the Savannah* or Ngugi in *A Grain of Wheat*? Or is the Francis Bacon-like brutality of *The Tax Inspector* more searing in effect, and as a result more thought-provoking? Both Achebe and Ngugi reinscribe women into the roles of caring mothers as archetypal hopes for the future; but because of the savagery of Carey's novel, it is difficult to see him as doing that.

The text as it stands seems to offer the birth of the baby, and Maria's reappropriation of it from Benny, not as a panacea so much as a temporary respite from some gruelling material, and is far from being an easy parable of redemptive change. This action is run in tandem with Gran Catchprice's abortive attempt to cleanse the earth of Catchprice Motors by blowing it up with gelignite and to purge history of Cacka and his children (259). In the event her destruction is as messy and inconclusive as Benny's abduction of Maria. At the end of both, the eldest and youngest Catchprices are presumably dead, but with no real sense of finality or potential for change.

This coincides with the contradictions evident between Carey's stated intentions when writing the novel and his awareness that the finished product was something different. He has spoken about wanting the book to affirm life through 'trying to oppose these two strong sexual urges – the birth and the sexual predator, the rapist';[23] 'I actually wanted to write a book affirming life through birth'.[24] But this doesn't represent the actual novel. As Carey has recognised, the redemptive imperative was overtaken by the necessity of being honest to the characters as they existed: 'I wanted birth to be so absolutely redemptive that it would change the poison person,' he has said, but 'in the end, when you look at it you can't be dishonest about what they [the characters] are going to do.'[25] The novel deliberately withholds any such idealised scenario in favour of remaining true to the political ambiguities it has investigated. It is this ambiguity which accounts for the disturbing power of the book. In terms of its political issues if not its fictional innovations, it is perhaps the most adventurous of Carey's career so far, and an indication that the acclaim for his work has in no way compromised the risks he takes with his fiction.

The Unusal Life of Tristan Smith (1994)
and The Big Bazoohley (1995)

> Why does it have to teach you? ... Why can't you just
> enjoy it? (*The Unusual Life of Tristan Smith*, 168)

THE Unusual Life of Tristan Smith is undoubtedly the strangest of Carey's novels. It marks a return to the overt alternative world-building found in the early stories with their fantastic and fable-like scenarios, and implicit in works like *Oscar and Lucinda*. It might be characterised as a cross between the dystopian science fiction of novels like *The Left Hand of Darkness* or *The Dispossessed* by Ursula Le Guin, for whose work Carey has expressed his admiration,[1] and the carnivalesque qualities of Robertson Davies's *The Deptford Trilogy* or *Nights at the Circus* by Angela Carter, who expressed her admiration for Carey's *Oscar and Lucinda*.[2]

The dystopian qualities are evident in the satirical contrast between the novel's two nations, Efica and Voorstand, modelled roughly on Australia and the USA, a contrast of two political states. On the surface, Voorstand epitomises a cruel and ruthless imperialist culture, using and abusing the smaller, less powerful Efica for its own ends, epitomised by the ELF project to thread 2,400 miles of insulated cable through Efica for defence purposes (33), and by the manipulation of Efican politics by the Voorstandish secret service (35). It has a corrupt culture embodied in the high-tech Voorstandish Sirkus, with its giant vid screens, a cultural hegemony which threatens to marginalise any Efican cultural activity by its sheer size (10) and which Felicity despises since it 'ran counter to everything we Eficans held so dear' (50).

It is individualistic and self-seeking whereas Efica is 'more humane, more bureaucratic' (46). Efica is small, insignificant and beleaguered, but it also embodies a communal state with a cultural integrity marked by Felicity's belief in Feu Follet's version of Sirkus and her work contributing to the creation of a national identity, 'inventing the culture of its people' (50, 53). Bill's decision to go and work in the Voorstand Sirkus is seen as a betrayal culturally as well as personally (50–2), which Felicity counteracts through her Brechtian agit-prop plays (55) and the performance of *The Caucasian Chalk Circle*. Tristan becomes the 'mascot' for this anti-establishment theatre, which forms an avant-garde 'not only artistically but also morally' (66), a subversive role which relates to what we will see as Tristan's personification of the marginalised experience of disability.

Yet as in Le Guin's work, what is also explored through this structural contrast are the contradictions involved within as well as between the two cultures. There are evident contradictions in Efican culture with its political divisions between the Voorstand-supporting Red party and the Blue party which Felicity tragically champions. The colour coding reverses the usual attribution to left and right: effectively the Reds are capitalists (33–4), while the Blues are idealist reformers (34) or Brechtian revolutionaries like Felicity. Efica is also riddled with Voorstandish subversions and agents like Gabe Manzini who takes advantage of Roxanna's desire for the good life. It suffers from a cultural cringe which is accompanied by a compensatingly fierce and insular pride (5, 9). Along with its history as a penal colony and its massacred indigenous peoples (9), this suggests analogies with Australia and the wider post-colonial experience. The eighteen islands of Efica constitute a hybrid culture with a hybrid English language, the 'soft, self-doubting Efican patois' (51). Significant neither as a military nor as an economic force (202), a strategic territory to be manipulated and used, they are 'the periphery shouting at the centre' (32). Such language is familiar from critical approaches to post-colonialism and, as has been increasingly the case in such debates, Carey's book explores the ambivalence of this dualism, the covert strengths of the periphery, the hidden weakness of the centre.

The oppressive Voorstand culture is shown as enticing, as Tristan's ambivalent relationship with the Mouse mask suggests, and vulnerable. When Felicity undertakes her election campaign for the Blues, she dresses Tristan 'in the visage of the enemy', the sharp-toothed Mouse (180), since she herself was originally a Voorstander and 'no matter what her critique of Voorstandish hegemony', she 'obviously held more complex feelings for Bruder Mouse than she had ever admitted ... she was a creature of her culture' (185). Like Maria in *The Tax Inspector* and Lucinda in *Oscar and Lucinda*, Tristan's mother is one of a number of strong women characters in Carey's work who challenge the roles and limitations imposed on them. Once Felicity has been assassinated, Tristan's first response is to grind the mask to dust (223); yet in the later stages of the novel, he adopts the persona of Bruder Mouse in the form of the gutted Simulacrum, subversively infiltrating himself into Voorstand culture and into the embrace of Peggy Kram.

Vincent, too, is both hostile to, and enamoured of, Voorstand culture, despite being a leading strategist for the Blues and devoted to freeing Efica of Voorstand influence (56–7). After Tristan's traumatic escape from the hospital, Roxanna urges the company to visit the Sirkus and Sparrow observes 'I don't doubt that it's reactionary ... What I want to know is: will it cheer me up?' (160). The Voorstand Sirkus is attacked as 'commercial' but it is also 'fun'. At the end of the show, Sparrow is converted and comes out celebrating the Voorstanders as 'a great people ... That's what we keep forgetting when we're trying to get their hands out of our guts. That's what a show like this teaches you. Theirs was a country that was founded on a principle. What you can still see in this Sirkus is their decency. I'd forgotten it. I spend all my time thinking about their hypocrisy. You don't see decency when their dirigibles are bombing some poor country who tried to renegotiate their Treaty.' Roxanna's reply is: 'Why does it have to teach you? ... Why can't you just enjoy it?' (168).

There are a number of different issues at work here. Not least is the question of the contradictory legacy of the imperial process, epitomised in the contemporary world by the significantly similar love–hate relationship between Americanised cultures and America itself. The hegemonic culture is hegemonic precisely because it achieves consent as well as enforcing coercion. Similar contradictions emerge during the approach to the crumbling splendour of Saarlim city (292–4) and Tristan's comments on Voorstand's ambivalent appeal: 'It was through your charm and your expertise that you conquered us, with your army, yes, and with the VIA, but you kept us conquered with jokes and dancers, death and beauty, holographs, lasers, Vids' (294). Peggy Kram later provides an insider's critique of Voorstand culture which reveals its hidden weaknesses and ambiguities, suggesting that 'the Great Historical Past' is being upheld merely by a few fanatics like herself, that Voorstanders 'were better then' and did not need to resort to brutality, and that Voorstand itself is in hock to 'foreign corporations' (406–7). But it is through her sexual relationship with Tristan that she is led to articulate this critique, and she herself is interestingly compromised through her seduction by the Mouse: her infatuation with the Simulacrum is shattered when she finds Tristan inside and the horror of her reaction fundamentally qualifies our view of her humanity as a character. This section of the book presents the spectacle of the upholder of the best past traditions of Voorstandish culture being subversively infiltrated by an 'Ootlander' disguised as one of the central emblems of her own culture, suggesting hidden weaknesses within hegemonic forces. In adopting the Mouse costume, Tristan enacts the kind of subaltern retaliation and destabilisation effected through a post-colonial 'mimicry' of dominant colonial forces such as that envisaged by Homi Bhabha, a mimicry which is 'at once resemblance and menace', a '*double* vision which in disclosing the ambivalence of colonial discourse also disrupts its authority'.[3]

Much of this accords with Carey's own sense of the major sources of origin for the novel, linking with the critique of America which threaded through 'American Dreams', *Bliss* and *Illywhacker*. The book was 'fuelled by a strong suspicion that America has sometimes meddled in the affairs of [Australia]' and that visitors from the 'peripheries' to 'the great metropolitan centres' often come with a love in their hearts which is contradicted by a feeling of not being known or understood. Added to this was a visit to Disneyland in Florida with his son to see Mickey and Minnie Mouse walking around 'like royalty' and seeming 'mythical and magical'. This led Carey to begin reimagining these icons as having 'deeper mythical, or ethical, or moral roots', and to begin reinventing America along the lines of a heretical Protestant sect which had believed animals had souls and for whom the animal icons were 'degenerate forms' of principles and beliefs from a more ethical past. He also began to imagine someone coming in from 'the periphery … from a small country who had been meddled with' by the more powerful country, who inhabits the skin of one of these icons and 'becoming powerful in the re-imagined America' by doing so. The literary analogies Carey has mentioned are with Kafka's invention in his novel *America*, and with the narrative voice of eighteenth-century travel writings.[4]

From such sources, Carey has created a narrative which entertains as well as it instructs. Roxanna's question, which forms the epigram for this chapter, raises issues designed to investigate the function of art itself. Her plea seems to encompass a call for art not to be seen simply as serious, for it to service pleasure, be escapist, and for that to be fundamental to its function and importance. At the same time, the capacity of art to take us out of ourselves, to heal through enjoyment, is being questioned: hasn't the Sirkus merely been an officially sanctioned analgesic, alleviating the pain but changing nothing? As my use of the epigram suggests, we might invoke Roxanna's response to the Sirkus in relation to Carey's novel itself. It is an example of almost pure storytelling. It displays all of Carey's capacity for narrative drive and for the deployment of hybrid forms. It mixes the fabulatory and fantastic with elements of the political thriller, as the book unravels the manipulations of the Voorstandish secret service around the Efican election which lead to the assassinations of Natalie and Felicity, the hazardous journey to Voorstand as Tristan is unwittingly implicated in a terrorist role through the undercover blunders of Jacqui, and the threat to

Tristan's life from Gabe Manzini. As in *Oscar and Lucinda,* these narrative convolutions generate a bizarre sense of characters being overtaken by the wider flow of events, of 'history lurking in the dark' (207).

This is utterly engrossing to the extent that it defies obvious thematic containment. It is easy to say whether or not one enjoyed reading it, but to say what it is 'about' is quite another matter. Perhaps that is partly because the novel hovers between a number of possibilities, none of which presides as the final interpretative template. The contrasts and contradictions explored between Efica and Voorstand suggest in part a political fable, yet the political narrative is hardly worked through fully enough. It always seems secondary to the elements of Tristan's unusual life, rather than integrated with it. For example, the brief glimpse we are given of Tristan's life between his mother's death and the trip to Voorstand suggests a growing involvement in pamphleteering and political confrontation in the form of the January 20 group (231); but this is undeveloped or sketchy, and plays no direct role in the latter part of the novel. If on the other hand the political elements are intentionally secondary, then one wonders about their function in this extravagant fantasy.

If an approach to the novel as political fable seems unsatis-factory, a more fruitful approach might be to consider it as what it ostensibly is, a myth-making fantasy. The fantastical elements are evident in the Sirkus culture Carey invents and in the fabulatory extravagance of the story itself. As Kate Kellaway suggested, the novel deals with 'the theatricality of appearances', and she links the theatre theme with Carey's experience deriving from his wife Alison Summers's profession as theatre director.[5] This world of masks, storytelling, performances and bodily functions, presents a mixture of the grotesque and the circus-like which might suggest analogies with the carnivalesque and the theories of Mikhail Bakhtin. The one mark of the carnival missing is actual laughter: *Tristan Smith* is not a comic novel, despite the claims of some reviewers,[6] and despite its opening epigram. There, Bruder Duck tells Bruder Mouse how he would change the minds of people in foreign countries over locking animals in cages: 'I would do doody and fall over ... I would make them laugh' (3). Rather than invoking sheer comedy, perhaps this serves to indicate more the idea of the humanising function of fictional entertainment, within which category this novel undoubtedly falls.

Unlike much science fiction or fantasy, Carey takes the risk of not revealing the full dimensions or constituent elements of his fictional world, indicating in interviews that much originally explanatory or expository material generated by the freedom and excitement of inventing a new world and naming things was either relegated to footnotes or cut out of the final version.[7] Galen Strawson pointed this out in a review for *The Independent on Sunday*, providing a judicious response to the effect of the novel:

> Many writers have created new worlds. Some seem to bring their world into being as they write, adding new facts and features seriatim. The most successful (like Tolkein [sic] in *The Lord of the Rings* and Frank Herbert in *Dune*) give the impression that they are describing a place that exists independently of their imagination. Peter Carey approaches this second category but falls short. This is not a failure but a choice: his working shows, given the way in which he takes pleasure in his invention. The explanatory footnotes are mock scholarship, and do not seriously deepen one's sense of a pre-existing world. The glossary of Efican and Voorstand English is hastily compiled. There are inaccuracies (of French), implausibilities (of geography), and at least one impossibility (of chronology). But the whole thing works. It releases an intense, disturbed energy. It runs as planned, a powerful jalopy, bright with scavenged chrome, fairy lights, and no brakes, carrying a story of considerable psychological brilliance.[8]

Carey's strategy is to assume a knowing audience for the narrative voice, an audience which is mostly familiar with the details of the cultures invoked, as with the address '[y]ou know this already, Meneer, Madam? Then skip ahead' (356). This is both effective and problematic. Its effectiveness is measured by the degree of absorption achieved by the narrative. The assumption of such an audience creates a sense of the pre-existence of this fictional world alongside our own. It makes it easier to generate narrative conviction, to suspend the reader's disbelief, if the raw mechanisms of the fictional illusion are not being continually exposed through narrative explanation. Instead Carey indulges in the device of footnoting the narrative, the source of the footnotes being both Tristan himself as narrator and an undisclosed editorial presence.

The problems of this strategy are paradoxically an accompanying lack of narrative conviction. The reader ends the book little wiser about the origins or nature of the 'full story' to this imaginary world. For example, although we are given some insight into the cultural mythology surrounding the Dog, the Duck and the Mouse, we are little wiser about the Dog and Duck by the close of the novel. Nor are we very certain about other aspects of the fictional scenario like the origins of the Sirkus. This is undoubtedly better than elaborate self-explanation, but it creates its own dissatisfaction in that we feel somewhat short-changed, as if we had been sent on a bit of a wild dog-duck-and-mouse chase, or heard a cock-and-bull story by a master story-teller. It seems Carey's imagination was fired by the story of Tristan within this framework and not by the framework itself.

Perhaps this point gives the book a truer emphasis. As with Herbert in *Illywhacker*, the heart of the book is Tristan Smith himself. As a narrator, Tristan is similar to Herbert in some ways. His story is more contained but similarly picaresque in manner, and it is his voice which dominates the tone and flavour of the book. In that the listener is revealed as complicit in the situation, the narrative voice's address to an audience is similar to *Illywhacker*'s: from the opening chapter, Tristan speaks to his readers as citizens of Voorstand, as 'Meneer, Madam' in the manner of the MC at the Water Sirkus (341), and this suggests that the novel is a performance or display, and Tristan has 'no choice' (6) but to perform. But it is also a clarification of the historical record as Tristan explains his behaviour in Voorstand to imaginary or real inquisitors, possibly the Bhurgercourt to which Peggy Kram gives her deposition (414).

Like most of Carey's central characters, Tristan is another

'odd-bod', to use the phrase describing Oscar. *The Tax Inspector* ends with a monstrous birth, and *The Unusual Life of Tristan Smith* begins with one. Tristan is subject to diverse congenital conditions: his mouth is a lipless rag with green bile bubbling from it; he has a leaking heart, a faulty duodenum, withered and twisted legs, clubbed feet, and a maximum height of three and a half feet. He is also a victim of personal betrayal, specifically by his father Bill, and as in *Oscar and Lucinda*, the theme of fathering and the relationship between father and son is strong in the book. Bill betrays Tristan's trust a number of times, as when he abandons him after Felicity 's death and Tristan calls him a traitor (308–11). Tristan inherits Wally as a surrogate father along with the extended family of the theatre, until finally Bill reassumes his role after Wally's death and the flight from Voorstand, with Jacqui as a potential surrogate mother (414). But the whole drive of the book is towards stressing that the sense of Tristan's monstrosity is a function of the attitudes and assumptions of his perceivers. In this regard the episode in the hospital in sections 37, 42 and 43 of Book One is one of the most painful moments, since Tristan is treated as sub-human by hospital staff, patients and the crowd gathered to watch his escape. Equally telling is the enamoured response of Mrs Kram to Tristan in the guise of Bruder Mouse as opposed to her horror at him once divested of the costume. The exception is the girl in the Zeelung hotel who gives him a flower: 'she saw that I was a human underneath my horror' (284).

The issue of severe disability is central to the novel and was the other crucial part of its genesis. According to the interview Carey conducted with Sue Wyndham, '[w]hen he was first thinking about the book, Carey saw a family pushing a badly deformed boy in a wheelchair near his home. At first he recoiled, but quickly realised he was forgetting the person inside the ugly body. At the same time, he had been reading *Beauty and the Beast* to his children. As those images merged together, he found he had the makings of his protagonist, Tristan Smith, a talented actor and passionate lover trapped in a useless body'.[9] Carey's account to Kate Kellaway was that he first saw 'a horribly deformed young man, only seeing afterwards what I'd seen – a sharp look of intelligence. I suppose I'm interested in the life you walk away from and discount.'[10] He has also associated this last element with his 'beginnings as a writer': 'Faulkner was one of my early influences, particularly *As I Lay Dying*. One of the things that attracted me to him was these people who you would walk by in the road and wouldn't pay any attention to, and in the book they produced this rich language and complicated interior lives.'[11] Perhaps this sheds some light on the inventive richness of the narrative language and voice: the novel is Tristan's interior and exterior life through his own utterance, and it is this which gives the book its imaginative exuberance.

Bizarre and intriguing as it is, *The Unusual Life of Tristan Smith* marks the continued adventurousness of Carey's career as a novelist. Like Tristan in the opening chapter, Carey felt himself to be 'up there on a tightrope' while he negotiated the great freedom of sheer invention which the book allowed.[12] On the final page of *The Unusual Life of Tristan Smith*, Tristan reveals, like the narrator's view of Lucinda at the end of *Oscar and Lucinda*, that 'although I did not know it, my unusual life was really just beginning' (414).

As if to echo that, Carey has published yet another innovation in his fictional practice, this time into children's literature. *The Big Bazoohley* takes the idea of adventurous risk-taking as its main idea. The Big Bazoohley of the title refers to the notion of life's big gamble, the main chance, whose existence nine-year-old Sam has absorbed from his gambler father and which Sam succeeds in pulling off. Like many other Carey characters, he does this through a process of self-transformation. For Crabs, or the narrator in 'American Dreams', or the characters in 'The Chance', or Herbert Badgery, or Benny, or even Oscar, self-transformation is a finally negative process. For Sam, as with Harry Joy, it ultimately has positive results, despite its painfulness on the way. Like Tristan in the simulacrum, Sam subjugates himself to absorption by a hateful disguise: he is transformed from being a normally grubby little boy into the scrubbed and pristinely clean Perfecto Kiddo, complete with velvet suit, manicured nails and super gelled curly hair. He undergoes this nauseating role-change in order to win the £10,000 prize in a cosmetic company's competition and thus save his beleaguered parents from bankruptcy. This whimsical and engaging tale contains many characteristic features of Carey's fictional world in miniature, not least the humorously self-referential role given to Sam's mother as the artist who creates magical paintings which are perfectly miniaturised versions of reality the size of a matchbox. Echoing Oscar and Lucinda, the strange Mr de Vere concludes the story by saying 'life is a gamble … There is no doubt about it. Love, business, art – you have to take a chance' (128). It seems as if Peter Carey would undoubtedly agree with him.

Jack Maggs (1997)

JACK Maggs begins in the best traditions of Victorian melodrama:

> It was a Saturday night when the man with the red waistcoat arrived in London. It was, to be precise, six of the clock on the fifteenth of April in the year of 1837 that those hooded eyes looked out the window of the Dover coach and beheld, in the bright aura of gas light, a golden bull and an overgrown mouth opening to devour him – the sign of his inn, the Golden Ox. (1)

The immediate attention to details – 'the red waistcoat', 'to be precise' – is notable, as is the style of narrative delivery. The narrator's manner is inflected with phrasings which are slightly colloquialised ('It was a Saturday night', 'looked out the window') and antiquated ('six of the clock'). After experimenting with a more deliberately antique narrative voice, adapted from accounts in eighteenth- and nineteenth-century criminal biographies, Carey wisely decided that would be 'anachronistic [...] a bit mannered',[1] opting instead for this mildly-flavoured historical feel. The precision of the timing is significant: the action of this fast-paced novel unfolds in the space of three weeks and insists on dates and times to stress the urgency of its central character's quest. The narrative's imaginative energy makes it, in Anthony Hassall's words, a 'cracking yarn'.[2] Place is also important: the main action is set in Victorian London in its heyday as the metropolitan centre of the British Empire. In order to recreate this London of the past convincingly, Carey researched the details to get a true sense of the place. Maps of the time provided precise information about street names, which are vividly inhabited with the vibrant life of this imaginary city, seen as if for the first time through the eyes of the newly-returned Jack Maggs: 'There was now a tobacconist in Great Queen Street, a laundry, and a narrow little workroom where glass eyes were made for dolls and injured gentlemen' (6). Of particular use were descriptions by foreign visitors to London. A peculiarity which intrigued Carey in such accounts was the effect of gas lighting: instead of being dark and gloomy as one might expect, one American traveller of the time, unused to street lighting at all, found the main London streets were 'blindingly bright',[3] as they are for Jack Maggs: 'This light had shone all the way from the Elephant and Castle: gas light, blazing and streaming like great torches' (2).

Of course the poorer sidestreets would not be, and this paradox is crucial. Like Joseph Conrad's *Heart of Darkness*, *Jack Maggs* juxtaposes the hidden and the visible to reveal a terrible social violence beneath the surface of the imperial ideal. London's glowing streets with their 'bright aura' mask a savage barbarity, captured emblematically in the inn sign of the 'overgrown mouth' ready to devour the golden bull. This is a story of dispossession, appropriation and retaliation. Jack Maggs is an orphan, betrayed and brutalised into a life of crime by an uncaring society, which, having made him a criminal, then punished him with imprisonment and transportation to Australia. He returns in search of his home and reparation, and his quest reveals a continuing mental bondage to illusions about England, his past, his 'family' and the other sources of his identity. Maggs undergoes an awakening from a somnambulism which acts as a major metaphor in the story. As the note in the novel's publication details explains, the epigraph derives from the popular nineteenth-century pseudo-science of mesmerism through 'magnetisation' as practiced by Armand Marie Jacques de Chastenet, Marquis de Puységur. Puységur (1751–1825), a disciple of Franz Anton Mesmer (1734–1813), discovered the technique of invoking a state of somnambulistic sleep and is recognised as one of the founders of modern psychotherapy.[4]

The extract from de Puységur's *Mémoires pour servir a l'histoire et a l'établissement du magnétisme animal* (first published 1784) outlines his view that a hypnotist has the power to bring his patient out of a magnetic state by an act of will. By contrast, Maggs increasingly realises that only he can liberate himself from his mesmerised subjection to England, to false notions of social responsibility and kinship, and even to his own fictional origins.

Characteristically, Carey crosses genre boundaries in this novel to create a distinctive hybrid narrative. Historical fiction, which he exploited so vividly in *Oscar and Lucinda,* now adopts the traditions of Australian convict literature epitomised by Marcus Clarke's classic novel *His Natural Life* (1885). Convict literature is a well-established form in Australian writing. Part of its significance lies in its 'revaluation of Australian history in which the convict experience is seen as significant in the development of the national psyche'.[5] This confrontation with the colonial past had long been suppressed in the popular mind. In his *Beyond the Fatal Shore* documentaries, Robert Hughes indicated the way in which the 'convict stain' was often a hidden history which many white settler families did their best to eradicate, although more recently it has often become a cause for commemoration.[6] Marcus Clarke's book was one of the first to address this suppression, being published originally as a serial in the Melbourne *Australian Journal* between 1870 and 1872. John Thieme calls it 'a study of the colonial psyche wrestling with the competing claims of English and Australian society'.[7] The revaluation of convict ancestry has continued in novels as diverse as Thomas Keneally's *Bring Larks and Heroes* (1967) and *The Playmaker* (1987), Patrick White's *A Fringe of Leaves* (1976), and more recently Richard Flanagan's *Gould's Book of Fish* (2001). Carey's novel takes a different angle and examines the impact of the imperial experience on the English national psyche. It allows the transported convict to return 'home' and confront the society which created him.

While using the historical and convict genres, Carey inflects them with postcolonial counter-discourse strategies and meta-fictionality. By doing so, the novel shows how the economic exploitation of class and colonialism are integrally linked to cultural domination, which effaces and appropriates identities, selves and histories. Carey uses his characteristic narrative tactics of short chapters, readily shifting tenses and interleaving threads, to create a vibrant interplay of themes and ideas as the postcolonial issues and fictional artifice feed into each other, while the layers of the story unfold with an appropriately mesmerising fluidity.

The convict is no less than a version of Magwitch from Dickens's *Great Expectations*. *Jack Maggs* is Peter Carey's *Wide Sargasso Sea*, an act of postcolonial retaliation against a parent culture. Like Jean Rhys's novel, it rewrites elements of a canonical text from the heart of the English literary tradition to reveal the hidden alternative history that cultural hegemony has effaced or suppressed. Carey 'willingly admits to having once or twice stretched history to suit his own fictional ends' in his Author's Note. *Wide Sargasso Sea* gives voice to the silenced and marginalised madwoman in the attic in *Jane Eyre*. *Jack Maggs* does the same for Magwitch. Carey describes *Great Expectations* as 'a way in which the English have colonized our ways of seeing ourselves. It is a great novel, but it is also, in another way, a prison. *Jack Maggs* is an attempt to break open the prison and to imaginatively reconcile with the gaoler.'[8] One of Carey's starting points for the novel was postcolonial theorist Edward Said's views on *Great Expectations* in *Culture and Imperialism*, in which Said sees the transported convict Magwitch as a metaphor for the relationship between England and its colonial offspring.[9] In his discussion, Said refers to Carey's work in a context which one can imagine triggered fruitful reflections in the novelist's mind. He quotes a passage from Robert Hughes's *The Fatal Shore*, where Hughes argues that in Magwitch 'Dickens knotted several strands in the English perception of convicts in Australia at the end of transportation. They could succeed, but they could hardly, in a real sense, return. They could expiate their crimes in a technical, legal sense, but what they suffered there warped them into permanent outsiders. And yet they were capable of redemption – as long as they stayed in

Australia.'[10] After referring to the writing of Australian historian Paul Carter, Said goes on:

> *Great Expectations* was not written with anything like the concern for native Australian accounts that Hughes or Carter has, nor did it presume or forecast a tradition of Australian writing, which in fact came later to include the literary works of David Malouf, Peter Carey, and Patrick White. The prohibition placed on Magwitch's return is not only penal but imperial: subjects can be taken to places like Australia, but they cannot be allowed a 'return' to metropolitan space, which, as all Dickens's fiction testifies, is meticulously charted, spoken for, inhabited by a hierarchy of metropolitan personages.[11]

Defying this prescription, by re-imagining him as Jack Maggs, Carey does allow Magwitch a future very different to that found in Dickens's original.[12] He is conditionally pardoned from his Australian prison and takes centre stage, to tell his story from his own point of view; he suffers the pain of being a 'permanent outsider' as well as being driven to murder, and yet he achieves a kind of redemption by virtue of what he learns during his encounter with his 'home'. Whereas Rhys's heroine writes back against the male character who dominated her in Charlotte Brontë's story, Carey audaciously has his hero confront the novelist who authored him, and rewrite his own creator.

Anthony Hassall points out that Carey's novel is not the only Australian reinvention of *Great Expectations*,[13] but it is certainly the most distinctive by its inclusion of a surrogate version of Dickens himself in the character of Tobias Oates, the novelist. While John Thieme has shown the extent of the engagement between Australia and Dickens and the numerous intertextual connections to be made between *Jack Maggs* and *Great Expectations*,[14] Hassall has indicated how the character of Tobias Oates has features in common with Charles Dickens, not least his love for his sister-in-law Mary Hogarth, his love of acting and obsession with mesmerism.[15] Dickens learned mesmerism from Dr John Elliotson, who popularised the practice in Victorian England in the 1830s and 1840s. As Carey discovered in his research for the novel, in addition to experimenting on his wife, Dickens developed an intense doctor-patient relationship with a Madame La Rue while in Italy in 1844: he put her into mesmeric trances in an attempt to heal her of 'a condition she had called *tic douloureux*, which I later gave to Jack Maggs'.[16]

But Carey's novel creatively sidesteps the direct connection with Dickens and *Great Expectations*. Like *Wide Sargasso Sea*, it is an autonomous work which functions entirely on its own terms. There is less to be gained from reading *Jack Maggs* in any detail against Dickens's novel than there is from considering its intrinsic issues, strategies and merits. Once we accept the starting point for this fictional reinvention, Jack Maggs and Tobias Oates function as convincing characters with their own imaginative sovereignty. They are also 'real life subject matter' and 'novelist in search of material', like Leopold Bloom and Stephen Daedalus in Joyce's *Ulysses*. Whereas Joyce shows up his budding novelist as out of touch with life and in need of the counsel Bloom can offer, Carey shows Oates to be a manipulative parasite, feeding from his subject under the pretence of helping him. This raises questions about the responsibility of the novelist to his subject matter that form part of a wider concern. Like the society which abandoned Maggs and the Empire which eats its own offspring, Oates is a false parent who refuses his responsibilities towards his own immediate and wider family. Family relationships, particularly parenting, orphaning and adoption, are to be understood literally and as metaphors for the responsibilities of society as a parent to its children. This preoccupation with orphans and abandoned children is a pattern that Carey recognises in his work and probably has 'psychological roots' in 'the trauma of going to boarding school',[17] of being 'sent away'.[18] It also has connections with the loss of his children with his first wife, who suffered an abortion and the death of twins during premature birth, an experience Carey has recounted in the autobiographical piece, 'A Small Memoir.'[19] But as so often, Carey insists that, when creating fiction, 'I never write close to life',[20] and that 'the purpose of my fiction is never therapeutic or confessional; I'll just use whatever's there.'[21] Instead, 'this denied trauma of my own echoes my country's trauma': 'Magwitch was behaving in a really Australian way. He's cast out, he's treated very badly, and all he can think to do, at the risk of his own life, is to go and live with his abusers.' This, Carey realised, 'was about *us*': Australians 'really were like abandoned children'.[22] It is, as Jack Maggs himself knows, 'a family matter' (48).

Jack Maggs is also an investigation of dispossession and delusion. Maggs returns to London seeking his home and harbouring contradictory desires for redemption, reconciliation and revenge. Both impulses are revealed as false. His first encounter is with his 'foster mother' (75), Mary 'Ma' Britten, who betrayed him into a life of childhood crime under the Fagin-like tutelage of Silas Smith. 'Ma' Britten, Mother Britain, embodies the failure of societal responsibility towards the orphan Maggs, representing the poor and the colonised. She is both 'the Queen of England' (92) and an abortionist. When Mary Britten asks Maggs 'What're you doing here in London?', his reply is 'It's my home […] That's what I want. My home' (5). As part of his deluded state, he later denies his Australian heritage, asserting 'you see, I am a fucking *Englishman*, and I have English things to settle. I am not to live my life with all that vermin. I am here in London where I belong' (128). What he has to settle is not merely his betrayal by England but also his own betrayal of his adoptive community in Australia.

One form of delusion is his view of Henry Phipps. Maggs explains in Chapter 71 how, while being transported by coach to begin his sentence, in his mind he impulsively adopted the orphaned Phipps as his 'son' (262), vowing to act as his benefactor in reparation for his own corrupted childhood. By becoming a benevolent substitute parent, he hoped to redress his own fate. An 'orphing' himself like Phipps and Oates, Maggs was 'betrayed' by his step-brother, Tom, 'to be cast out of my dear England'. He sees Phipps as what he himself might have been before being 'trained to be a varmint' and vows to 'weave him a nest so strong that no one would ever hurt his goodness' (263–4). His error is indicated by his mistaken assumption that the miniature portrait he keeps is of Phipps when in fact it is King

George IV dressed as a commoner (262), the very King who was responsible for Maggs's transportation and floggings: as Mercy Larkin points out, 'it were the King who lashed you' (318). He shows Oates the miniature vowing 'I will not abandon him' (264). Yet already at the beginning of the novel, having received a letter from Maggs warning of his impending arrival, Phipps has abandoned Maggs and gone into hiding at his club (267). By the end of the novel, despite having benefited substantially from Maggs's 'convict gold' (256), Phipps betrays Maggs and attempts to murder him. As an unjust society reveals its distorted inheritances, the idea of the 'benefactor' becomes increasingly ironic.

In his quest for his lost 'home' and 'son', Maggs takes a job as a footman for Percy Buckle, next door to the house he himself owns. He is forced to steal across the rooves to break in to the property he has purchased as part of his legacy to his son. In a reminder of his criminal childhood, Maggs's view of his 'home' from its rooftops (34) suggests how he does and does not belong, as his elevated views of England are increasingly revealed as illusory. Like a somnambulist, he is trapped in a dream of England, a fiction as vivid as those created by Oates, an illusion which re-enacts his exclusion from wealth and privilege.

By contrast, the real England is revealed as the inferno to which Maggs and Oates return after their nightmare visit to Gloucestershire: 'The London they left behind had been a sunny place where daffodils grew in the window boxes. The London they returned to seemed hellish' (291). Like Conrad, Carey exposes the violence beneath the colonial illusion, suggesting that the darkness originates not in the colonies but in the heart of imperialist London itself. When Phipps is on his way to murder Maggs, the realities are evident in the streets being dug up for new sewers:

> The trench was criss-crossed with new black pipes, and below this grid of iron was a further shadowy world of excavated arches leading to God knows what place. [...] Great wooden beams criss-crossed the street, like intrusions in a nightmare. Others had been propped against the walls of shops. These beams were joined together like

inverted, lopsided *A*'s, and something in their rude design brought to mind the gallows. A kind of fog now rose from the excavation, and in the penumbra of the gas light Henry Phipps imagined he saw a man's body hanging from a beam, suspended above the pit. (320–1)

The significance of this is evident in the following chapter when Maggs recalls the triangle to which he was strapped for flogging in New South Wales. Colonial violence ghosts the metropolitan centre. It was to distract himself from the pain while being whipped that 'the wretched man would begin to build London in his mind' (321): not 'Mary Britten's meat-rich room at Pepper Alley Stairs, but rather a house in Kensington whose kind and beautiful interior he had entered by tumbling down a chimney, like a babe falling from the outer darkness into light. Clearing the soot from his eyes he had seen that which he later knew was meant by authors when they wrote of England, and of Englishmen' (322). The London glimpsed here he first saw in his criminal exploits as a child with his 'Benefactor' (75), Silas, who took him 'further and further from the London that I knew' (96) over the roof tops and down the chimneys of the houses of the rich. During the first of these expeditions, the six-year old Maggs, 'imagining I was about to go to school' (95), enters this rich world thinking 'I was tasting what my future would be' (96). But that inheritance is not to be his, and the 'lessons' Silas promised prove to be assignments in burglary. Maggs, the working-class orphan, the eventual Australian, is a victim not merely of the actual oppressions he suffers, but also of a fictional England of the mind, an imaginary community which in reality is a nation of inequality whose injustices of class and colonialism are interwoven.[23]

Carey insinuates as much through an ironic linguistic echo. While Buckle is galvanising Phipps to murder his benefactor in order to secure possession of the property Maggs has leased for him, he tells Phipps 'Your house is not your own [...] It is the property of Jack Maggs. I have seen the title again this morning, and as far as I can tell it is still in his name' (270). Maggs's dream of creating the English gentleman from a convict inheritance exposes the origins of middle-class wealth in colonial and class exploitation. When Buckle's maid-servant, Mercy, reveals that Phipps is Maggs's son, Buckle is astonished and asserts 'But Mr Phipps is a gentleman', and he goes on to condone Phipps's hatred of Maggs:

> It is beyond belief. The convict owns the house next door? Pretends to be my footman, but owns the freehold? [...] It's convict gold, that's what it is. [...] who can blame the gentleman? Dirty money. Thievery. Murder. Of course he would hide. He don't want Jack Maggs trampling through his life. But what if the rascal cuts off all his funds? Disinheritance: it may be on the cards, Mercy. It must be on the cards, by gosh. (256)

But if Maggs were arrested, the property 'would be subsumed *nullus contredris* [...] It would be taken from him, as a felon' (270). Buckle's Latin phrase, the narrator tells us, is a fraudulent invention to mask his own lack of knowledge of the law, but it also recalls the doctrine of *terra nullius* whereby Australian indigenous peoples were defrauded of their inheritance and land. Similarly, the dispossession of the lower classes and of the colonies has created the wealth and wealthy of England and sustains their privilege. Maggs's illusions about Phipps, the son who attempts to murder him to keep the life-style bequeathed by his bene-factor, are part of his class-colonial blindness, a ragged-trousered philanthropy. Yet paradoxically, as Robert Tressell's novel reveals, while complicit in their own oppression, the dispossessed might yet disinherit the ruling class they work so hard to maintain.

The novel thus exposes the deceptions practiced by the imperial fiction of England on its offspring and the double complicity of oppressor and oppressed. Maggs gradually wakes from his self-deceiving fantasies of England to the violent realities of the London that made and betrayed him to criminality and then punished him for it. In a moment of sympathy with Maggs, Buckle tells Oates of his own sister who was transported to Australia, like Maggs: 'God help us all, that Mother England would do such a thing to one of her own' (89). The idea of the nation which has betrayed its children resonates through these orphaned characters, Maggs, Phipps, Oates, and all are implicated.

The other side to this is Magg's rejection of New South Wales and his family there. He vehemently denies being 'of that race [...] [t]he race of Australians' (312–13), but he learns his real sense of belonging from the aptly-named Mercy, Buckle's maid. She points out that, just as Maggs had been betrayed and orphaned, so he is in danger of doing the same to his own sons. Mercy herself was abandoned by a parent when her mother forced her into prostitution to save the family from starvation. She was rescued from her fate by the newly-enriched Buckle, who had himself come into an unexpected inheritance. This transformed him from 'a humble grocer in Clerkenwell' into 'the owner of a gentleman's residence at 29 Great Queen Street', but like Phipps, 'he was no more a gentleman' by this legacy than Maggs (9). The corrupt and corrupting social contradictions of wealth in Victorian London are shown in Buckle's betrayal of his guardianship: acting initially as Mercy's 'benefactor' (71), he abused her innocence still further by turning her into his mistress, his 'Good Companion' (115–16), a role she accepted in the hope that she might finally marry her master, like Pamela in Richardson's novel (151). Nevertheless, as she reminds him later in the novel, 'You've ruined me.' (299) Her involvement with Maggs stems from an increasingly genuine concern and 'charity' stirred by her 'knowledge of his ill-usage'(158). Her compassion becomes a moral tutelage as she insists that Maggs is in danger of disinheriting and abandoning his real children in favour of a fallacy. Mercy forces Maggs to face up to his responsibilities to his adopted country and his 'real children' (312), instead of remaining in the grip of self-deception: 'You were their da, but you had an aim to find a better class of son' (318).

The metafictional strategies of the novel are integral to this exposure of colonial delusions. They call attention to the process of fictional invention, not just as lying, as in *Illywhacker*, but as appropriation, theft. Just as England stole Magg's birthright by making him a thief, so Tobias Oates colonises Maggs for his own imaginative purposes, stealing Maggs's life for his fiction. Carey too performs a kind of theft in appropriating elements of Charles Dickens's *Great Expectations*, and in creating a novelist-character, Oates, modelled on Dickens. This transformation is partly a matter of play, and there are some nice jokes in the book as when Maggs finds himself on Carey Street (39). But it obviously has its serious side. This Magwitch escapes the grip of his creator to the extent of manacling him in his own trousers and threatening his life. His also escapes his own demise both in the original Dickens novel and in Oates's vindictive vision in his book, *The Death of Jack Maggs*. Maggs wakes from his somnambulist dream-fiction of England to re-write his own script and escape from his seemingly determined role, like Antoinette in *Wide Sargasso Sea*. Antoinette breaks with her part in *Jane Eyre* and the colonial script overlaying her life when she escapes imprisonment and, certain of her purpose at last, walks off down the corridor sheltering her candle. Some readers take this as indicating that she will fulfill her fate in *Jane Eyre* by burning down Thornfield and dying in the conflagration. But Rhys's adoption of the present tense and the artistic choice to end the novel at this moment of undefined intent also allow us to imagine Antoinette escaping the pre-determined chain of events into the blank page of the future. Jack Maggs, by contrast, is already having his script changed at the very beginning of Carey's novel where the other passengers in the coach from Dover busily 'imagined him' (1) in a variety of alternative guises. His suppressed voice is released from its original master text, allowing Maggs to adopt the classic position of autobiographical fiction and give his own account of his life. He writes, rather than merely being written.

Throughout the book, there is an intense awareness of story-telling, the writing process, and the capacity of both to deceive or liberate. This persistent attention stresses the relativity of any narrative, the multiple viewpoints on events. Maggs's version of his life appears in his journal and, appropriately enough for a counter discourse, it is written in mirror writing and invisible ink. The journal takes up chapters 21, 26–7, 43, 58–60 and 65. It is Maggs's 'secret history' (150), detailing his apprenticeship in crime under Silas Smith's tutelage and the tragedy of his love for Sophina, who was forced by Ma Britten to abort their baby and died on the gallows. It performs a number of functions: it is an invitation to 'imagine what it was' to live Maggs's early life (92). It is also his attempt at self-explanation, his bid for recognition by Phipps and England as a 'real' person with his own history, and not least, an act of fictional self-creation, liberation and defiance. Notably, it is Maggs who first writes down Tobias Oates, not the other way round. Maggs comes into contact with Oates at Buckle's dinner party. While Oates tells 'a strange tale' of Partridge the 'Thief-taker' (26), who then appears as a character in Chapter 67, we are given a description of Oates which Maggs composes later in his journal. Maggs' life will be stolen and colonised by Oates's imagination to form the basis for his novel *The Death of Maggs*, but the character appropriates and describes his own author first.

The most intriguing writing scene is in the coach, ironically-named the *True Briton*, on the trip to Gloucester in Chapters 62–63. With the 'real' Jack Maggs sitting opposite, Oates takes out his portmanteau and begins to compose the first chapter of the novel he thinks of as *Jack Maggs*, but which will eventually become *The Death of Maggs*, all the time 'not unaware that the subject of his tale was seated staring at him' (223). As Oates writes, we read the opening passage of that fictional novel, but what we encounter is neither the opening of the novel by Peter Carey that we are reading, nor of Dickens's *Great Expectations*. Instead, it is a third possible version of the Magwitch/Maggs story, whose existence we never gain access to, though we do get to read this draft first chapter in Chapter 74 (274–8) when Maggs and Oates are escaping in the punt after Maggs has killed the Thieftaker. As he writes, Oates is interrupted by the 'real life' going on around him in the coach, not least by Maggs, who demands to see his notebook and finds the sketches for the novel about his life: 'Jack Maggs frowned, as if dimly perceiving the unhappy fate before him on the page' (227). That fate would be a fictional capture as complete as the imprisonment from which he has had a conditional pardon, and Maggs disassociates himself from Oates's embryonic version of himself: 'I'm not your comic figure, Mr Oates' (228).

As with much post-colonial writing, this self-conscious narrative calls into question the reliability of written texts as embodiments of any kind of truth. We are also made acutely aware of the novelistic process in action, of the transformative power of writing and the written to reveal and veil. As the journey continues, Oates rethinks the opening of his novel, crosses out the entire chapter he has written and begins again: he draws on what Maggs has just told him of his nostalgic love of England and finally discovers the 'real' opening with which *The Death of Maggs* would begin when finally published thirty years later (231). This version shares with Peter Carey's actual opening the red waistcoat Maggs wore as he arrived in London on page 1. Meanwhile, a family called Harris gets on the coach, including two males with gargantuan beards, one of whom amuses his children by strapping his beard down to his stomach with his belt. Oates is fascinated by this and within a few paragraphs has metamorphosed it into his embryonic novel as an account of a storm at sea in which the Maggs character is pinned to the deck while '[b]eside him lay a man named Harris with a sodden grey beard upon his cold and lifeless chest' (231–2). But the real Maggs retaliates by grabbing Oates's head and demanding back the secrets he has stolen. He then takes possession of Oates's quill pen to write an entry in his own journal; and later it is Jack Maggs who straps his supposed creator's hands into his trousers with his own belt.

There are also numerous digressive stories within stories in the novel. In addition to Maggs's journals and Oates's drafts of his novel, we have episodes in which Maggs tells his own story orally to Oates. In the punt on the River Severn, Maggs describes how he first met Phipps, beginning in the best traditions of nineteenth-century fiction: '"It were a rainy autumn day," Maggs said at last. "A cold miserable sort of day, with a bitter wind blowing low and hard across the marshes"' (262). The effects of this proliferating spiral of story-telling are comparable with Italo Calvino's engrossing metafiction *If On a Winter's Night a*

Traveller, in which various stories start, never to end, and the novel's real 'story' is the reader's search for the story. Calvino's book is playful entertainment which displaces the reader's sense of narrative control. Carey's destabilises the power of creator over creation, coloniser over colonised, conscious over unconscious. Maggs's return is the return of repressed.

The relationship between Maggs and Oates lies at the heart of this intertwined investigation of colonial, familial and fictional responsibility. They echo each other in strangely resonant ways to expose the secrets and corrosive guilt which infect English culture. They shadow and double each other, suggesting respectable society's complicity in injustice as the links between the themes of class and colonisation, responsibility and betrayal, legacies and retaliations become increasingly intricate. Both orphans, they are driven to compensate for their sense of deprivation by a desire for love and belonging. Maggs's urge to protect Phipps and 'weave him a nest so strong that no one would ever hurt his goodness' (264) is matched by Oates's 'mighty passion to create that safe warm world he had been denied', having had 'no proper family himself' (36). But they both carry secrets, a word which gathers a whispering intensity as the book progresses. Driven by the painful legacies of his own childhood, Oates's 'unholy thirst for love' leads to criminal incest with his sister-in-law Lizzie: 'he was in love with his wife's sister […] She was eighteen years old, he defiled her' (37–8). Oates's guilt about this extends to the illness of his own baby, whose 'innocent body' he feels he himself has infected (189). The tragic outcome of his relationship with Lizzie echoes Maggs's love for Sophina: both women abort their children and then themselves die.

Oates himself is a thief in that he burgles Maggs's life-history. Carey has said that he became interested by 'this sort of oppositional force […] where the writer was a thief and the thief would be a writer'.[24] Maggs has already had his life stolen through his criminalisation and transportation; he now has it purloined for fictional purposes. When in Chapter 7 Maggs suffers an attack of *tic douloureux* and is hypnotised by Oates for the first time, he feels afterwards that '[h]e was burgled, plundered, and he would not tolerate it' (32). As a result, Maggs pursues Oates and strikes a bargain to submit himself to his experiments with hypnosis. Oates proposes to be 'the surgeon of this soul' (54), and during these proto-psychoanalytical sessions, Oates creates Maggs's inner world for him, echoing suggestions that Freud himself was a kind of fiction writer. Oates convinces Maggs that his malady is caused by a psychological "Phantom" (47), which Maggs takes to be the embodiment of the violent floggings he suffered as a transported prisoner. In actuality it is an 'invention' created by Oates (203), who holds Maggs a hypnotised "prisoner" (54) while he drafts the beginnings of his novel. Later he describes his free access to Maggs's mind to the initially sympathetic Buckle in terms of breaking into 'a treasure house' (87). When Buckle challenges Oates 'Did you never imagine yourself in his position?', Oates can only see from the egocentric position of the novelist: 'Buckle, dear Buckle. It is my business to imagine everything' (88). The word 'business' has multiple resonances. In his trip to Brighton to cover the story of the fire Oates demonstrates his compassion in his response to the victims – 'he was fiercely protective of abused children' (130) – and at the same time imagines using the experience of viewing the bodies as a source for the ending of his novel about Maggs (133), as well as providing much needed copy for the *Chronicle*. He then sells the copyright to *Jack Maggs* even before he has written the novel. In practicing mesmerism on Maggs, Oates keeps 'two sets of books [...] as in all crooked businesses' – one suitably 'fabricated by the writer to hide the true nature of his exploration', the other his appropriation of Maggs's 'hidden history' (91). For Oates, 'the Criminal Mind' is 'a world as rich as London itself', and Maggs becomes synonymous with the London Oates exploits for his own fictional creations: 'What a puzzle of life exists in the dark little lane-ways of this wretch's soul, what stolen gold lies hidden in the vaults beneath his filthy streets' (90). But what worries him is that in 'stumbling through the dark of the convict's past' he finds himself looking into 'a mirror held up to his own turbulent and fearful soul' (91). The death of Buckle's senile butler Spinks in the aftermath of the quarantine episode leaves Oates himself 'by some trick of Fate, suddenly the criminal' (183), possibly 'a murderer' (180).

During the trip to Gloucester, the shadowing becomes more malevolent, as Oates finds that he cannot shake Maggs: 'He began to walk out into the High Street, but found Jack Maggs strolling close at his side. When he turned one way, Jack turned with him; and when he turned the other, he was beside him there also' (233). Maggs becomes Oates's alter ego, Mr Hyde to his Dr Jekyll. From a psychoanalytical viewpoint, Maggs is the projection of repressed desires, of the destabilising effects of the unconscious, the uncanny double, which Freud saw as 'that impulse towards self-protection which has caused the ego to project such a content outward as something foreign to itself.'[25] Just as Maggs reveals the true source of the wealth which supports the gentleman Henry Phipps, so he emerges as the hidden subject of English culture, the discontent at the heart of civilisation. If Oates infects Maggs with his 'Phantom', Maggs returns the complement by becoming Oates's *doppelganger*. In defiance of the novelist's fiction-making capacities, and those of imperial England more generally, Maggs tells Oates 'you can't imagine who I am' (252) and as if to demonstrate the limits of Oates's power and the reality of the fiction, he murders the charlatan Thieftaker. In the aftermath, Maggs and Oates become locked together as fellow conspirators (258) in a struggle for survival, fighting for their freedom and at the same time battling with each other for their own identities. In one of the most powerful and atmospheric sections of the novel on the boat out on the River Severn, they bond in a kind of perverse mateship (265–7), until, after reading the novelised version of his life and the notes for his death, Maggs accuses Oates of being a 'damned little thief' (279). When Oates proclaims that the Jack Maggs of his novel is merely a character who bears the real Maggs's name, Maggs makes the ultimate retort: 'You are just a character to me too, Toby' (280) and proceeds to manacle Oates with his own belt (284). The novelist is thus confronted with the rebellion of the character he has colonised, an assertion of authentic self and identity which transforms the power relationship between the two of them.

This turbulent novel accelerates into a gripping climax and an abrupt, though powerful and moving, ending. Key strands and threads of plot and theme are re-run to give a vivid sense of the interplay between reality and fiction, choice and chance, fate and freedom. Having realised her sister is pregnant by her husband, Mary Oates visits 'Ma' Britten to purchase abortion pills and unwittingly shadows Jack Maggs's journey in the very opening pages of the novel: 'their paths were so close that she must, from time to time, have brought her stout little heel down on the same spot of pavement where Jack Maggs's hessian boot had trod' (287). When Maggs insists that Oates should administer Lizzie with the abortion pills he has obtained from 'Ma' Britten, Oates demands to know 'Why would you have me tread this path [...] the very path that brought you and Sophina so much pain and anguish?' (303). Rather than controlling Maggs as a fictional character, it is 'the Criminal Mind which now controlled Tobias' (304). Lizzie re-enacts the role of Sophina by undergoing an abortion and death and feels that 'her life had always been travelling towards this point' (306), as if trapped in a deterministic pre-existing script. While she is made to destroy her baby, Maggs forces Oates 'to destroy his own creation' (306) by burning the notes and drafts of his novel, and in a telling echo of Maggs's sooty childhood, all three characters are engulfed by the imagery of destruction and corruption as the wind blows down the chimney: 'Elizabeth Warriner, Tobias Oates, Jack Maggs – they all stood as the black ash fell around them' (307). The charm of mesmerised predestination is broken as Phipps, incited by Buckle, attempts to murder his benefactor. In this climactic moment, as Phipps shoots and Mercy intervenes to save Maggs at the cost of her wedding finger being blown off, Lizzie dies.

Some critics have felt the ending of the novel, in which Maggs and Mercy escape back to Australia to build a new life together, fails to do justice either to the problems of the colonial legacy of settler culture in Australia, particularly with regard to the indigenous peoples, or to the issues of gender raised by Mercy's relationship with Maggs, such as her role as 'a force of nature' (324). Máire ní Fhlathúin argues that Carey shows no wish to condemn patriarchal or imperial law and that, far from escaping England, Maggs rebuilds it in Australia through his businesses, his pub, his presidency of the Cricket Club.[26] But the sudden compression of events in the final section creates a striking effect of fictional distancing: after the brutal events in London, the new lives of Mercy and Maggs in Australia read like a fairy tale, deliberately unreal, while Oates is left cleaning up after Lizzie's death, burning the bloodstained sheets and seeing in their flames the ghosts that will continue to haunt him and which he will weave into his own Jack Maggs. Carey's novel insists that '[t]his Jack Maggs was, of course, a fiction' (326), yet the 'real' Jack Maggs's new life and identity as an Australian are an equally fictional success story. Maggs eludes his seemingly determined role in Oates/Dickens's novels only to be reinvented as a fiction at the end of Peter Carey's. Mercy's role, too, is equally idealised and is offset against the book Oates eventually publishes in which there is 'no young woman to help the convict recognize the claims of Richard and John to have a father kiss them good night' (327). Perhaps that is why this self-declaringly fictional resolution ends with Mercy being obsessed by Oates's eventual novel, and at the same time rewriting it by cutting out the dedication to Buckle, showing that what is fictional can be changed in reality.

In a novel obsessed with reinvention, it seems appropriate that the transported character who discovers the power to translate and transform himself, and potentially transform the colonial relationship with England, should then be captured by his own reinvention. It is also appropriate to a novel which is really *about* England, that England itself should remain obsessed and haunted by the nightmares of its colonial past.

True History of the Kelly Gang (2000)

In *Jack Maggs*, an orphan becomes a criminal; in *True History of the Kelly Gang*, Carey's second Booker Prize winning novel, Ned loses his father and is abandoned by his mother to become a highwayman and killer. Significant sections of *Jack Maggs* are given over to Maggs's justification of himself to his adopted son, while the majority of *True History* is Ned's letter of self-explanation to his daughter whom he has never seen. Both these historical novels explore what Carey has called the 'patterns [...] of abandonment, orphans' in his work.[1] They retell the stories of marginalised characters, outsiders and outlaws, fictional in *Jack Maggs*, fact in *True History*, in reinvented voices as Carey intervenes into existing texts to reimagine them. *True History* has been called 'a virtuoso feat of ventriloquism'[2] and a 'fully imagined act of historical impersonation',[3] as if it were a conjuring trick, but it is more like a performative act of habitation, occupation, identification. Carey conjures Ned Kelly's flesh and bones onto the page with the tactile intensity of lived experience, through a remarkably vivid narrative voice, Kelly's own. Ned speaks directly, with a fervour that embodies his reckless character, and this creates a sense of narrative urgency enhanced through minimal punctuation, as in the headlong opening: 'I lost my father at 12 yr. of age and know what it is to be raised on lies and silence my dear daughter you are presently too young to understand a word I write but this history is for you and will contain no single lie may I burn in Hell if I speak false' (7).

This abrupt style is both characterful and true to the original. One of the sources of Carey's inspiration was Kelly's famous Jerilderie Letter[4] that Carey first came across in the mid-1960s, in which the historical Ned Kelly wrote his own account of his actions. Carey describes it as 'an extraordinary document, the passionate voice of a man who is writing to explain his life, save his life, his reputation.' He was impressed by its 'howl of pain' against injustice, but even more enthralled by the style: 'all the time there is this original *voice* – uneducated but intelligent, funny and then angry, and with a line of Irish invective that would have made Paul Keating envious. […] it was Kelly's language that drew me to this story. In those eccentric sentences was my character's DNA.'[5] The quality of the original Ned Kelly's invective can be judged from his attack on 'the brutal and cowardly conduct of a parcel of big ugly fat-necked wombat headed big bellied magpie legged narrow hipped splaw-footed sons of Irish Bailiffs or english landlords which is better known as Officers of Justice or Victorian Police'.[6] And since it echoed the kind of speech Carey was familiar with from his home town of Bacchus Marsh, he found that he could 'inhabit this voice like an old, familiar shoe.' It also linked with Carey's desire to emulate his familiar reference point, William Faulkner's *As I Lay Dying*, and give 'rich voices to the poor': 'I have always had a passion to write like this, to make a sort of poetry from the uneducated voice, to give a speech to the speechless.'[7] Reading the letter during the 1960s, the period when he was being introduced to the writings of Joyce and Beckett as well as Faulkner, Carey found it possible 'to misread this document […] as almost a modernist text.'[8]

Carey keeps specific elements of the Jerilderie Letter, adapting sections to fit his own accounts of episodes such as the McCormick's horse and Wild Wright.[9] But whereas the actual Jerilderie Letter was addressed to a contemporary newspaper audience, and possibly to the future, Carey changes the intended audience of his invented version. This narrative may be addressed to the daughter he will never meet, but Ned writes in the belief that he *will* meet her, and be able to re-read what he has written (202). Like Jack Maggs's journal, the tone is one of self-explanation, but more emotive given the attachment Kelly has to the absent and orphaned daughter and the dramatic irony of his fate.

Of course, the novel is not 'the real thing': Carey has described it as 98 per cent imagined,[10] and it is a testimony to the vividness of his imagination that many readers probably believe Kelly's life to have been as the novel presents it. In so far as this is a problem, it is partly one of lost knowledge: outside Australia Ned Kelly's name may be well-known but his story is not, and even inside Australia, the 'real facts' are often subsumed by the myth. For Carey's novel, there are a number of repercussions. One response is simply to say, as with *Jack Maggs*, that the novel can function independently of its sources as a fully-imagined fiction, which it does. This is history reinvented as fiction in an utterly engrossing and convincing manner. But whereas *Jack Maggs* relied on another fiction for its source, which it then transformed, *True History of the Kelly Gang* takes actual history as its premise, and this has different effects. We might well read *Jack Maggs* without reference to Dickens's *Great Expectations* or even in ignorance of it, but it is possibly more difficult to ignore historical events.

If we do compare the novel with what is known about Kelly's life and character we encounter the familiar problem, which the novel itself raises, of the degree to which historical accounts can themselves be taken as trustworthy. Early in the novel, Constable O'Neill tells Ned that 'children should know their history' (11) and then proceeds to give a very biased version of the events leading up to Ned's father's transportation. Ned's own account is undoubtedly an 'alternative history' like Jack Maggs's, aiming to counteract received versions: 'that true & secret part of the history is left to me.' (199) But if we place Carey's Ned Kelly by the side of historical descriptions of the actual Ned Kelly, we get a contrasting picture. Carey's Ned Kelly is an in-depth self-portrait of a man driven to crime through injustice and persecution. While he is evidently a racist and a sexist, as well as homophobic, he is nevertheless a character whom we admire for his stoicism, determination, defiance, capacity for love, and whose violence we understand as emerging from the damage and misunderstandings that result from the society he lives in. The historical Ned Kelly is a less endearing character by virtue of his own testimony as much as anything else. On the surface at least, the Jerilderie Letter displays a more crassly violent psychology at work, as shown in what Alex McDermott, recent editor of the letter, calls the 'extremity of threat, and the rhetoric of blood [...] the ferocity and anger' in Kelly's invective.[11] By comparison, Carey's novel offers a fully imagined subjective reality as a source for the words we read.

Given this, what is the purpose of Carey's reinvention of Kelly? It has a double intention. Partly it is a revaluation of national icon, but it also has the effect of demythologising Kelly. This is entirely appropriate since Ned Kelly's status as an Australian national icon is both indisputable and problematic. Carey has argued that 'the sort of space Kelly occupies in the national imagination' is akin to that of Thomas Jefferson in America. Kelly's status as a principled and courageous rebel is, as Carey realises, one reason why 'Australians still respond to him so passionately': 'he was not brutalised or diminished by his circumstances. Rather, he elevated himself, and inspired a parti-cular people with his courage, wit and decency [...] He was proof that our dismal history need not be read pessimistically.'[12] Justice and injustice are recurrent choruses throughout Ned's account of his life, as is the celebration of courageous resistance against oppressive authority which has made the Kelly legend such a hallmark of the mythic Australian levelling spirit. As he reminds his daughter, 'you must also remember your ancestors would not kowtow to no one and this were a fine thing in a colony made specifically to have poor men bow down to their gaolers' (151). Kelly embodies what Eric Hobsbawm calls the 'social bandit', one of the 'bandit-heroes' who reflect a longing for 'freedom, heroism and the dream of justice' amongst the poor and embody their yearning for 'the fellowship of free and equal men, the invulnerability to authority, and the championship of the weak, oppressed and cheated'.[13] He is an altruistic criminal and at the same time raises questions about who imposes the label of 'criminal' on whom.

But as Phil Shannon points out, the reputations of such social bandits 'may depend on a fair helping of embellished myth and selective idealisation'.[14] This double perspective is crucial to Carey's novel. The point of the Jefferson comparison is not that Kelly himself can be thought of as equivalent to Jefferson: Jefferson was both a revolutionary and a professional man, a lawyer who drafted the Declaration of Independence and later became President; whereas Kelly may have been a rebel but he was not a revolutionary, remained outlawed and died as a result. As Carey says, it is the 'space' he holds in the national story that is equivalent, and that is what generates the controversy. For Carey, the significance of the Kelly myth for contemporary Australia is that it poses a question: 'who are we Australians that this man should be our greatest hero?'[15] By both celebrating and demythologising Kelly, the novel asks what Kelly's status as national icon says about the identity of the Australian settler culture. Ned's attempt to tell his daughter his version of the truth and dispel the 'lies and silences' (7) parallels contemporary Australia's attempt to do the same, and with the same problematic contradictions. As Carey puts it, 'one of the conditions of being an Australian right now is having the notion that we've been brought up with lies and denial about all sorts of things. As a nation we are totally obsessed with finding out what really did happen.'[16]

As Graham Huggan has shown, one major area of contradiction which Carey's novel exposes is the ambiguity of cultural memory in relation to national myths such as Ned Kelly. Huggan argues that the danger of such myths is that they can be used to manipulate historical awareness and privilege one social group at the expense of others. He points out that 'the national narrative embodied in Kelly [...] is embarrassingly exclusive' when compared to the 'memory work' being done on the history of Aboriginal dispossession and genocide.[17] For John Kinsella, Carey's novel comes dangerously close to such exclusivity: 'the more I let Peter Carey's novel *True History of the Kelly Gang* sink in, the more uncomfortable I feel. This fictionalisation of the life of Ned Kelly participates in the creation and continuation of so many national myths that I begin to comprehend why it is that right-wing groups in Australia connect with Australian literary identities like Henry Lawson and Banjo Paterson.' Kinsella recognises that Carey has 'factionalised […] with critical awareness', but concludes: 'The novel is a work of pure advertising. […] What worries me is the ends a book like this may be put to. It doesn't create anything new, doesn't adequately address the problem of racism outside the Irish-British condition, and doesn't really challenge the notions of narrative that inform it.'[18]

By contrast, Huggan believes that Carey's novel counteracts 'the romantic impulse toward anti-imperial nostalgia' which might allow the Kelly legend to be manipulated in favour of a limited view of the national story. From the beginning, Carey 'emphasises the ambivalent and, above all, commodified status of Kelly as national icon and anti-imperial resource', factors which compromise any unqualified use of the Kelly story. The opening section, for example, describes the 'wholesale souveniring' (4) which occurred in the aftermath of the Kelly Gang's last stand against the police at Glenrowan.[19] Huggan's awareness of the Kelly story as commodity immediately places the story in question, and we find that the same kind of destabilisation occuring throughout Ned's own narrative.

As with any dramatic monologue worth its salt, Ned's narrative is imbued with unconscious ironies, which let us see more in what he says than he can. Carey uses Kelly to explore injustice and dispossession, and at the same time puts him, and the mythologising and idealisation of him, in question. Ned is an unreliable narrator with a restricted view of events and we should beware of taking his version as the only one. Ned might think his story is about fundamental binaries of right and wrong, but as Andrew Riemer perceptively points out, if 'the political attitudes embedded in Ned's narrative are simple and uncomplicated: villains and heroes, tribalism and the conflict of comic-strip creatures […] Carey's novel, on the other hand, is far less schematic. Evidence of that may be found in the carefully modulated variations of tone and diction Carey slips into Ned's artless narrative.' The result is an ironic narrative effect which both engages us with Ned as a character and distances us from him, a double perspective which suits a contemporary Australian expatriate's re-telling of this national myth. Riemer argues that '[a]s a political ideal, of the kind commemorated by bombastic monuments in many parts of the world, Ned Kelly is hollow or, at best, compromised. His significance for contemporary Australians lies in those far more modest human values: a kinship with the land, a capacity for love which Carey has tucked into the corners, so to speak, of this retelling of an all-too-familiar tale', and that Carey might have needed his 'voluntary exile' in New York 'before the supremely iconic figure of Ned Kelly could come into focus for him.'[20]

For Carey, in addition to the Jerilderie Letter, the spark for tackling the subject was partly occasioned by a fortuitous exhibition of Sidney Nolan's Ned Kelly paintings at New York's Metropolitan Museum some years prior to writing the novel. Having seen the paintings previously and 'liked them', Carey was anxious as to whether they would translate to the fashionable New York cultural scene, only to find himself impressed by their being 'beyond fashion, imbued with an apparent awkwardness, artlessness illuminated by enormous grace.' In championing the paintings and the Ned Kelly story to American friends, Carey found himself struck by 'what a strange, powerful thing this was', finding that '[a]bsence simplified the story', freeing it of the commercial heritage culture which encumbers it in Australia and allowing him the different perspective from which to interrogate the legend.[21]

Carey was well aware that this iconic figure has been tackled in other literary versions,[22] notably Robert Drewe's *Our Sunshine* (1991), as well as a novel by Jean Bedford about Ned's sister (*Sister Kelly* 1982) and a play by Douglas Stewart (*Ned Kelly* 1940). Robert Drewe's novel, currently being made into a film by Gregor Jordan to be released in 2003, is equally significant in demythologising the Kelly legend.[23] It too raids sections of the Jerilderie Letter, though without attempting to recreate the voice itself.[24] In Carey's novel, Ned writes his life-story in the belief that 'if a man could tell his true history to Australians he might be believed' since 'Australians they knew full well the terror of the unyielding law the historic memory of UNFAIRNESS were in

their blood' (299). Ned's account is his alternative history, a reply
to the authorised versions of the history of the British Empire
and of the ruling class of the penal colony of Australia: 'I wished
only to be a citizen I had tried to speak but the mongrels stole my
tongue when I asked for justice they give me none.' (328) It too is
a recovered history to counteract the enforced erasure of memory
and tradition which accompanied penal transportation: 'That is
the agony of the Great Transportation that our parents would
rather forget what come before so we currency lads is left alone
ignorant as tadpoles spawned in puddles on the moon' (278).[25] But
it is also an account of the active creation of history, however
distorted and troubled. When one of the Kelly gang begins to
sing 'some mournful song in the old language I told him to be
quiet we would write our own damned history from here on' (245).

Ned's story is a 'true history' in the sense that it follows the
events of Kelly's actual life as far as they are known, and the
novel deliberately fosters the illusion of historical authenticity in
a number of ways. The title, with its assertive lack of the definite
article, invokes the flavour of the authentic eye-witness narrative
testimonies or memoirs, such as became common in the seven-
teenth and eighteenth centuries. A 'true history' was a reliable
chronicle, asserting its authenticity against fable and myth, as
with Jose de Acosta in 1590, who would not respect Plato's
authority 'as I will beleeve he could write these things of the
Atlantis island for a true Historie, the which are but meere
fables'.[26] The tradition dated from classical models like the True
Historie of Lucian the Somosatenian that formed an inspiration
for Rabelais and Swift's *Gulliver's Travels*, and became incorporated into such historically-based works as George Ferrers's *A
mirour for magistrates: being a true chronicle historie of the
vntimely falles of such vnfortunate princes and men of note* of
1559. Many such accounts were a mixture of fact and fiction, and
the 'true history' became one element in the development of the
modern novel. An early example was Aphra Behn's *The Unfor-
tunate Happy Lady: A True History* (wr. pre-1685; pub 1698 or
1700), and the form was used through the eighteenth and
nineteenth centuries, often mixed with picaresque and epistolary

genres. *True History of the Kelly Gang* uses these forms too: Ned's 'parcels' are letters addressed to his daughter, so that his story is told in epistolary fashion, while the plot of the novel follows his adventures chronologically from childhood, blending the picaresque with the autobiographical *bildungsroman*. Using all these genre modes, *True History of the Kelly Gang* not only re-writes a national icon; it effectively re-writes the founding elements of the English novel tradition.

As well as professing to be an authentic historical testimony, *True History of the Kelly Gang* takes the form of 'parcels' of documents, each with a bibliographical description of contents, paper and condition, such as might be done by a manuscript collection in a library, to add to the flavour of authenticity. The irony is that whilst this scholarly paraphernalia and the actual writing are fictions, the basic life and events are historical fact. And whereas in *Jack Maggs* the writing strategies were developed in a deliberately self-conscious manner, here Carey carefully avoids deliberate metafictional play to generate a sense of historical testimony that can then be interrogated. The inclusion later in the narrative of newspaper reports of the Kelly Gang's most famous raids on the banks at Euroa and Jerilderie alongside Ned's own critical annotations, expressing 'the outlaw's growing anger that he should be denied a national audience' (301), intensify the awareness of competing versions of history rather than calling the text's fictional status into question. They also give a sense of Ned's insight into the way his life was being constructed and distorted as a media event.

The history dealt with in this historical novel is not over; it is a continuing legacy, as the epigraph from William Faulkner suggests: 'The past is not dead. It is not even past.' If *Jack Maggs* looks at the effects of the colonial enterprise on England, *True History of the Kelly Gang* shows the realities of colonialism as lived inside of the colony itself. What the novel reveals is a multiple colonisation. The aftermath of the original penal colony is reflected in a hierarchy of oppressions that continue the penal system under another guise. As Judith Kapferer argues: 'The surveillance of convict society by the military provided a framework for the foundation of a local constabulary, while the rules and regulations of the prison system were the foundation of the bureaucratic order of the State.'[27] Ned is more blunt: 'we was being ruled by warders there were no more justice than in the days of yore' (303). Most marginal to the novel are the indigenous peoples, derided as 'blacks' in the 'nigger show' of the cattle sale in Parcel 1 (15). Most powerful are the increasingly rich Protestant English squatters and settlers, backed by a supportive police force and government: 'Through his connections in government the squatter Whitty had been permitted to rent the common ground and as a result a poor man could no longer find a place to feed his stock in all the drought stricken plains [...] there was men so enraged by these abuses that they put the squatter's oats under the torch in revenge' (188). For Carey, there are contemporary analogies here: he describes Ned's background as 'a rural underclass that's probably not all that different to contemporary urban underclasses.'[28] The novel is about 'a war between the rich and the poor',[29] about issues of social criminalisation and definitions of criminality, and continues Carey's engagement with political issues of dispossession and injustice.

The focus of Ned's sense of injustice are the families of Irish transportees, a vivid feature of the original Jerilderie Letter.[30] From the outset, the fortunes of the Kelly family are shown as a product of the prejudice and vilification that poor Irish transportees, such as Ned's own father, were subjected to. In his opening paragraphs, Ned declares that his account aims to help his daughter 'finally comprehend the injustice we poor Irish suffered in this present age' which he assumes will seem 'far away in ancient time' to her (7), though for the contemporary reader the problems generated by the English colonisation of Ireland continue to resonate. In Ned's first view of a police camp he is faced by 'a huge red jowled creature the Englishman' who seemed 'the most powerful man I ever saw and might destroy my mother if he so desired. Approach says he as if he was an altar' (8). Ned's rage is aimed at the privileged class whose wealth is gained at the expense of his own people and who effectively drive Ned himself to crime by depriving him of the opportunities to attain even a basic standard of living. At school Ned realises 'Them scholars were all proddies they knew nothing about us [...] each day they learned from Mr Irving that all micks was a notch beneath the cattle' (27).

He is aware of 'what contentment the colony might provide if there is ever justice' (108). But the denial of a share for his family fuels Ned's increasing desire for retribution: 'When our brave parents was ripped from Ireland like teeth from the mouth of their own history and every dear familiar thing had been abandoned on the docks of Cork or Galway or Dublin then the Banshee come on board the cursed convict ships [...] and there were not a English eye could see her no more than an English eye can picture the fire that will descend upon that race in time to come' (87). Ned's father dies 'bulging with all the poisons of the Empire' (34), leaving Ned the legacy of 'that flame the government of England lights in a poor man's guts every time they make him wear the convict irons' (156). One of the contradictions of colonialism is shown to be the double-edged effect of penal oppression and criminalisation: 'The Queen of England should beware her prisons give a man a potent sense of justice' (284). As a result, Ned has ample recruits for his gang: 'The British Empire had supplied me with no shortage of candidates' (328).

Ned's reaction against the persecution suffered by his family and community, as in his response to Whitty's impounding of selectors' livestock (190–1), is through acts of criminal defiance and revenge in the first place, but they have a potential for something more. His real impulses are to belong and to speak out against injustice: 'I wished only to be a citizen I had tried to speak out but the mongrels stole my tongue when I asked for justice they give me none' (328). When the Kelly Gang begins to form almost through a process of osmosis, the pleasure of stealing from the rich is accompanied by a commitment to the formation of a new community: 'they come not to avoid honest graft the opposite when you stayed with me and Dan you would leave your grog behind and work beside us from dawn to dusk thus in the middle of that wilderness we cleared the flats and planted crops. We was building a world where we would be left alone'

(194). This offers a glimpse of a possible future that could not occur given the conditions of the time, but also acts as a premonition of the new nation in the process of being formed, to which the Kelly Gang myth has made its contradictory contribution. The embryonic community later convenes spontaneously to celebrate the birth of Ned's daughter, and its significance is made explicit: 'we was them and they was us and we had showed the world what convict blood could do. We proved there were no taint we was of true bone blood and beauty born' (323). It is Ned's vision of 'true Australian coin' (340). For Carey the Kelly story is in part an answer to the question posed by the notion of the 'convict seed': 'Can you have a decent society when you begin with these people?' Ned proves that he is 'not caught up in this deterministic notion at all' and by doing so shows 'he is us in a way',[31] redeemed from a false view of the convict stain.

As these examples show, Ned acts as a powerful voice against colonial injustice, but he is by no means merely a mouthpiece. Carey creates a complex picture of Ned as both culpable and admirable, which invites a contradictory empathy with this violent criminal. Ned is shown, among other things, to be doggedly hard-working (48–9), innocently trusting (63), stoical, heroic, admirably principled, chauvinistic, violent, driven, angry, loving, brooding, and 'straight as a die' (144), all at once. We are given a vivid insight into the circumstances, prejudice, inequality, harassment, accidents and misunderstandings that led to Ned's increasing criminalisation. Faced by a policeman with a raised gun during the Stringybark Creek incident, Ned 'squeezed the fateful trigger what choice did I have?' (239). At the same time, for Carey it is important to remember that 'people were oppressed and people were cruelly treated, and just the same many of them were criminals as well.'[32] We are sufficiently distanced by this double perspective to view Ned's actions critically, as indeed he himself does looking back on his earlier life. For example, leading up to his revenge on Bill Frost, the manipulation of his innocence by Harry Powers is balanced by Ned's later realisation that rather than follow Powers's example, 'I would of proved my manhood better by turning back to Greta' (114).

Appropriately for the man who famously died with the words 'Such is life' on his lips (352),[33] Ned is dogged by a sense of fatalism and destiny. Unlike Jack Maggs, Carey's Ned Kelly seems trapped by the script history has written for him and, despite his hope that he will be able to read his account in the future with his daughter in America (202), he is all too aware of his coming doom: 'Thus troubles rushed towards us like white ants hatching on a summer night' (220–1). The framing of the novel enforces this sense of turbulent destiny. The picaresque plot begins in the thick of the defining moment in Kelly's career as an iconic outlaw, Ned's final confrontation with the police and his appearance in home-made metal body armour with the famous bucket-shaped helmet. He proclaims himself 'the Monitor', after the iron warship he read about in a newspaper report (324), with an ironic echo of his achievement in becoming ink monitor at school. He seems invincible, only to be brought down by his defenceless legs. The story then hurtles the reader through the agonising series of misadventures which comprise Ned's short life, towards its inevitable conclusion. As it does so, Ned has growing delusions of power and control over a situation whose outcome he does not know but which we do. Ned might believe 'the police was actors in a drama writ by me' (304) and feel himself 'the terror of the government being brung to life in the cauldron of the night' (317) as he writes his various letters and accounts of his actions, but both the novel and history prove him wrong, disturbing the grip of his narrative on the reader and increasingly putting a different viewpoint on events. Yet the voice of Ned himself rides and survives these events, giving his account a strangely uplifting feel.

As with Mercy Larkin's effect on Jack Maggs, Ned learns the true value of compassion and love from his passion for Mary Hearn. His relationship with Mary shows Ned's most humane side, and forms an all too brief idyll in his violent career. It is Mary who encourages him to compose his account for the public record but more poignantly to give their embryonic daughter 'the proper story of her da and who he is and what he suffered' (265). At the heart of the novel is a family saga, which again offers a different view on the legend. Ned wants to establish a firm relationship with the daughter he will never see and clarify her view of him. But he is also haunted by the ghosts of his own parents. Even after his death, his father remains an abiding presence such that 'there would never be a knot I tied or rabbit I skun or a horse I rode that I did not see those small eyes watching to see I done it right' (37). The patriarchal legacy between father and son is the customarily contradictory one of anxiety, guilt (39), hostility, and repressed or unacknowledged affection. Ned feels he has 'lost' his father (18) in a number of ways – because of the story O'Neill tells about his father's treachery to his Irish community (12), because of the episode of his father wearing the dress (14–19) which Ned only understands later, and not least because his father dies – but his feelings are complex and ambiguous, as his heartfelt cry at the end of 'Parcel 1' testifies: 'were this not he who give me life now all dead and ruined? Father son of my heart are you dead from me are you dead from me my father?' (33).

Ned's relationship with his mother is equally complicated, and classically Oedipal. Carey realised that because of its status as myth, '[w]e Australians have not even begun to imagine the emotional life of the characters in our great story.'[34] He makes good that deficiency in his portrait of the passionate attachment between Ned and Ellen Kelly: 'it is no secret that Ned Kelly's father died when he was 12, that he was the eldest boy, that he took responsibility for his family and became "the Man". Ned and his mother were very close all his life, and his actions in his last two years seem largely motivated by his desperation to get her out of jail. Ellen Kelly was a wild woman. She had lovers, husbands, children by numerous fathers. If we only imagine her son as a hero, then we cannot allow him to be jealous of these men. But if we allow ourselves to think of him as a growing boy we can permit him to be human.'[35]

Ellen provides the only haven for Ned and the rest of the children so that even in the middle of misfortune, listening to her traditional Irish stories '[w]e was far happier than we knew' (156). But she too betrays him in a number of ways – by selling him into apprenticeship with Harry Powers (68, 89–90), by having a constant train of inadequate, corrupt or disastrous suitors, and by misjudging Ned on a number of occasions. His response is a testimony to the depth of his feelings for her, as he explains to his daughter: 'I were even angrier that my ma should have judged me so poorly and my hands was shaking and my feelings jumping like a slice of bacon on the pan. [...] More than food I yearned for your grandma to apologise for her injustice' (147). Throughout their disagreements and divisions, Ned comes to realise 'how deep I loved her we was grown together like 2 branches of an old wisteria' (192). As Andrew Riemer points out, Ellen Kelly emerges in the novel increasingly as 'a figure of tragic stature, despite (or rather as a consequence of) the severe limitations of diction and eloquence Carey took on when assuming Ned's voice.'[36] As she declares to her son in a rare moment of hysterical despair: 'You don't know nothing about my adjectival life she said you don't remember what its like to live here with the adjectival squatters impounding every adjectival chook and heifer they can snaffle and the traps always knocking on my door hoping to take away my children' (170). Her strength and capacity to endure the terrible events which have befallen her are the corollary to her fierce determination and readiness to act in defence of her family. It is she who triggers the shooting of Fitzpatrick by hitting him with a shovel when she hears of his betrayal of her daughter Kate, thereby becoming the catalyst for the downfall of her son as well as her own imprisonment. His desperation to get his mother released fuels Ned's increasingly frantic attempts to write and be heard. As Carey indicates, 'one can think of this story as being all to do with a mother and her son. He was signing letters at the end saying "I am a widow's son outlawed and must be obeyed".'[37]

The family and its wider community are placed in the context of lingering traditions of the Irish transportees. Traditional Irish stories and practices resonate through the lives of the characters, from the tales of Banshees (86–8), encounters with the Devil (75) and substitute children (112), to Steve Hart's attempts to re-enact the activities of Irish rebels. Hart disturbs

Ned by appearing at various times in women's dresses, as Ned believes his own father had done. Ned's feelings of losing his father date from the moment he discovers his father's trunk with dresses in it (18), but the true meaning of this transvestism doesn't become clear until Mary explains the activities of the Children of Molly or Sons of Sieve (271–3) that Hart is attempting to revive. Carey apparently got the idea for this thread of the novel from Sidney Nolan's painting *Steve Hart Dressed as a Girl* 1947, which was based on historical sources for the Kelly story.[38] Anne Marsh has argued that the inclusion of transvestism is a 'queering' of the Ned Kelly legend, in which case it could be seen as part of a destabilisation of the myth.[39] But the novel questions the legacies of the past rather than endorsing them. This Irish folklore and tradition are seen as a living transmission, but also as a bondage, a malevolent Banshee curse that thrived in the new colony while the beloved and productive St. Brigit wasted away (88). In Hart's case, Mary sees his reversion to the transvestism of the Sons of Sieve as the legacy of a destructive terrorism that must be abandoned if the Kelly Gang are to win the hearts of the community: 'I will tell you boys if you wish to ride around in this costume the people will not love you. You must ease their lives not bring them terror' (278). Both Ned and Mary Byrne agree that 'this queer boy's daydreaming were no defence at all' (196) and 'won't solve nothing' (271) in the new conditions of the colony, but this resolve is balanced by the tragedy of Ned's alternative assertion of individual freedom against the injustice of the new society. While current problems can only be solved in the new Australian context, rather than by a return to the past, the past remains a haunting legacy shadowing the present. As Graham Huggan argues, 'Kelly's perception of ancestral memory itself is presented as being deeply riven […] The narrative is consistently *doubled*, as the subjective recounting of Australian colonial history encounters half-buried memories of an Irish ancestry – an ancestry that clearly causes Kelly as much pain as pride'.[40]

This family saga is placed in the wider context of Ned's connection to the land. Throughout *Kelly Gang*, as Riemer suggests, 'a touching sense of kinship with an often inhospitable environment emerges from Ned's brief and seemingly matter-of-fact descriptions'.[41] The harshness of the Australian outback and its effects on the lives of the poor settlers is ever-present, as is the corresponding dream of a beneficent, potentially attainable land of plenty. Ned is aware of 'what contentment the colony might provide' (108), and the early sections follow the family's search for the rich and fertile paradise Ned's mother promised them after his father's death (37). But this kinship goes further. The Australian outback forms a continuum for the action, almost to the extent of becoming a character in the novel. Ned describes his surroundings in a frequently throwaway manner but often to great dramatic effect: 'That hill were too much effort even for the bitter winds which turned around and come howling back towards our hut below' (13). Such down-to-earth descriptions are true to the original style of the Jerilderie Letter: 'the ground was that rotten it would bog a duck in places' (1); but Carey gives his Ned Kelly an imagined depth which the original letter ironically lacks. Ned's way of seeing the world is distinctively shaped by the environment in which he grows up. The narrative voice is the prism by which the reader views Ned's world through his own eyes, as he celebrates both the beauty and the harshness of the Australian landscape in a lyrical style: 'we was silent on our blankets looking out across the mighty Great Divide I never seen this country before it were like a fairy story landscape the clear and windy skies was filled with diamonds the jagged black outlines of the ranges were a panorama.' (124–5). Ned registers the tactile actuality of his surroundings through all his senses: 'though it were not warm the sweet scents of the dark clung to me like cobwebs [...] although I couldn't see a thing I heard a bandicoot with its snout in the leaves beside the track' (133). At the same time, the natural and social environments translate themselves into Ned's evaluations of people and the events of his life. He describes his father as 'a stubborn ironbark cornerpost you could strain a fence with 8 taut lines and never see it budge' while his Uncle James 'were dug too shallow or placed in sandy soil' (40). Once involved with Harry Powers, Ned realises 'I were a rabbit in his snare but did not know it yet' (119), while he describes his early encounter with the police and the rich squatter, McBean, in the following terms: 'I knew I had helped steal the horse and timepiece from the Police Commissioner's friend but understood so little of that class that I couldn't imagine so much as McBean's feather pillow. I were a plump witchetty grub beneath the bark not knowing that the kookaburra exists unable to imagine that fierce beak or the punishment in that wild and angry eye' (135–6). Ned's life and feelings interact with his environment to such a degree that the one becomes the correlative for the other, as when he describes his youthful anger as a green log brought to fierce flame (162). In fact, in the celebratory scene accompanying the news of his daughter's birth, Ned equates his own words with the prolific inevitability of the natural world itself: 'The words must be said and say them I did beneath the dazzling Milky Way the skies spilled like broken crystal across the heavens' (323).

To counteract this exuberance with the inevitability of history, Carey boxes Ned's narrative in with a prelude and an aftermath, both ostensibly written by historical third parties. The pace of Ned's narrative intensifies as he struggles against time and events to describe the creation of the famous armour, culminating in the tragic events at the Glenrowan hotel where the Kelly Gang are surrounded and Ned himself captured. But the story of the siege itself, described in the prelude and aftermath, takes us outside Ned's own voice into a third-person narrative. The contrast between the prelude version of Ned's capture and the final version emphasises the difference between the myth and the reality. The prelude presents the image of Ned in the armour as almost invincible, the Monitor, while the final version reveals that 'he was not the Monitor, he was a man of skin and shattered bone' (349).

The final section also reveals with the benefit of hindsight how local schoolmaster Thomas Curnow befriends and betrays Ned, and paradoxically becomes both custodian and critic of his legend. Curnow provides Ned and his accomplices in the hotel with a momentary glimpse of their emerging mythic status as he appropriates the St Crispin's day speech from Shakespeare's *Henry V*, in a miniature act of post-colonial counter discourse. But like Oates with *Jack Maggs*, Curnow appropriates Ned's writings and effectively becomes the editor for the manuscript we have just read, as he 'continued to labour obsessively over the construction of the dead man's sentences' (350). The text itself is exposed as an act of capture. As Graham Huggan astutely points out, '[t]he manuscript emerges in this context as another souvenir': Curnow turns Kelly into a commodity and occupies his words so that 'the voice through which [the narrative] claims to speak is never Kelly's own.'[42] Through this strategy, Carey displaces the reader's reliance on and absorption by Ned's voice, leaving us to ask with Spivak, 'Can the subaltern speak?'[43] Curnow also challenges Ned's version of the fledgling nation and community, the 'true Australian coin' (340), and the 'ever-growing adoration of the Kelly Gang' (350), revealing the ongoing debate about Australian national identity in relation to the Kelly story: 'What is it about we Australians, eh? he demanded. What is wrong with us? Do we not have a Jefferson? A Disraeli? Might not we find someone better to admire than a horse-thief and a murderer? Must we always make such an embarrassing spectacle of ourselves?' (350). Compromised and complicit, like Ned himself, Curnow's questions disturb the emotional hold of Ned's narrative on the reader, raising vital reservations about the function of the Kelly myth. The final description of the hanging, meanwhile, is delivered by another third-person narrator, this time in the form of a flat, unemotional account of the execution. Both narratives dislocate us from our involvement in Ned's voice in such a way as to put it into necessary perspective and question the potential use of the Kelly myth as part of a nostalgic and elitist view of national identity.

Such ambivalence has always been part of the response to the Kelly story. Judith Kapferer quotes Bernard Smith's response to one of Sidney Nolan's paintings: 'It is ... by no means easy to decide whether Nolan intends Kelly to be read as a hero or clown and the ambiguity is well pointed, because Australians in general have never made up their minds either; he is an

ambiguous figure, in the national imagination as in Nolan's art.'
But as Kapferer goes on to argue, definitions of Kelly's identity
are always in the service of ideologies with other motives: 'Those
men whose bodies become captured by repressive apparatuses of
the state – bushrangers, swagmen, striking workers – are doubly
captured when their very images are also appropriated by the
ideological apparatuses of that same state to which their lives
were so often forfeit.'[44]

What is remarkable about Peter Carey's novel is the linguistic and imaginative flair with which he recreates Ned Kelly's
life, his context and most of all his voice. Thoroughly convincing,
this novel is Carey's most dazzling fictional imagining to date. It
deservedly received high praise from reviewers and won a number
of pre-eminent awards, notably the Booker Prize in England, the
Commonwealth Writers Prize, the Townsville Foundation for
Australian Literary Studies Award and the Victorian Premier's
Literary Award.

Critical overview and conclusion

THIS book has given a reading of Peter Carey's work stressing the different aspects in the political concerns of his fiction, an approach which has so far not had widespread treatment by other critics, and indicating his critiques of multinational capitalism, the legacies of colonial history, exploitative power relationships, and sexual roles as of particular interest. While doing so, it has picked up on the main trends in Carey criticism, especially views of Carey as a fabulist or surrealist, as a post-modernist and as a post-colonial writer, to present him as a hybrid who exploits the literary, formal and thematic ambiguities afforded by this mixture, rather than offering easily decodable narratives. This chapter collates some of the existing criticism of Carey's work in relation to these approaches, and gives a summary of the positions outlined in reviews of the individual volumes of fiction.

Much early criticism of Carey concentrated on the fantastic and weird elements in his stories. The use of the terms fabulist and surrealistic to describe his work has been frequent, but also contested. Early reviewers tended to use them in an unexamined way to describe the bizarre sides of Carey's imaginings, although Brian Kiernan denied the appropriateness of 'surreal' since 'that would imply Freudian assumptions and allow symbolic decoding'.[1] Subsequent criticism has tended to elaborate Kiernan's position. Bruce Clunies-Ross claimed that Carey's stories are surrealistic only 'in the precise sense of the word', which he takes to be the delineation of the menace beneath the surface of everyday life, rather than the exploration of the unconscious;[2] while Greg

Manning has insisted that the specifically psychoanalytic basis for surrealism is inappropri-ately limiting in the case of Carey's stories.[3] Nevertheless, as I suggested in chapter 1, there is a context of Australian surrealism which has some bearing on the fiction writing of the 1960s and 1970s to which Carey's early work belongs.

The use of the term 'fabulist' has been equally ambivalent.[4] An early essay by Bruce Bennett hailed Carey as 'a true fabulator' and invoked Robert Scholes's definition of the term in his book of 1967.[5] Kate Ahearn contested this assignation, arguing that rather than employing the 'ethically controlled fantasy' of the fabulist, Carey's work was 'more like straight parable', with allegorical and didactic meanings. Her essay ended with a response from a bemused-sounding Peter Carey: 'the stories were never intended as didactic and, far from being attempts to communicate a discovered fact, were the result of purely intu-itive processes. I began both stories ['Crabs' and 'Peeling'] with-out knowing how they would end. I am still at a loss to think of how they could be didactic.'[6] Kiernan argued that the stories are 'not fables or allegories that parallel the real world in their own terms'; instead they are 'pure fictions à la Borges', their 'point' being 'the grotesque association of images within the story rather than any outward reference'.[7] This view seems to coincide with Carey's own in a suggestion worthy of Bob Dylan in its evasiveness that '[t]he stories are only about what they seem to be about'.[8] The analogy with the work of Borges led to a highly favourable comparison by *The Bulletin* reviewer of *War Crimes,* who placed it alongside the Australian publication of Borges's *The Book of Sand,*[9] although in terms of overt influence, Carey has declared himself fortunate to have read Borges 'later rather than earlier'.[10]

There has been diverse criticism examining the post-modern playfulness and self-conscious fictionality of Carey's work. Helen Daniel's reading of *Illywhacker* is, in common with the rest of her book *Liars,* dedicated single-mindedly to the playful strategy of the novelist/narrator as liar and the fabricatory effects that allows. Her article in *Southerly* formed the basis of her chapter on Carey in *Liars*. There, she celebrates the novel rather uncritically as 'a constant delight' for its yarning quality which she associates with the comic picaresque narratives of Peter Mathers. She describes and lists the proliferating narratives and characters in the book, characterising it as 'an extraordinary blend of comic vignettes, absurdist notions, zany fictions and convincing images of time and place ... a vast and generous novel in which wondrous scenes abound'.[11] But Brian Edwards has argued against the 'totalising rhetoric' of Daniel's critical template.[12] Edwards's Derridean-influenced article usefully sets Carey's text off against Murray Bail's post-modern play in *Homesickness* (1980) and *Holden's Performance* (1988) and examines Carey's post-modern exploration of construction and bricolage particularly through a focus on language and writing. Margaret Harris has made interesting intertextual analogies with George Eliot's *The Mill on the Floss*[13] to demonstrate the post-modern qualities of *Oscar and Lucinda*, while Wenche Ommundsen has used that novel to investigate the validity of the term 'metafiction'.[14] In his thorough treatment of the storytelling theme in *Bliss*, A.J. Hassall compares the book with David Malouf's *Child's Play* (1981), which he sees as an example of a post-modern fiction abandoning the referential, whereas Carey avoids doing that despite playing 'elegant metafictional games'.[15] Hassall's essay has been incorporated into his informative book on Carey's work, and his approach tends to foreground the post-modern strategies in the novels and stories, while paying attention to a wide variety of thematic angles and acknowledging the post-colonial elements.

The overlap between post-modernism and post-colonialism in Carey has been investigated by a number of critics. Tony Thwaites has provided an interesting 'double' reading of *Illywhacker* as a 'metalinguistic' novel about the Great Australian novel,[16] providing an ironic view of the very project it seems to undertake, while M.D. Fletcher has examined the novel alongside the theoretical material in *The Empire Writes Back* to find a post-colonial combination of 'metafictional devices with political engagement',[17] although he tends to concentrate on the devices rather than the engagement. Kirsten Holst Petersen has argued that Carey's post-modernism is used in the service of his post-colonialism, 'to emphasise the mainly political and ideological points' he wishes to make.[18] Graham Huggan has investigated the post-colonial use of allegory as a mode of counter discourse in relation to *Oscar and Lucinda*, and examined analogies with Günther Grass's *The Tin Drum*,[19] while David Callahan looks at Carey's treatment of Gosse as evidence of a new authority and ease in the relation of post-colonial culture to its colonial progenitors.[20]

Karen Lamb considers the production and reception of Peter Carey as an Australian author in her interesting, if patchy, book *Peter Carey: The Genesis of Fame*, which Graeme Turner has developed in an essay looking at Carey's position as a 'national' author.[21] Lamb provides a valuable, if sometimes slightly inaccurate,[22] survey of critical responses to each of the novels. She also outlines arguments which are worth developing. She sees reviewers suggesting that Carey fails to resolve the problems of realism and fabulism, whereas the fabular elements in his work 'could have unyoked it from the conventional expectations of longer narratives'. In her elliptical and condensed manner, Lamb takes the responses to *Illywhacker* as symptomatic of the contradictions in Carey's literary ascendancy. The book won prizes in Australia and some enthusiastic celebrations as 'a barometer of Australianness', but was first published in England and received its highest accolades abroad. This colonial approval leads Lamb to question the 'historical nostalgia' behind the novel's early reception and posit that a 'starker, more post-modern and political reading' might complicate such a response, wondering whether the book possesses 'the political motivation of parody' since the 'elision between post-colonial and post-modern energies' in the novel causes 'critical uncertainty' about its project. *Illywhacker* exploits the playfulness of a post-modern fiction and presents its play with Australian myths as an exposé of post-colonial lies, but in undertaking both at the same time, Lamb seems to argue, and in aiming for a kind of novel capable of achieving international recognition, Carey is in danger of subverting his critical edge.[23] On this political view of Carey, Ken

Gelder interestingly emphasises the novel's 'construction of the history of capitalism in Australia' suggesting that it 'speaks from its position in capitalism and tries to express itself as both product or commodity (for consumption) and anti-product (as text, difficult to consume)'.[24]

Carey's move to New York, his prolific writing and prize-winning career and his international impact perhaps explain the emergence of a Carey backlash in some Australian circles. Part of this may be a genuine sense that Australian writing and publishing is still at the mercy of the imperialistic effects of Western culture. When *Illywhacker* was published by Faber in London in 1985, the University of Queensland Press, which had published Carey's previous works, had to buy the Australian rights. This prompted 'a bitter debate' at the 1986 Adelaide Writer's Festival where UQP's Laurie Muller 'accused overseas publishers of luring successful Australian writers away from the Australian publishers who gave them their start'.[25] George Turner 'cannot forgive [Carey] for his statement at the Booker Prize dinner, that "Australia is hedonistic and intrinsically corrupt and probably always has been", and feels that this 'explains much about his writing'.[26] Not surprisingly, Carey's own reaction has been to point to the American capacity to 'celebrate success' rather than 'dump on it'.[27]

Other criticism has come in the form of suggestions that Carey has lost touch with his initial inspiration. Armanda Lohrey was initially excited by the brilliant and disturbing capacity of Carey's early stories, but feels that his subsequent career has been a 'regression', a 'retreat from his earlier vision and the technical innovation that accompanied it'.[28] Van Ikin has maintained a similar belief that Carey's best work is to be found in the 'spare, chilling shorter fictions',[29] while Stephen Muecke criticised Carey for a 'conservative attitude to literature' by virtue of his apparent endorsement of nineteenth-century fictional conventions.[30] Ken Goodwin's piece in *New Literature Review* is an interesting, if partial, interrogation of Stephen Muerke's partisan post-structuralist view of Carey,[31] and generally, far more of the criticism of Carey's work has celebrated it as innovatory and exciting, although few of the articles on his work do complete justice to either its range or character.

Given the limited number of large-scale critical works on Carey so far, it is also worth documenting some of the review responses to individual works as they appeared.

The Fat Man in History volume was hailed by many reviewers as outstanding, a landmark in Australian literature, a verdict which was reinforced by the publication of *War Crimes* in 1979, which won the NSW Premier's Literary Award for 1980. There were some dissenting voices: the book received a dismissive review from Morris Lurie,[32] who as a result was read 'a stern lecture' by Barry Oakley.[33] But generally Carey was seen as 'the most spectacular talent to emerge in the 1970s'.[34]

Initial reaction to *Bliss* was favourable if mixed. Graham Burns was unsettled by the uneven tone of the novel which left the reader unclear how seriously to take it. Along with the 'two-dimensional' quality of the character of Harry and the tediousness of Honey Barbara, Burns suspected that the 'hippie complacencies' of her outlook and the ending were also Carey's own.[35] Peter Pierce found the ending transformed the book into 'a disappointingly mawkish fable of re-integration'.[36] Despite seeing the novel as 'a brave book', John Tranter criticised it for its 'tangled plot' and its 'unconvincing paean to vegetarian food, hippy communalism and tree-worship', as well as 'an apparent lack of moral range and depth': 'what brand of eschatology sees unethical advertising as its main focus of evil, and vegetarian communalism as its only salvation? At times Carey seems like an aqualung diver without enough weights on his belt, trying to reach the depths, but bobbing back up to the surface again.'[37] John Ryle saw Carey being lured from his true strengths as a writer of bleak, doom-laden stories 'into this sentimentality by a nostalgia for happy endings'.[38] For Helen Daniel, the ending was 'a cop-out';[39] while Rory Barnes found the ending 'surprisingly mundane' for Carey, 'too soft, too romantic'.[40] Susan McKernan pointed out that 'Carey's imagination only slackens when Harry finds his way to the pure life of the bush', partly because Carey 'loves the crazy world of modern capitalism' and 'cannot help suggesting that it is more fun than digging holes and eating honey'.[41] A number of reviewers noticed the ending relied too often on what Martin Duwell called 'the rhapsodic tone derived from Garcia Márquez'.[42] Lee noticed 'small echoes ... not only in the Columbian setting but also in elements of its phrasing'.[43] Some critical reviewers of the novel felt that *Bliss* was technically structured as a loose collection of 'thematically very disparate short stories, yoked together by an inadequate narrative structure',[44] a criticism which was inevitable given the understandable but incorrect perception of Carey as a short story writer until the publication of this apparent first novel.[45] In fact, Carey had been carrying the idea for the book around since the late 1960s and tried it out as a short story a number of times.[46] Antonella Riem Natale argued for a much more integrated view of the 'stratification of stories' in *Bliss*, suggesting that Harry's developing maturity is inextricably connected with his abilities as a teller of stories.[47]

Illywhacker appeared in 1985 to very mixed critical responses. Many reviewers felt Carey had overstretched himself. Peter Goldsworthy felt that the book was 'overall just boring', seeing it as evidence of Carey's decline from being the writer of 'carefully crafted' stories, a victim of the 'bad praise' and 'indiscriminate hype' of the early 1970s when critics were on the look-out for great Australian Writers.[48] Van Ikin again shared this sense that Carey's real strength lies in his 'breathtaking talent as a writer of spare, outre short stories' and that he has been misled into believing that more means better. By comparison with the 'sparkling élan of Carey's speculative fictions', he 'found [*Illywhacker*] a chore to plough through' and felt the book trod 'an uneasy path between authenticity and fantasy'. Its indictment of Australia's manipulation from overseas or its contemporary malaise he thought much less scathing than the 'fierce anger' of David Ireland's bleakly abstract *The Flesheaters* (1972) or Xavier Herbert's massive epic *Poor Fellow My Country* (1975).[49] Elizabeth Webby felt that 'inside this fat novel was a great short story crying to get out'. She admired the way the 'idiomatic narrative cracks along at a rapid pace', but its mixture of history and fantasy lacked 'the bite of a Salman Rushdie'. In an intriguing analogy with Herbert's shift from shacks to the emporium, she suggested that Carey 'has progressively moved up-market', from what he has called the 'strange little shacks' of the short stories 'which you can always pull down if they don't work' to the 'modest bungalow' of 'War Crimes', the split-level of *Bliss* and the high-rise of *Illywhacker*,[50] implying that, like Herbert, Carey was trapped within the international market ambitions of his novel. Adrian Mitchell also disliked what he identified as the 'carelessness' of a novel that was 'too big' and which allowed its different lines of interest to take over the direction so that the ideas 'aren't integrated with the characters'.[51]

Many other reviewers found much to celebrate, though praise was often qualified. Geoffrey Dutton was one of the most unreserved, finding the novel 'astonishing', convincingly constructed by 'a master craftsman' and 'new'.[52] Andrew Hislop felt the book 'overreaches itself' and that the earlier 'humorous zest' is 'not sustained', reducing 'a broad, rollicking historical canvas to a cramped, futuristic vision' with 'menacing symbolic luggage'. Nevertheless, he admired the 'dazzling heterogeneity' of Carey's 'parables of a "colonised" culture', and made inter-esting points about the proliferation of immigrant experi-ences documented in the novel, and the links between coloni-sation and the 'politics' of machinery.[53] Peter Pierce argued that the fact that the book 'flags somewhat' was a deliberate intention, since Herbert's story is partly about 'how he was superseded by less exuberant and less resilient generations'. He saw the book in an Australian picaresque tradition represented by Henry Lawson's stories, the 'inveterate truthfulness'[54] of Joseph Furphy's *Such Is Life* (1944) and an oral-narrative tradition represented by American novelist Thomas Berger's *Little Big Man* (1964).[55] John Hanrahan found the novel 'consistently entertaining' and 'a lot of fun' but felt disappointed because 'Carey loses his way in the second half'. Carey's characters 'evaporate' and the well-observed details of situation disintegrate as they 'crash into a concrete wall of symbolism'. Nevertheless, Hanrahan applauded Carey for having 'an eye and an ear that gets scenes just right', testifying from the personal experience of the portrait of his home village in Victoria, and for having 'caught the rhythms of speech beautifully', even if the book ends 'with simple formulae'.[56] Marion Halligan admitted to having long admired 'the special quality' of Carey's imagination, which she describes interestingly as 'lateral ... a way of seeing elements and connections freshly, a whole new way of percep-tion, often disturbingly surreal'. *Illywhacker* she found not lateral so much as 'baroque, indeed rococo'; she felt that the allegorical theme of Australia as a pet shop selling its treasures off to foreign money was 'too heavy' and undermined the true appeal of the book as 'a collection of terrific yarns'.[57] Laurie Clancy, too, admired Carey's 'glorious invention' and found the writing 'the finest and most sensuous' that Carey had done, particularly by contrast with the 'no more than functional' prose of the earlier work. But he was disappointed overall by the way Carey failed to sustain his inventive energy as a result of the 'desperate improvisation' of the structure.[58] Howard Jacobson felt reading the novel was 'not unlike spending a week in the company of the best kind of Australian' and recommended it as an experience that 'will give you the feel of [Australia] like nothing else I know'.[59]

Much of the reception accorded to *Oscar and Lucinda* was suitably laudatory for a book which garnered four major prizes. Annette Stewart claimed it Carey's 'best novel to date ... an entirely satisfactory homogeneous whole' which thereby contradicted criticisms of Carey's earlier novels as fragmentary or merely sequences of short stories. Its strengths she located in the 'deeply imagined and felt way' in which Carey rendered the nineteenth-century context of his 'romantic thriller'.[60] Don Anderson agreed that this novel has 'outshone even his own prior creations', outdoing John Barth with his imaginative virtuosity and stylish writing.[61] For Elizabeth Riddell the book was 'a marvellous piece of story-telling',[62] while Margaret Harris celebrated the pleasures which this 'thoroughly post-modernist fiction' brought through its 'arcana and esoterica'.[63] D.J. O'Hearn saw it as 'a monumental masterpiece' and disagreed with critics who 'seem piqued that he has written a novel in the old style: discursive, unselfconscious, with rounded characters and narrative'.[64] Perhaps he had in mind less favourable reviews such as Gerard Windsor's berating of Carey for being 'slack, even boring' in his realism.[65] Howard Jacobson detected problematic elements of style and tone which undermined the coherence of the novel, setting a gauche sentimentality against a bleak nihilism in an unconvincing way.[66] More damningly but with little argument, Mary Rose Liverani dismissed the book 'a numbing work of misanthropy and self-loathing which ... could well be the next great Australian movie'.[67] C.K. Stead argued more perversely that the novel suffered from a contradiction between its nineteenth-century realism and its metafictionality, such that it was contrived and unconvincing, and remarked that 'something unsavoury ... infects the whole novel' with an 'anal vision'.[68] With some degree of back-handed praise, Lorna Sage celebrated the novel as 'deeply unoriginal' with a 'softness at the centre' distinc-tively its own.[69] Matthew Da Silva took up some of the reservations of reviewers and has argued for an incoher-ence in the novel deriving from the isolation of characters from their contexts.[70]

It has become almost a commonplace to assume that the reviews of *The Tax Inspector* were favourable in America and the UK, but were damning or bad in Australia. There were some complimentary Australian reviews, such as Diana Giese's; but many were highly critical. Writing in *The Sydney Morning Herald* under the title 'Brutish and Nasty' with its Hobbesian analogy, A.P. Riemer called the book 'generally unpleasant', wondered whether Carey had become hooked on *Twin Peaks*, admitting that he could not disguise his 'distaste' for much of the book, despite its verve and pace.[71] Despite his conclusion that Carey has merely 'stumbled' in his artistic progress, Peter Pierce called the book 'sour', merely 'a competent thriller', 'bleakly reductive', 'perfunctory' in presentation, 'half-hearted', with 'rickety scaffolding' and 'little imaginative inwardness'. By the end of his review, Pierce appears as one of the very 'jackals' whom he anticipates will be circling Carey as he comes home to Sydney 'to present a sour prospectus, cum indictment, of the city'.[72]

That indictment hit home perhaps because of the accuracy of Carey's vitriolic thumbnail sketches of aspects of Sydney. As Richard Glover has pointed out, Chez Oz is 'the real restaurant, accurately described' and Balmain is 'precisely recorded'.[73] In the run-up to the Olympic 2000 bid, having Carey coming back from his 'moral holiday'[74] in New York with this acidic view of a poisoned city perhaps seemed too much like an act of bad faith, despite the fact that the novel is no more grim that his earlier stories, as Karen Lamb points out in her useful if highly abbreviated comments. Lamb goes on to explain this adverse reaction further. What she calls 'Carey's most socially relevant novel to date' is also the one in which he 'demythologises the Australian dream of freedom – self-employment' and exposes other cherished myths – the lone battler scenario in which anyone can make it, the freedom-loving ingenuity which can lead to 'a self-serving petty criminality'.[75]

This might be the origin of that sense of 'betrayal' which Graeme Turner has noted in responses to the book. This is best epitomised by the paranoia evident in a *Sydney Morning Herald* story which opens 'Would you buy a used car from this man? Peter "I was born in Bacchus Marsh" Carey has been talking to *The New York Times* about us again.'[76] Turner perceptively com-ments that the Australian reviews were generally 'not so much bad as bewildered'.[77] Helen Daniel displayed this position, seeing the novel as an artistic retreat and a desertion of national responsibility.[78] Certainly other reviewers like Laurie Clancy found difficulty in locating 'the centre of the novel', seeing an overall lack of coherence with many of the episodes as either irrelevant or, as with the ending, downright implausible.[79] This critical confusion was notable even in fairly positive reviews: Veronica Brady seemed to have enjoyed the book to the extent of calling it 'fundamentally cheerful … a story about human resourcefulness'.[80]

The criticisms of the novel also touched on some significant areas of debate. Fuller criticism came from Robert Dixon in the review and article considered earlier,[81] which offer thought-provoking insights. While relishing the 'comminatory tone' of the book, Angela Carter detected a 'programmatic quality' which makes the novel 'miss a tragic resonance' as Carey 'takes the Catchprices seriously as an idea, but he doesn't take them seriously enough as people'.[82] Eden Liddelow's view of Carey's 'white trash novel' located an absence of notable Carey features which readers might expect: 'the dazzling concept', 'the sense of joy and human potential', 'the ironies, the imaginative leaps, above all the humour'. For Liddelow, this was a moralistic novel with types rather than characters, which 'sacrifices variety and wit and courts dullness from film noir', 'scraping the bottom of the naturalistic barrel' in its filmic naturalism.[83] But we also notice here an example of the critical nostalgia and 'conservatism' which Graeme Turner has pointed to in responses to Carey's later work.[84] What reviewers seemed to want was another prize-winning great Australian novel set safely in the past with humour and distance, rather than the savage piece Carey had written, and which Philip Hensher has described more recently as 'spectacular' and 'underrated'.[85] It is a novel which will no doubt continue to generate very different responses in readers.

Philip Hensher's comment comes in his review of *The Unusual Life of Tristan Smith*, in which he rightly takes the opportunity to celebrate Carey's indefatigable inventiveness 'in never writing the same book twice': even 'the apparently familiar genres don't erase the sense that Carey starts each novel with an absolutely blank sheet, and takes nothing for granted', while at the same time creating works which are 'stamped with a powerfully distinctive personality' belonging to 'one of the most recognisable and elegant stylists in fiction now'. While not giving *Tristan Smith* an unconditional endorsement, Hensher adds with suggestive economy that 'what sticks in the mind is the disturbing idea that the imperial enterprise and the force of the imagination are the same thing'. Peter Kemp also celebrated this novel as 'energetically audacious', calling it a 'ripplingly substantial achievement', a 'gorgeous carnival of conjuring up' in the way Carey gives his imaginary world 'fabulous actuality'. Like Hensher, Kemp makes analogies with Dickens which were very appropriate given Carey's next project.[86] Most reviews of the novel have endorsed Carey's daring flamboyance even while almost inevitably questioning some of the elements of the book. Galen Strawson saw it as 'a powerful jalopy, bright with scavenged chrome, fairy lights, and no brakes, carrying a story of considerable psychological brilliance'.[87] Geraldine Brennan found it 'spellbinding ... rattling, witty, profound'.[88] In a long, resumé-laden article surveying Carey's whole career, April Bernard sees the novel as 'a savage and hilarious satire, told, in the manner of *Gulliver's Travels*, as a fable set in mythical lands', while beneath the indictment of 'the Disneyization of the world's culture', she detects 'a simple folk tale' endorsing the 'heart's affection for love and loyalty and truth'.[89] Taking a more complex view, Andrew Riemer has argued that although it is inevitable 'that this rich and sprightly novel, where Carey's imagination soars and dances, will be read as a political allegory', to read it in the 'rigorously political manner' demanded by some of Carey's earlier work would 'diminish the richness and complexity'. He stresses the playful extravagance of the analogies between events in the novel and actuality, which are 'almost always designed to make simple one-to-one substitutions inappropriate': 'even in the few places where the novel threatens to decline into a kind of agitprop simplicity, considerable irony and ambivalence seem almost always to operate'. Riemer makes the interesting analogy between Tristan and Oskar from Günther Grass's *The Tin Drum*, and feels that the novel is Carey's 'richest and most satisfying work so far'.[90]

More recent readings of Carey's work have supported this view. Graham Huggan's critical study of Carey (1996) offers a very lively, acute and illuminating coverage of the works from a thematic viewpoint. Huggan examines Carey's engagement with consumer capitalism and an intensifying media-dominated culture by looking at the nightmarish, the grotesque and the monstrous in the fictions. His thematic chapters are on dreams and secrets, the magical power of signs, the rage for structure, past and futures, and monsters; and he weaves together illustrations from the whole range of Carey's work up to 1996, illuminating them with flexible reference to current arguments, theories and approaches. Of the essays and articles that have appeared since the first edition of this work and which are not mentioned in the additional chapters, the following are particularly notable. Bill Ashcroft (1996) and Ian Adam (1994) have both investigated Carey's treatment of history in *Illywhacker* and in *Oscar and Lucinda* in relation to postcolonial arguments. Heinz Antor (1998) has analysed *Illywhacker* for both its postcolonial and post-modernist aspects; while Simon During (2000) has placed *Oscar and Lucinda* in the context of arguments about its relation to the literary system of prize-winning novels and arguments about literary value. Barbara Bode (1995) has provided a useful essay on child sexual abuse in *The Tax Inspector*, and *The Unusual Life of Tristan Smith* has received interesting attention from Peter Pierce (1996) and Carrie Dawson (1997). Carey himself has done an interview with Ray Willbanks (1997) which provides a fascinating insight into how he begins to construct his imaginary worlds, using the opening of *The Tax Inspector* as an example, and providing useful angles on *The Unusual Life of Tristan Smith*. He has also published three autobiographical pieces of note: 'A Small Memorial' (1995) dealing with his feelings about the abortions his first wife underwent in the 1960s, *30 Days in Sydney* (2001) describing a return visit to his home city, and a letter to Robert McCrum (2001) documenting his response to the World Trade Center attack.

The diversity of responses to Carey's work suitably match the diversity of the fictions themselves. Their changing shapes and scope affords the exhilarating spectacle of an author who is constantly daring himself to risk everything on yet another imaginative gamble, and who promises to keep his reading public equally intrigued and entertained in the future.

Notes

Chapter 1

1 Van Ikin, Answers to seventeen questions: an interview with Peter Carey, *Science Fiction: A Review of Speculative Literature*, 1, 1, 1977, 33.

2 Translated as 'the trial of the real world' in André Breton, *Manifestos of Surrealism*, trans. Richard Seaver and Helen R. Lane, Michigan, Ann Arbor: University of Michigan Press, 1972, 47. See chapters 2 and 8 for the Australian context of surrealism.

3 Ikin, Answers to seventeen questions, 34.

4 Robert Ross, 'It cannot *not* be there': Borges and Australia's Peter Carey, in Edna Aizenberg (ed.), *Borges and his Successors: The Borgesian Impact on Literature and the Arts*, Columbia, Miss.: University of Missouri Press, 1989, 50.

5 All references to Carey's major works will be to bracketed page numbers from the following British editions: *Collected Stories*, London: Faber, 1995; *Bliss*, London: Pan-Picador, 1982; *Illywhacker*, London: Faber, 1990; *Oscar and Lucinda*, London: Faber, 1989; *The Tax Inspector*, London: Faber, 1991; *The Unusual Life of Tristan Smith*, London: Faber, 1994; *The Big Bazoohley*, London: Faber, 1995.

6 Captain Moonlite (1842–80) was an Irish-born bush ranger turned bandit in the 1860s – see William H. Wilde, Joy Hooton and Barry Andrews (eds), *The Oxford Companion to Australian Literature*, Melbourne: Oxford University Press, 1986, 488 – while Frank Hardy has written powerful political novels. Ironically, he has also offered a critique of Carey as a post-modernist adman who decided to manufacture books: 'He set out to win a prize and he did. It's packaging.' Louise Kennedy, Frankly speaking, *The Canberra Times*, 23.8.1992, 23.

7   Joanna Penglase (co-writer) and Don Featherstone (co-writer and director), The most beautiful lies: a film about Peter Carey, BBC1 *Omnibus*, 1986–7. Also Packed lunches – writer's talks: interview with Peter Kemp, ICA audio-tape, 12.3.1994: 'I do like the idea of fiction as invented, made up – a totally plastic world'.

8   Penglase and Featherstone, The most beautiful lies.

9   Richard Yallop, A mild colonial boy is bound for Eton, *The Age*, 1.12.1993, 1.

10 Candida Baker, Peter Carey in *Yacker: Australian Writers Talk About Their Work*, Sydney: Picador, 1986, 70.

11 Richard Glover, The tallest story of them all, *The Sydney Morning Herald* Saturday Review, 29.6.1985, 39; Alan Attwood, Is this man mad? The marvellous mind of Peter Carey, *Time*, 22.2.1988, 55.

12 Glover, Tallest story of them all, 39, for example.

13 David Sexton, Review in *The Literary Review*, June 1985, 38.

14 Gerry Turcotte (ed.), *Writers in Action*, The Writer's Choice Evenings, Sydney: Currency Press, 1990, 19.

15 Ray Willbanks, *Speaking Volumes: Australian Writers and their Work*, Ringwood: Penguin, 1992, 44.

16 *Ibid.*, 44.

17 Turcotte, *Writers in Action*, 19.

18 Alison Summers, Candid Carey, *The National Times*, 1–7.11.1985, 32.

19 Baker, *Yacker*, 71.

20 John F. Baker, Peter Carey, *Publishers Weekly*, 13.12.1991, 38; the bracketed addition was indicated by Peter Carey in a fax to the author, 28 August 1995.

21 Peter Carey, Letter to Brian Kiernan, 5.3.1976, MS Dr Brian Kiernan, 7017, correspondence, National Library of Australia.

22 Sexton, *The Literary Review*, 39.

23 Carey, Letter to Kiernan, 5.3.1976.

24 Sexton, *The Literary Review*, 38.

25 *Ibid.*

26 Tony Thwaites, More tramps at home: seeing Australia first, *Meanjin*, 46, 3, 1987, 403.

27 Karen Lamb, *Peter Carey: The Genesis of Fame*, Sydney: Angus & Robertson, 1992, 8, n. 16.

28 Anthony J. Hassall, *Dancing on Hot Macadam*, St Lucia, Queensland: University of Queensland Press, xiv – see Lamb, *Peter Carey*, 9 for a brief description.

29 Hassall, *Dancing on Hot Macadam*, 187.

30 Andrew Olle, Interview with Peter Carey, 26.9.88, Australian Broadcasting Corporation tape 89/10/1559–2.

31 Peter Carey, Statement, *Australian Literary Studies*, 8, 2, 1977, 183.

32 Lamb, *Peter Carey*, 8; see also p. 10 for description.

33 Olle, Interview with Peter Carey.

34 Sue Woolfe and Kate Grenville, *Making Stories: How Ten Australian Novels Were Written*, St Leonards, NSW: Allen and Unwin, 1993, 41.

35 Willbanks, *Speaking Volumes*, 45.

36 Lamb, *Peter Carey*, 11; elsewhere called *In Loving Memory of Luke McClosky*, see Carey, Statement, 186.

37 Lamb, *Peter Carey*, 11.

38 Jan Garrett, Interview with Peter Carey, 8.10.1979, Australian Broadcasting Corporation tape 80/10/1043–5.

39 John Anderson (1893–1962) was the initiator of the Sydney Freethought group. See William H. Wilde, Joy Hooton and Barry Andrews (eds), *The Oxford Companion to Australian Literature*, Melbourne: Oxford University Press, 1986, 26.

40 Frank Moorhouse, What happened to the short story?, *Australian Literary Studies*, 8, 2, 1977, 181.

41 Valerie Lawson, Peter Carey: advertising doesn't hurt him a scrap, *The Sydney Morning Herald*, 5.9.1981, 47.

42 Baker, *Yacker*, 74–5.

43 Hassall, *Dancing on Hot Macadam*, 171, n. 24.

44 See Baker, *Yacker*, 74–5; Turcotte, *Writers in Action*, 17.

45 Kate Grenville, From *The Getting of Wisdom* to *Illywhacker*: the library and our literary heritage, *Australian Library Journal*, 38, 1.2.1989, 64.

46 See John Docker, *In a Critical Condition*, Ringwood, Victoria: Penguin, 1984, 83–109. I am grateful to John Thieme for this point.

47 Ken Gelder and Paul Salzman, *The New Diversity: Australian Fiction 1970–88*, Melbourne: McPhee Gribble, 1989, 15; Michael Wilding, The tabloid story, in Michael Wilding (ed.), *The Tabloid*

Story Pocket Book, Sydney: Wild and Woolley, 1978, 304–6.

48   Grenville, From *The Getting of Wisdom to Illywhacker*, 62.

49   Patrick White, The prodigal son, *Australian Letters*, 1.4.1958, 39.

50   Wilding, The tabloid story, 307.

51   Michael Wilding, A Random House: the parlous state of Australian publishing, *Meanjin*, 34, 1, 1975, 106.

52   Carl Harrison-Ford, How good is the boom in Australian fiction?, *The Australian Author*, 7, 2, 1975, 4.

53   Brian Kiernan, *The Most Beautiful Lies*, Sydney: Angus & Robertson, 1977, xii.

54   Diana Giese, Brave new world of publishing, *The Canberra Times*, 10.9.1989, 18.

55   Lamb, *Peter Carey*, 14.

56   Laurie Hergenhan (ed.), *The Penguin New Literary History of Australia*, Ringwood, Victoria: Penguin Australia, 1988, 540.

57   *Ibid.*, 455.

58   Wilding, *Tabloid*, 295–6, 302.

59   Wilding, *Tabloid*, 304–5.

60   Frank Moorhouse, What happened to the short story? *Australian Literary Studies*, 8, 2, 1977, 179.

61   Carey, Statement, 187.

62   John Maddocks, Bizarre realities: an interview with Peter Carey, *Southerly*, 41, 1, 1981, 32–3.

63   Robin Ravlich, Interview with Peter Carey, 22.10.1979, Australian Broadcasting Corporation tape 88/10/1864–2.

64   Helen Frizell, Reputation – and power, *The Sydney Morning Herald*, 23.9.1980, 7.

65   Jane Singleton, Interview with Peter Carey, 8.7.1985, Australian Broadcasting Corporation tape 85/10/798–4.

66   Neil Shoebridge, Reborn agency aims to stand alone, *Business Review Weekly*, 3.8.1990, 85–6; additional information from Peter Carey in a fax to the author, 28 August 1995.

67   Baker, *Yacker*, 66.

68   Van Ikin, Peter Carey: the stories, *Science Fiction*, 1, 1.6.1977, 20, 22. The term 'speculative fiction' was probably first used by Robert A. Heinlein in *Of Other Worlds*, ed. Lloyd Arthur Eshbach, 1947. Thanks to Andy Butler for pointing this out. For Carey's acceptance

of the term see Ikin, Answers to seventeen questions, 36: 'of course they're speculative fiction, and I react very well to the idea of them being recognised as such'.

69 Bruce Clunies Ross, Lazlo's testament, or structuring the past and sketching the present in contemporary short fiction, mainly Australian, *Kunapipi*, 1, 2, 1979, 116, mentions this.

70 There is a useful comparison of Carey and Bail focusing on 'Report on the Shadow Industry' in the acute early review of *The Fat Man in History* by W. Green in *Westerly*, 4, 1975, 73–6. A treatment of metafictionality in Carey stories, in particular 'Do You Love Me', can be found in Ken Gelder and Paul Salzman, *The New Diversity: Australian Fiction 1970–88*, Melbourne: McPhee Gribble, 1989, 116–17, and in Hassall, *Dancing on Hot Macadam, passim*.

71 See Michael Wilding's selected stories, *Great Climate*, London: Faber, 1990.

72 Frederic Jameson, Postmodernism and consumer society, in Hal Foster (ed.), *Postmodern Culture*, London: Pluto, 1985, 111–25. Pastiche is considered as offering 'a key to destabilisation and deconstruction of a repressive European archive' by some post-colonial critics – see Helen Tiffin, Introduction, in Ian Adam and Helen Tiffin (eds), *Past the Last Post: Theorizing Post-Colonialism and Postmodernism*, Hemel Hempstead: Harvester Wheatsheaf, 1991, x.

73 Frederic Jameson, *Postmodernism, or the Cultural Logic of Late Capitalism*, London: Verso, 1990.

74 Jean-François Lyotard, *The Postmodern Condition*, trans. G. Bennington and B. Massumi, Manchester: Manchester University Press, 1984.

75 John Frow, What was post-modernism?, in Adam and Tiffin, *Past the Last Post*, 148.

76 You've got nothing to lose – advertising, 27.4.75, Australian Broadcasting Corporation tape 75.10.916 contained the earliest radio interview with Carey in which he discussed the ambiguities of being a writer and an advertiser. Unfortunately the tape has been lost.

77 Plinio Apuleyo Mendoza and Gabriel García Márquez, *The Fragrance of Guava*, trans. Ann Wright, London: Verso, 1983, 35–6.

78 Willbanks, *Speaking Volumes*, 56–7.

79 See chapters 2 and 8 for a discussion of this.

80 *Surrealism: Revolution by Night*: Canberra: National Gallery of

Australia, 1993, 216, 321. Peter Carey has pointed out in correspondence with the author that there was no relation between the
names of the character and the painter, although he knows James
Gleeson's work – (fax from Peter Carey, 28 August 1995).

81   Homi K. Bhabha, *The Location of Culture*, London: Routledge,
1994, 25.

82   Janet Hawley, How an ad man found bliss, *The Age*, 26.9.81, 26; see
also Turcotte, *Writers in Action*, 20, Willbanks, *Speaking Volumes*, 54.

83   Harrison-Ford, How good is the boom in Australian fiction?, 7.

84   See Bill Ashcroft *et al.* (eds), *The Post-Colonial Studies Reader*,
London: Routledge, 1995, 117–50 and Adam and Tiffin, *Past the
Last Post, passim*, for examples of the debates over the possible
relationships between post-modernism and post-colonialism.

85   Summers, Candid Carey, 32. In a fax to the author, Peter Carey
commented that 'socialist' seemed 'a rather moderate, centrist description', suggesting that his actual outlook is more radical that
that implies (28 August 1995).

86   The text of *Illusion* is in the National Library of Australia manuscript collection (MS 5062) on open access. The narrator (Kevin) is
enrolled to investigate a missing person, adopting a voice and appearance derived from Dashiel Hammett and Raymond Chandler
detective stories as done on screen by Humphrey Bogart. This allows for a humorous pastiche effect along with other elements such
as the corrupt uranium dealer, the Fat Man, echoing *The Maltese
Falcon* and lines of classic film dialogue such as the 'hill of beans'
speech from *Casablanca*. A chorus figure, the newspaper seller, reveals 'mysterious deaths' as he sells the newspaper 'Illusion'.
Along with songs, a slide show 'as close to hard-core porn as possible', on-stage sorcery and a figure called the Glowing Man, we
learn of the multinational and state supported underworld of uranium production and smuggling in what is undoubtedly a fairly
wayward, though intriguing, script.

87   *Bliss*, 113.

88   Turcotte, *Writers in Action*, 19–21, and Willbanks, *Speaking Volumes*, 44.

89   Packed lunches – writer's talks: Interview with Peter Kemp, ICA
audio-tape, 12.3.1994.

90   Woolfe and Grenville, *Making Stories*, 39.

91   *Ibid.*, 35, 44.

Chapter 2

1   The term used by Darko Suvin in *Metamorphoses of Science Fiction: On the Poetics and History of a Literary Genre*, New Haven, Conn.: Yale University Press, 1979, 4, to describe the intellectual and imaginative challenges to normative world views generated by the transformative effects of science fiction narratives. Thanks to Andy Butler for suggesting this link. All references to Carey's stories will be to the volume *Collected Stories* except in one case where the story has not been included in that volume.

2   Michael Morton-Evans, Carey reaches a blissful peak in his literary career, *The Australian*, 26.7.1984, 8.

3   Jan Garrett, Interview with Peter Carey, 14.10.1981, Australian Broadcasting Corporation tape 82/10/619–2.

4   See Ruth Ronen, *Possible Worlds in Literary Theory*, Cambridge: Cambridge University Press, 1994.

5   Joanna Penglase, (co-writer) and Don Featherstone (co-writer and director), The most beautiful lies: a film about Peter Carey, BBC1 *Omnibus*, 1986–7.

6   Graeme Turner, American dreaming: the fictions of Peter Carey, *Australian Literary Studies*, 12, 4, O1986, 434–5.

7   Thomas E. Tautsky, 'Getting the corner right': an interview with Peter Carey, *Australian and New Zealand Studies in Canada*, 4, 1990, 29–30.

8   D. Vines, Review of *The Fat Man in History*, *Blacksmith*, 2, 1975, 54 points this out.

9   Jean Baudrillard, *America*, London: Verso, 1988, 77, quoted in Don Anderson, 'I'm going to America in my mind': the American presence in Australian writing, 1960–90, in Margaret Harris and Elizabeth Webby (eds), *Reconnoitres: Essays in Australian Literature in Honour of G. A. Wilkes*, Sydney: Sydney University Press, 1992, 178. For the notion of the simulacrum mentioned later in this section see Jean Baudrillard, *Simulations*, trans. Paul Foss, Paul Patton and Philip Beitchman, New York: Semiotext(e), 1983.

10   Penglase and Featherstone, The most beautiful lies.

11   Alice Munro, *Lives of Girls and Women*, Harmondsworth: Penguin, 1982, 249.

12   Graeme Gibson, Interview in *Eleven Canadian Novelists*, Toronto: Anansi, 1973, 256.

13   Anderson, 'I'm going to America in my mind', 184.

14   Peter Carey, Statement, *Australian Literary Studies*, 8, 2, 1977, 184.

15   John Fiske, Bob Hodge and Graeme Turner, *Myths of Oz: Reading Australian Popular Culture*, Sydney: Allen and Unwin, 1987, 121–2.

16   Bail's story was included in *Contemporary Portraits*, St Lucia, Queensland: University of Queensland Press, 1975, reprinted as *The Drover's Wife*. The comparison is explored by Nigel Krauth, Peter Carey: a portrait of electricity, *Australian Book Review*, 133, 1991, 18.

17   Murray Bail, *Homesickness*, Melbourne: Macmillan, 1980, 112.

18   *Ibid.*, 81.

19   *Ibid.*, 61–4.

20   Anderson, 'I'm going to America in my mind', 184.

21   John Pilger, *A Secret Country*, London: Vintage, 1990, 164–70. Baudrillard begins his *America* with a chapter on the desert as an emblem for his view that 'the whole of America is a desert' (99) in which 'the cities are mobile deserts' (123).

22   Robin Ravlich, Interview with Peter Carey, 22.10.1979, Australian Broadcasting Corporation tape 88/10/1864–2.

23   Jan Garrett, Interview with Peter Carey, 8.10.1979, Australian Broadcasting Corporation tape 88/10/1043–5: during the interview, Carey commented 'hello Bart, if you're listening'.

24   John Maddocks, Bizarre realities: an interview with Peter Carey, *Southerly*, 41, 1, 1981, 39–40.

25   Joseph, Conrad, *Three Short Novels*, New York: Bantam, 1963, 75.

26   See pp. 314, 320, 323, 325, 327, 329, 333.

27   Jan Garrett, Interview with Peter Carey, 8.10.1979.

28   See obituary articles in *The Guardian*, 30.11.1994, G2 8, 17.

29   Phillip Neilsen, Peter Carey: author's statement, *Australian Literary Studies*, 10, 1, 1981, 191–2. See Albert Speer, *Inside the Third Reich*, London: Phoenix, 1995, 221–6. In his fictionalised version of Speer's Berlin in the novel *Fatherland* (1992), Robert Harris has this great cupola gathering the breath of its multitudes to form clouds and rain in the same manner as in Carey's story – Robert Harris, *Fatherland*, New York: Harper Collins, 1992, 29. See also Albert Speer, *Spandau: The Secret Diaries*, London: Collins, 1976.

30   See Ken Gelder and Paul Salzman (eds), *The New Diversity: Australian Fiction 1970–88*, Melbourne: McPhee Gribble, 1989, 114.

31   Kenneth Gelder, Sex in Australian fiction 1970–1987, *Meanjin*, 47, 1, 1987, 125.

32   Gelder and Salzman, *The New Diversity*, 114.

33   See *ibid.*, 175–7.

34   I stress this in contrast to Trudi Tate's reading which, in its manner of talking about 'Nile', seems to assume at times that that 'she' is 'real' – for example 'The events that follow are implicitly the woman's fault for transgressing the narrative rules he has established', etc. See Trudi Tate, Unravelling the feminine: Peter Carey's 'Peeling', *Meanjin*, 46, 3, 1987, 394–9.

35   Invoking here a Freudian model of the polymorphously perverse infant prior to social gender allocation – see Sigmund Freud, *On Sexuality: Three Essays on the Theory of Sexuality and Other Works*, trans. James Strachey, ed. Angela Richards, Harmondsworth: Penguin, 1977.

36   Marjorie Garber, *Vested Interests: Cross-dressing and Cultural Anxiety*, New York: Routledge, 1992.

37   A pun picked up by David Gilbey in his review of *The Fat Man in History* in *Southerly*, 44, 1977, 469.

38   Recent post-colonial theorists like Homi Bhabha, *The Location of Culture*, London: Routledge, 1994, have attempted to refine or challenge the binary metaphor of dominance which has described the colonial and post-colonial situation in terms of a colonial centre enforcing power on colonised margins. Others like Diana Brydon and Bill Ashcroft have adapted from French post-structuralists Deleuze and Guattari the model of 'the rhizome', an interlinked system of roots and growths in which no one channel can be said to have priority – see Graham Huggan, Decolonising the map: post-colonialism, post-structuralism and the cartographic connection, in Ian Adam and Helen Tiffin (eds), *Past the Last Post: Theorising Post-Colonialism and Post-modernism*, Hemel Hempstead: Harvester Wheatsheaf, 1991, 122.

39   In *The Pleasures of Exile* (1960), George Lamming set out his influential rereading of *The Tempest* as a colonial text and, in doing so, indicated how the colonisation process was transformative for the coloniser as well as the colonised, who together formed a reciprocal relationship emblemised by Prospero and Caliban in Shakespeare's play.

Chapter 3

1   Graham Burns, Romantic pursuits, *Australian Book Review*, 41, 1982, 28; Rory Barnes, Salvation on Bog Onion Road, *The National Times*, 11–17.10.1981, 42; Peter Pierce, Finding their range: some recent Australian novels, *Meanjin*, 40, 1981, 526.

2   Kate Ahearne, Stephen Williams and Kevin Brophy, An interview with Peter Carey, *Going Down Swinging*, 1, 1980, 49.

3   Anthony J. Hassall, *Dancing on Hot Macadam*, St Lucia, Queensland: University of Queensland Press, 71.

4   Karen Lamb, *Peter Carey: The Genesis of Fame*, Sydney: Angus & Robertson, 1992, 28.

5   See chapter 5, 102–3.

6   See G. Leech and J. Svartvik, *A Communicative Grammar of English*, Harlow: Longman, 1975, 73 – thanks to Michael Lumsden for this reference.

7   Gabriel García Márquez, *One Hundred Years of Solitude*, London: Picador, 1982, 9.

8   See pp. 10, 14, 16, 18, 20, 27, 37, 51–2, 63–5, 67–74, 148, 150, etc.

9   John Ryle, Magic and poison, *The Times Literary Supplement*, 20.11.1981, 1350.

10   Jean-Paul Sartre, *Being and Nothingness*, London: Methuen, 1966, 70, note 9. This experience has similarities with 'congruence' as described by psychotherapist Carl Rogers – see Carl Rogers, *On Becoming a Person: A Therapist's View of Psychotherapy*, London: Constable, 1961, 61.

11   See Antonio Gramsci, *Selections from Prison Notebooks*, ed. and trans. by Quentin Hoare and Geoffrey Nowell Smith, London: Lawrence and Wishart, 1978, 12.

12   Douglas Kellner, *Critical Theory, Marxism and Modernity*, Cambridge: Polity Press, 1989, 181, 158. Kellner argues for the term techo-capitalism to describe the present configuration which exhibits 'growing concentration and centralisation of capital, organised in transnational conglomerates in a global system in which new advanced technologies like satellite television, computers and information, scientific and technical knowledge, and forms of consumer and mass culture are international in scope, disseminated throughout the world by transnational capital and techo-elites. Techno-capitalism depends on an increasingly high-velocity form of capital in which money, ideas, images, technologies, goods and

services can be rapidly moved from one part of the world to another … Techno-culture represents a configuration of mass culture and the consumer society in which consumer goods, film, television, mass images and computerised information become a dominant form of culture throughout the developed world which increasingly interpenetrate developing countries as well' (180–1). See also Kellner's recent book *Media Culture: Cultural Studies, Identity and Politics Between the Modern and the Post-modern*, London: Routledge, 1995.

13   A view associated with Norman Mailer – see Don Anderson, Introduction, in Peter Carey and Ray Lawrence, *Bliss: The Screenplay*, St Lucia: University of Queensland Press, 1986, 19–20.

14   Ken Gelder suggests Alice Dalton is a derivative parallel to Big Nurse in the Kesey – Ken Gelder, Bliss and punishment, *The CRNLE Reviews Journal*, 1, 1983, 48. Ken Gelder has also suggested analogies with other Australian fiction such as Dal Stivens's *A Horse of Air* (1970) or Walter Adamson's *The Institution* (1974) which both have central characters incarcerated in mental hospitals, while David Ireland has explored the analogies between a corrupt culture and institutionalisation in *The Flesheaters* (1972) – see Ken Gelder, The novel, in Laurie Hergenhan (ed.), *The Penguin New Literary History of Australia*, Ringwood, Victoria: Penguin Australia, 1988, 507.

15   Ray Willbanks, *Speaking Volumes: Australian Writers and their Work*, Ringwood, Victoria: Penguin, 1992, 48.

16   Thomas E. Tausky, 'Getting the corner right': an interview with Peter Carey, *Australian and New Zealand Studies in Canada*, 4, 1990, 30.

17   Graham Burns, Romantic pursuits, *Australian Book Review*, 41, 1982, 28.

18   Susan Sontag, *Illness as Metaphor*, London: Allen Lane, 1979, 87, 85, 70–1.

19   Philip Neilsen, Waiting for the barbarians: an interview with Peter Carey, *Literature in North Queensland*, 15, 3, 1987, 69.

20   David Sexton, Interview with Peter Carey, *The Literary Review*, June 1985, 40.

21   Neilsen, Waiting for the barbarians, 70.

22   Jan Garrett, Interview with Peter Carey, 14.10.1981, Australian Broadcasting Corporation tape 82/10/619–2.

23   See chapter 8 for a summary.

24 Neilsen, Waiting for the barbarians, 70; see Karen Lamb, *Peter Carey: The Genesis of Fame*, Sydney: Angus & Robertson, 1992, 25, note 3 for other earlier titles for *Bliss: A Wonderful Fool* and *Knocking on Heaven's Door*.

25 Jill Neville, Carey leaps crannies in a single bound, *The Sydney Morning Herald*, 10.10.1981, 44.

26 Carey and Lawrence, *Bliss*, 14.

27 *Ibid.*, 15.

28 For an approach which places *Illywhacker* in a Bakhtinian context see Ronald Blaber and Marvin Gilman, *Roguery: The Picaresque Tradition in Australian, Canadian and Indian Fiction*, Springwood, NSW: Butterfly Books, 1990.

Chapter 4

1 See Lauri Muller, Publishing in crisis, *Australian Bookseller and Publisher*, 65, 956, December 1985–January 1986, 13–14.

2 See Mark Rubbo, Starters and writers, *Australian Book Review*, 75, 1985, 2.

3 David Sexton, *The Literary Review*, June 1985, 41.

4 From *Following the Equator: A Journey Around the World* (1897), also published as *More Tramps Abroad*.

5 Thomas E. Tausky, 'Getting the corner right': an interview with Peter Carey, *Australian and New Zealand Studies in Canada*, 4, 1990, 31.

6 Carey has acknowledged that Anderson is an invention (John Baxter, Interview with Peter Carey, 28.5.1985, Australian Broadcasting Corporation tape 86/10/462–2).

7 In 1992 the Australian High Court ruled on the case of Eddie Mabo and Others versus the State of Queensland, ten years after the action had been initiated: the judgement gave recognition to Aboriginal claims of native title and rejected the notion of Australia as having been *terra nullius* at the time of colonisation. See Merete Falck Borch, Eddie Mabo and Others v. the State of Queensland, 1992. The significance of court recognition of landrights in Australia, *Kunapipi*, 14, 1, 1992, 1–12 and Tim Rowse, Mabo and moral anxiety, *Meanjin*, 52, 2, 1993, 229–52.

8 Tausky, 'Getting the corner right', 32.

9   William H. Wilde, Joy Hooton and Barry Andrews (eds), *The Ox-
    ford Companion to Australian Literature*, Melbourne: Oxford
    University Press, 1986, 661 – quoted from letter by Furphy to A. G.
    Stephens, 1897; see Paul Sharrad, Responding to the challenge:
    Peter Carey and the reinvention of Australia, *Span or Journal of
    the South Pacific Association for Commonwealth Literature and
    Language Studies*, 25, 1987, 37, n. 1 for links with *Such is Life*.

10 See Salman Rushdie, *Midnight's Children*, London: Picador, 1982,
    166. See also Rushdie's essay 'Errata': or unreliable narration in
    Midnight's Children, in *Imaginary Homelands: Essays and Criti-
    cism 1981–1991*, London: Granta, 1991, 22–5.

11 Baxter, Interview.

12 Wilde *et al.*, *Oxford Companion to Australian Literature*, 286.

13 Candida Baker, Peter Carey in *Yacker: Australian Writers Talk
    About Their Work*, Sydney: Picador, 1986, 61.

14 John Hanrahan, A dealer in dreams, visions, images and lies, *The
    Age* Saturday Extra, 6.7.1985, 14.

15 Elizabeth Webby, A great short story trapped in a fat novel, *The
    Sydney Morning Herald*, 13.7.1985, 47; Martin Duwell, The lie of
    the land, *Overland*, 101, 1985, 93.

16 Ray Willbanks, *Speaking Volumes: Australian Writers and their
    Work*, Ringwood, Victoria: Penguin, 1992, 51.

17 *Ibid.*

18 *Ibid.*

19 Antoni Jach, An interview with Peter Carey, *Mattoid*, 31, 2, 1988,
    28.

20 Willbanks, *Speaking Volumes*, 52.

21 See Michael Heyward, *The Ern Malley Affair*, St Lucia: University
    of Queensland Press, 1993.

22 Peter Fuller, Carey gives the lie to some old lies, *The Canberra
    Times*, 21.8.1985, 27.

23 Baxter, Interview.

24 Sharrad, Responding to the challenge, 38, n. 6.

25 Adrian Mitchell, Weaving a tangled web of lovely lies, *The Week-
    end Australian Magazine*, 6–7.7.1985, 15.

26 John Pilger, *A Secret Country*, London: Vintage, 1990, 345.

27 *Ibid.*, 313, 317, 318.

28 Zee Edgell, *Beka Lamb*, London: Heinemann, 1985, 35–7.

29   Willbanks, *Speaking Volumes*, 49.

30   Sexton, *The Literary Review*, 40.

31   Richard Glover, The tallest story of them all, *The Sydney Morning Herald*, 29.6.1985, 39. See Pilger, *A Secret Country*, chapter 5 for coverage of this event.

32   Webby, A great short story, 47.

33   The original arcade inspiration came from a pet shop above Dymocks book shop in George Street, Sydney, and from the Strand arcade between Pitt and Castlereagh Streets; see Willbanks, *Speaking Volumes*, 50. The Herbert Badgery sections of the Penglase/Featherstone video about Carey, 'The most beautiful lies' give a good impression.

34   Tausky, 'Getting the corner right', 32.

35   Tony Thwaites, More tramps at home: seeing Australia first, *Meanjin*, 46, 3, 1987, 402.

36   See Peter Marshall, *Demanding the Impossible: A History of Anarchism*, London: Fontana, 1993, 409.

37   Chomsky adopted the phrase from Walter Lippmann, reversing its political direction, in his *Deterring Democracy*, London: Vintage, 1992, 367; see also 348.

38   Baxter, Interview.

39   Martin Duwell speculates that the use of the word 'Professor' might be a deliberate Americanization of the more specialised Australian usage (Duwell, The lie of the land, 93).

40   Thwaites, More tramps at home, 406.

41   Pilger, *A Secret Country*, 352.

Chapter 5

1   Margaret Harris, Eminent Victorians?, *Southerly*, 49, 1, 1989, 109.

2   Thanks to Jo Chipperfield for this inventive suggestion.

3   Geoffrey Dutton, Carey and the cringe, *The Weekend Australian Magazine*, 20–1.2.1988, 7.

4   Joanna Penglase (co-writer) and Don Featherstone (co-writer and director), The most beautiful lies: a film about Peter Carey, BBC1 Omnibus, 1986–7.

5 Sue Woolfe, and Kate Grenville, *Making Stories: How Ten Australian Novels Were Written*, Sydney: Allen and Unwin, 1993, 38.

6 David Sexton, *The Literary Review*, June 1985, 41.

7 Patricia Rolfe, The making of Oscar, *The Bulletin*, 23.2.1988, 69.

8 The extra chapter, called 'A degree from Oxford' and numbered 74, contains an account of Lucinda's meeting with Mr d'Abbs in which she convinces him of Oscar's adequacy as a potential employee – see Peter Carey, *Oscar and Lucinda*, New York: Harper and Row, 1988, 286–9, and *Oscar and Lucinda*, London: Faber, 1995.

9 A flaw acknowledged by Carey: 'I changed the dates half-way through and forgot I had done it' (Thomas E. Tausky, 'Getting the corner right': an interview with Peter Carey, *Australian and New Zealand Studies in Canada*, 4, 1990, 35).

10 Sexton, *The Literary Review*, 39.

11 See Bruce Woodcock, *Male Mythologies: John Fowles and Masculinity*, Hemel Hempstead: Harvester, 1984, for a discussion of the way in which such post-modern strategies relate to the deconstruction of gender roles.

12 The obsession with glass goes back to the stories like 'Fragrance of Roses' with its description of the 'intricately wrought glasshouse, as delicate and weblike as the glasshouse in Kew Gardens in London' (295), and to *Bliss*; Carey's conception for the design of a house with Margot Hutcheson was of 'a lot of glass' (Janet Hawley, How an ad man found bliss, *The Age*, 26.9.1981, 26).

13 Laurel Graeber, Belief in the ultimate gamble, *New York Times Book Review*, 29.5.1988, 19; the extract from the drafts of *Oscar and Lucinda* quoted in Woolfe and Grenville (44) has the injunction 'READ PASCAL' – see chapter 1, p. 15 above.

14 Woolfe and Grenville, *Making Stories*, 39.

15 Paul Davis and John Gribbin, *The Matter Myth: Towards Twenty-first Century Science*, London: Viking, 1991, 219–25.

16 Thanks to Jo Chipperfield for this phrase.

17 For a discussion of the philosophical aspects of fictional worlds, see Ruth Ronen, *Possible Worlds in Literary Theory*, Cambridge: Cambridge University Press, 1994.

Chapter 6

1   Karl Marx, *Capital*, vol. 1, intro. Ernest Mandel, trans. Ben Fowkes, Harmondsworth: Penguin/London: *New Left Review*, 1976, 799.

2   Jen Craig, The real thing, *Southerly*, 52, 1, 1992, 152.

3   Phillipa Hawker, Carey's contemporary angels have the potential for destruction, *Australian Book Review*, 133, 1991, 17.

4   Barry Oakley, Gothic splendour, *The Weekend Australian*, 27–8.7.1991, 1.

5   Diana Giese, Diving deep into the dreams of damaged lives, *The Weekend Australian*, 27–8.7.1991, Review, 4.

6   Michael Heywood, Australia's literary ambassador, *The Age*, 25.7.1992, 8.

7   See Michel Foucault, *The History of Sexuality: An Introduction*, Harmondsworth: Penguin, 1978, 109–10, 129–30 on incest and the regulation of sexuality in the family.

8   John F. Baker, Peter Carey, *Publishers Weekly*, 238, 54, 13.12.1991, 37; Candida Baker, Carefree Carey, *The Age Magazine*, 27.7.1991, 3.

9   Peter Pierce, A stumble, no more, *The Bulletin*, 13.8.1991, 112.

10 Robert Dixon, The logic of the excluded middle, *Literature in North Queensland*, 18, 2, 1991, 136, 139–40.

11 Robert Dixon, Closing the can of worms: enactments of justice in *Bleak House*, *The Mystery of a Hansom Cab*, and *The Tax Inspector*, *Westerly*, 37, 4, 1992, 38, 43–4.

12 Robert Dessaix, Interview with Peter Carey, 25.8.1991, Australian Broadcasting Corporation tape 91/10/1249–1.

13 Homi K. Bhabha, *The Location of Culture*, London: Routledge, 1994, 9.

14 Mark Lawson, Sniffing the air at home and away, *The Independent on Sunday*, 25.9.1991, 18.

15 Definitions of the terms psychopathic and psychotic can be found in *The Oxford Companion to the Mind*, ed. Richard Gregory, Oxford: Oxford University Press, 1987, 651–3, 657–8.

16 Carol Ann Duffy, *Selling Manhattan*, London: Anvil, 1987, 29.

17 Karen Lamb, *Peter Carey: The Genesis of Fame*, Sydney: Angus & Robertson, 1992, 54.

18 Dessaix, Interview; see also Richard Glover, Peter Carey's Sydney

Babylon, *The Sydney Morning Herald*, 27.7.1991, 35.

19   See Anthony J. Hassall, *Dancing on Hot Macadam*, St Lucia, Queensland: University of Queensland Press, 157 for context.

20   Dessaix, Interview.

21   Chris Floyd, Review, *Span*, 33, May 1992, 180.

22   See Hassall, *Dancing on Hot Macadam*, 164, 185.

23   Glover, Peter Carey's Sydney Babylon, 35; see also Carey's letter to Hassall in Hassall, *Dancing on Hot Macadam*, 185.

24   Baker, Carefree Carey, 3.

25   Bron Sibree, Novel difficult to live with, difficult to write: Carey, *The Canberra Times Magazine*, 27.7.1991, C7.

Chapter 7

1   Carey has said that Le Guin is 'an astonishing writer in anybody's language and if I was half as good as she is I'd be very happy indeed', in Van Ikin, Answers to seventeen questions: an interview with Peter Carey, *Science Fiction: A Review of Speculative Literature*, 1, 1, 1977, 36. See also Bruce Woodcock, Radical Taoism: Ursula K. Le Guin's science fiction, in Gina Wisker (ed.), *It's My Party: Reading Twentieth Century Women's Writing*, London: Pluto, 1994, 193–211.

2   Angela Carter, Only a surface paradise, *The Guardian*, 29.8.1991, 22.

3   Homi Bhabha, Of mimicry and man: the ambivalence of colonial discourse in *The Location of Culture*, London: Routledge, 1994, 86, 88. Bhabha's view is summarised by Graham Huggan as follows: 'The destabilising process set in motion by colonial mimicry produces a set of deceptive, even derisive, "resemblances" which implicitly question the homogenising practices of colonial discourse' (Graham Huggan, Decolonising the map: post-colonialism, post-structuralism and the cartographic connection, in Ian Adam and Helen Tiffin (eds), *Past the Last Post: Theorizing Post-Colonialism and Post-modernism*, Hemel Hempstead: Harvester Wheatsheaf, 1991, 126). The mouse costume itself might be associated with Baudrillard's writings on the Simulacrum, although Carey's use of the idea here has less in common than in the case of the model in 'American Dreams' – see note 9 for chapter 2, above.

4   Packed lunches – writer's talks: interview with Peter Kemp, ICA audio-tape, 12.3.1994.

5   Kate Kellaway, Every man is a theatre, *The Observer Review*, 11.9.1994, 18.

6   Susannah Frankel found the book 'hilariously funny' (*Time Out*, 7–14.9.1994, 47).

7   Packed lunches – writer's talks.

8   Galen Strawson, A little yearning is a dangerous thing, *The Independent on Sunday*, 4.9.1994, 34.

9   Sue Wyndham, Peter Carey: an unusual life, *The Australian Magazine*, 20–1.8.1994, 45. See also ICA audio-tape account.

10 Kellaway, Every man is a theatre, 18.

11 Wyndham, Peter Carey: an unusual life, 45.

12 ICA audio-tape.

Chapter 8

1   Alan Attwood, What the Dickens?, *Sydney Morning Herald*, Good Weekend section, 2.8.1997, 24.

2   Anthony J. Hassall, A tale of two countries: *Jack Maggs* and Peter Carey's fiction, *Australian Literary Studies*, 18, 2, 1997, 129.

3   Peter Carey at the launch of *Jack Maggs*, Sydney 11.8.1997.

4   See Robert H. Wozniak, Mind and Body: René Descartes to William James, online at: http://serendip.brynmawr.edu/Mind/Trance.html.

5   William H. Wilde *et. al.*, *The Oxford Companion to Australian Literature*, Melbourne: Oxford University Press, 1991, 178.

6   Robert Hughes, *Beyond the Fatal Shore*, BBC2, 2000.

7   John Thieme, *Postcolonial Con-texts: Writing Back to the Canon*, London: Continuum, 2001, 119.

8   Interview with Peter Carey online at: www.randomhouse.com/boldtype/0399/carey/interview.html.

9   Attwood, What the Dickens?, 23.

10 Edward Said, *Culture and Imperialism*, London: Vintage, 1994, xvi; Robert Hughes, *The Fatal Shore: A History of the Transportation of Convicts to Australia 1787–1868*, London, Pan, 1987, 586.

11   Said, *Culture and Imperialism*, xvii

12   As Anthony Hassall points out (134), there is a sub-genre of Australian fiction chronicling 'disillusioned returns to the motherland', best represented by Henry Handel Richardson's novel trilogy *The Fortunes of Richard Mahony* (1917–29).

13   Hassall, A tale of two countries, 130 fn. 3.

14   Thieme, *Postcolonial Con-texts, passim.*

15   Hassall, A tale of two countries, 130. See also James Bradley, Bread and sirkuses: empire and culture in Peter Carey's *The Unusual Life of Tristran Smith* and *Jack Maggs, Meanjin*, 56, 3–4, 659–61.

16   Ramona Koval, The unexamined life *Meanjin*, 56, 3–4, 1997, 671.

17   Koval, The unexamined life, 674.

18   Desmond Christy, Inner conviction, *The Guardian Review*, 11.6.1998, 8.

19   Peter Carey, A small memoir, *The New Yorker*, September 1995, 54–63; Attwood, What the Dickens?, 26.

20   Koval, The unexamined life, 671.

21   Attwood, What the Dickens?, 24.

22   Christy, Inner conviction.

23   Sigrun Meinig (An Australian convict in the great English city: Peter Carey's *Jack Maggs, Southerly*, 6, 3, 2000, 59) suggests that 'the binary oppositions *within* London mirror the familiar ones that contrast the centre with the margin', and quotes Judith Walkowitz's view (in *City of Dreadful Night – Narratives of Sexual Danger in Late-Victorian London*, Chicago: University of Chicago Press, 1992, 26) that the East and West sides of London 'doubled for England and its Empire'.

24   Ramona Koval, The unexamined life, 671.

25   Sigmund Freud, from 'The Uncanny' 1919, printed in Julie Rivkin and Michael Ryan, *Literary Theory: An Anthology*, Oxford: Blackwell, 2001, 163.

26   Máire ní Fhlathúin, The location of childhood: 'Great Expectations' in post-colonial London, *Kunapipi*, 21, 2, 1999, 90.

Chapter 9

1   Ramona Koval, The unexamined life, *Meanjin*, 56, 3–4, 1997, 674.

2   Andrew Riemer, Ironclad irony, *The Sydney Morning Herald*, 14.8.2000, online: www.smh.com.au.

3   Anthony Quinn, Robin Hood of the outback www.nytimes.com/ books/01/01/07/reviews/010107.07quinnt.ht. Such enthusiasm is not the case for all readers, however, as the following responses by panel members in the BBC 'People's Booker' discussions testified: '*True History of the Kelly Gang* reads like a book that is very pleased with itself. Look at me, the book says: I can reproduce a vernacular that suggests the narrator is ignorant at the same time as it announces the Cheshire-Cat-genius of its author. It wears its stylish erudition on its sleeve and after two hundred pages or more it all gets to be rather tiresome' (Peter Wild, BBC Arts User); 'It's a bit of a rant … I wouldn't recommend this to a friend unless I hated them just a little bit' (Alain de Botton) see online: www.bbc.co.uk/arts/ booker/carey.shtml.

4   Alex McDermott (ed.), *The Jerilderie Letter*, London: Faber, 2001. For information on Ned Kelly's life see Ian Jones, *Ned Kelly: A Short Life*, Port Melbourne: Lothian Books, 1995. Websites include: www.ironoutlaw.com/. The Jerilderie Letter can be accessed along with other Kelly documents on the State Library of Victoria website at http://www.slv.vic.gov.au/slv/exhibitions/treasures/jerilderie/.

5   Robert McCrum, Reawakening Ned, *The Observer*, 7.1.2001, 19.

6   McDermott, *The Jerilderie Letter*, 63–4.

7   McCrum, Reawakening Ned, 19.

8   Interview for BBC World Service *Meridian Masterpiece*: www.bbc.co.uk/worldservice/arts/highlights/010803_carey.shtml.

9   Compare Carey 159 with McDermott 56, and Carey 161–2 with McDermott 9–16. Actual or adapted phrases are sometimes included, such as 'it caused my fist to come into collision with McCormick's nose and he lost his equilibrium and fell prostrate' (*KG* 159); 'my fist came in collision with McCormack's nose and caused him to loose his equilibrium and fall prostrate' (McDermott 5–6).

10 BBC2 People's Booker broadcast, 6.10.2001.

11 McDermott, *The Jerilderie Letter*, xxv, xxvii.

12 McCrum, Reawakening Ned, 19.

13 Eric Hobsbawm, *Bandits*, London: Weidenfeld and Nicolson, 1969, 13, 112–13.

14　Phil Shannon, Ideological gunfighters for the poor, online at: www.greenleft.org.au/back/2001/447/447p25.htm.

15　BBC2 People's Booker 6.10.2001.

16　Stuart Wavell, What kind of notorious outlaw wears a frock?, *The Sunday Times* News Review, 7.1.2001, 7.

17　Graham Huggan, Cultural memory in postcolonial fiction: the uses and abuses of Ned Kelly, *Australian Literary Studies*, 20, 3, May 2002, 149.

18　John Kinsella's On Peter Carey's *True History of the Kelly Gang*, online at www.johnkinsella.org/reviews/carey.html: Kinsella interestingly points out that 'One of the websites dedicated to Ned Kelly, tied up in the kind of Australian republicanism too often intertwined with xenophobia, carries a warning that people must not read Carey's book as fact. The site decries the book's elements of transvestism, Ned Kelly having a child, and so on. Details, it claims, that don't match the "true history"! On one level this is missing the point, but on another it is also a rebuttal of the hype that goes behind such a work.'

19　Huggan, Cultural memory in postcolonial fiction, 153, 146.

20　Riemer, Ironclad irony.

21　McCrum, Reawakening Ned, 19.

22　Alan Attwood, What the Dickens?, *Sydney Morning Herald*, Good Weekend section, 2. 8, 1997, 26.

23　See Huggan for a discussion of Drewe's novel and Carey's in relation to their treatments of the Kelly story and the issues of cultural memory.

24　One example is the McCormack episode and is comparable with Carey's version quoted in footnote 9: 'The horse jumps forward and my fist comes into collision with McCormack's nose and causes him to lose his equilibrium.' (Robert Drewe, *Ours Sunshine*, Victoria: Penguin, 2001, 31.)

25　'currency lads' are 'born of the colonies rather than in Ireland' – Kinsella.

26　Jose de Acosta, *The Naturall and Morall Historie of the East and West Indies*, translated by Edward Grimston (London: V. Sims. 1604). See online: http://cwx.prenhall.com/bookbind/pubbooks/faragher6/medialib/chapter1/1.html. 'The Jesuit priest Jose de Acosta (1540–1600) spent seventeen years, from 1570 to 1587, in Spanish America, working in areas as widely separated as Peru and Mexico. His book Historia natural y moral de las Indias (1590) is invaluable for Acosta's astute observations of the native cultures of the Americas and the dramatic effects of colonization … Acosta was first to propose that the Americas had been populated by migration from the Old World.'

27   Judith Kapferer, *Being All Equal: Identity, Difference and Australian Cultural Practice*, Oxford: Berg, 1996, 50.

28   *Meridian Masterpiece.*

29   *Meridian Masterpiece.*

30   See McDermott, *The Jerilderie Letter*, 65–72.

31   *Meridian Masterpiece.*

32   *Ibid.*

33   These famous words became the title for an equally famous early Australian novel by Joseph Furphy, published in 1903.

34   McCrum, Reawakening Ned, 19.

35   *Ibid.*

36   Riemer, Ironclad irony.

37   Wavel, 'What kind of notorious outlaw wears a frock?' The 'coffin letter' Ned sends, from which this quotation comes (328–9) is a virtual transcription of the end of the Jerilderie Letter (*JL*, 81–3).

38   Wavel, 7 and Anne Marsh, Ned Kelly by any other name, *Journal of Visual Culture*, www.sagepub.co.uk/journals/details/issue/sample/ao22422.pdf: 'Nolan read everything that he could about the Kelly Gang, including the official police records which document Hart's transvestism (Andrew Sayers, *Sidney Nolan: The Ned Kelly Story*, New York: Metropolitan Museum of Art, 1994, 9). Elizabeth McMahon says that: 'Legend has it that Hart's horsemanship was such that he won the Greta races wearing feminine garb and riding side-saddle, as he is posed in Nolan's painting' (Elizabeth McMahon, Australia crossed over; images of cross-dressing in Australian art and culture, *Art and Australia*, 34, 30, 1997: 375).'

39   Marsh, Ned Kelly by any other name.

40   Huggan, Cultural memory in postcolonial fiction, 147.

41   Riemer, Ironclad irony.

42   Huggan, Cultural memory in postcolonial fiction, 148–9.

43   Gayatri Chakravorty Spivak, Can the subaltern speak?, in Cary Nelson and Lawrence Grossberg, *Marxism and the Interpretation of Culture*, Basingstoke: Macmillan, 1988.

44   Judith Kapferer, *Being All Equal*, Oxford, 59.

Chapter 10

1   Brian Kiernan, Short story chronicle, *Meanjin*, 34, 1975, 39.

2   Bruce A. Clunies Ross, Laszlo's testament; or, structuring the past and sketching the present in contemporary short fiction, mainly Australian, *Kunapipi*, 1, 2, 1979, 121.

3   Greg Manning, Reading lesson: 'The Fat Man in History', teaching and deconstructive practice, *Span or Journal of the South Pacific Association for Commonwealth Literature and Language Studies*, 21, 1985, 40–1.

4   Michael Wilding, The tabloid short story, in Michael Wilding (ed.), *The Tabloid Story Pocket Book*, Sydney: Wild and Woolley, 1978, 305. The term 'fabulation' was coined by Robert Scholes, *The Fabulators*, New York: Oxford University Press, 1967 – see Graeme Turner, American dreaming: the fictions of Peter Carey, *Australian Literary Studies*, 12, 4, 1986, 432.

5   Bruce Bennett, Australian experiments in short fiction, *World Literature Written in English*, 15, 1976, 359–66.

6   Kate Ahearne, Peter Carey and short fiction in Australia, *Going Down Swinging* (Melbourne), 1, 1980, 16–17.

7   Kiernan, Short story chronicle, 39.

8   Michael Morton-Evans, Carey reaches a blissful peak in his literary career, *The Australian*, 26.7.1984, 8.

9   Geoffrey Dutton, A 'crime' that is utter creativity, *The Bulletin*, 4.12.1979, 66–7.

10 Kate Ahearne, Stephen Williams and Kevin Brophy, An interview with Peter Carey, *Going Down Swinging*, 1, 1980, 50.

11 Helen Daniel, 'The liar's lump' or 'A salesman's sense of history': Peter Carey's *Illywhacker*, *Southerly*, 47, 2, 1986, 158, 166, and Helen Daniel, Lies for sale: Peter Carey, in Daniel, *Liars, Australian New Novelists*, Ringwood, Victoria: Penguin, 1988, 168, 176.

12 Brian Edwards, Deceptive constructions: the art of building in Peter Carey's *Illywhacker*, *Australian and New Zealand Studies in Canada*, 4, 1990, 39–56 – see also Robert R. Wilson, Theory as template: the new Australian novel, *Mattoid*, 33, 1989, 169; Greg Manning, A litany of lies: a look at Australia's new fiction, *The Age Monthly Review*, 8, 3, 1988, 5–6.

13 Harris, Eminent Victorians?, *Southerly*, 49, 1, 1989, 11–13.

14 Wenche Ommundsen, Narrative navel-gazing, or, how to recognise

a metafiction when you see one, *Southern Review*, 22, 3, 1989, 264–74.

15   Anthony J. Hassall, Telling lies and stories: Peter Carey's *Bliss*, *Modern Fiction Studies*, 35, 4, 1989, 644. See Anthony J. Hassall, *Dancing on Hot Macadam: Peter Carey's Fiction*, St Lucia: University of Queensland Press, 1994.

16   Tony Thwaites, More tramps at home: seeing Australia first, *Meanjin*, 46, 3, 1987, 403–5.

17   M.D. Fletcher, Post-colonial Peter Carey, *Span or Journal of the South Pacific Association for Commonwealth Literature and Language Studies*, 32, 1991, 12.

18   Kirsten Holst Peterson, Gambling on reality: a reading of *Oscar and Lucinda*, in Giovanna Capone (ed.), *European Perspectives: Contemporary Essays on Australian Literature*, *Australian Literary Studies* Special Issue, 15, 2, St Lucia: University of Queensland Press, 1991, 110.

19   Graham Huggan, Is the (Günther) Grass greener on the other side? Oskar and Lucinde in the New World, *World Literature Written in English*, 30, 1, 1990, 1–10.

20   David Callahan, Peter Carey's *Oscar and Lucinda* and the subversion of subversion, *Australian Literary Studies*, 10, 1981, 178–80.

21   Graeme Turner, Nationalising the author: the celebrity of Peter Carey, *Australian Literary Studies*, 16, 2, 1993, 131–9.

22   Karen Lamb, *Peter Carey: The Genesis of Fame*, Sydney: Angus & Robertson, 1992. For example, Lamb attributes the interview quotation on pp. 36–7 to the wrong source: it actually comes from the interview with Richard Glover in *The Sydney Morning Herald*, 29.6.1985, 39.

23   Lamb, *Peter Carey*, 28, 33–41.

24   Kenneth Gelder, History, politics and the (post) modern: receiving Australian fiction, *Meanjin*, 47, 3, 1988, 558.

25   Laurie Hergenhan, *The Penguin New Literary History of Australia*, Ringwood, Victoria: Penguin Australia, 1988, 460.

26   Carolyn Bliss, The revisionary lover: misprision of the past in Peter Carey, *Australian and New Zealand Studies in Canada*, 6, 91, 45.

27   John F. Baker, Peter Carey, *Publishers Weekly*, 238, 54, 13.12.1991, 37.

28   Amanda Lohrey, The dead hand of orthodoxy, *Island Magazine*, 27, 1986, 20–1.

29   Van Ikin, Peter Carey in L. Henderson (ed.), *Contemporary Novelists*, Chicago: St James Press, 1991, 177.

30   Stephen Muecke, Wide open spaces: horizontal readings of Australian literature, *New Literatures Review*, 16, 1988, 7.

31   K.L. Goodwin, Muecke's map for reading Australian literature: some alternative legends, *New Literatures Review*, 17, 1989, 80–7.

32   Morris Lurie, A fat man's festival of short stories, *Nation Review*, 29 November–5 December, 1974, 204: Lurie granted the book a short paragraph, commenting bitchily 'myths and parables, I suppose, but lacking that reverberation that grants meaning, and all done in rhythmless broken toothed prose, oh so deadly serious and symbolic'.

33   Morris Lurie, Letter to Kiernan, 10.4.1976, MS Dr Brian Kiernan, 7017, correspondence, National Library of Australia.

34   Craig Munro in Gelder and Salzman (eds), *The New Diversity: Australian Fiction 1970–88*, Melbourne: McPhee Gribble, 1989, 15.

35   Graham Burns, Romantic pusuits, *Australian Book Review*, 41, 1982, 28.

36   Peter Pierce, Finding their range: some recent Australian novels, *Meanjin*, 40, 1981, 526.

37   John Tranter, Hell without logic loses credibility, *Age*, 3.10.1981, 27.

38   John Ryle, Magic and poison, *The Times Literary Supplement*, 20.11.1981, 1350.

39   Helen Daniel, *Liars: Australian New Novelists*, Ringwood, Victoria: Penguin, 1988, 165–6.

40   Rory Barnes, Salvation on Bog Onion Road, *The National Times*, 11–17.10.1981, 42.

41   Susan McKernan, Recent fiction, *Overland*, 88, 1982, 58.

42   Martin Duwell, The lie of the land, *Overland*, 101, 1985, 93.

43   Lee, 28.

44   Tranter, Hell without logic loses credibility, 27.

45   See Lamb, *Peter Carey*, 27.

46   Candida Baker, *Yacker: Australian Writers Talk About Their Work*, Sydney: Picador, 1986, 67.

47   Antonella Riem Natale, Harry Joy's children: the art of story telling in Peter Carey's *Bliss*, *Australian Literary Studies*, 16, 3, 1994, 342–3.

48   Peter Goldsworthy, The novella in *Illywhacker*, *Island Magazine*, 24, Spring 1985, 57.

49   Van Ikin, Mixed blessings, *Phoenix Review*, 1, Summer 1986/7, 126.

50   Elizabeth Webby, *Illywhacker*: a great short story trapped in a fat novel, *The Sydney Morning Herald*, 13.7.1985, 47.

51   Adrian Mitchell, Weaving a tangled web of lovely lies, *The Weekend Australian Magazine*, 6.7.1985, 15.

52   Geoffrey Dutton, Unlocking the showman's 'beautiful lies', *The Bulletin*, 16.7.1985, 90.

53   Andrew Hislop, Whoppers and warnings, *The Times Literary Supplement*, 3.5.1985, 492.

54   Tom Collins, Introduction, *Such Is Life*, North Ryde, NSW: Eden, 1989, vi.

55   Peter Pierce, I dips me lid to a glorious vagabond, *The National Times*, 5.7.1985, 30.

56   John Hanrahan, A dealer in dreams, visions, images and lies, *The Age Saturday Extra*, 6.7.1985, 14.

57   Marion Halligan, Peter Carey's palace of delight, *The Canberra Times*, 24.8.1985, B2.

58   Laurie Clancy, Some beautiful lies: our history mythologised, *Australian Book Review*, 73, 1985, 14–15.

59   Howard Jacobson, Dirty very old man, *New York Times Book Review*, 17.11.1985, 15.

60   Annette Stewart, The Booker Prize, *Quadrant*, 251, 12, December 1988, 66.

61   Don Anderson, Peter Carey does a wonderful thing, *The Sydney Morning Herald*, 20.2.1988, 71.

62   Elizabeth Riddell, Desire, gambling and glass, *Australian Book Review*, 98, 1988, 14.

63   Margaret Harris, Eminent Victorians?, *Southerly*, 49, 1, 1989, 110–11.

64   D.J. O'Hearn, Plotting (2): a quarterly account of recent fiction, *Overland*, 114, 1989, 52.

65   Gerard Windsor, Peter Carey's old-fashioned special effects, *The Bulletin* 23.2.1988, 70 – quoted in Harris, Eminent Victorians? 110.

66   Howard Jacobson, A wobbly odyssey, *The Weekend Australian Magazine*, 20–1.2.1988, 13.

67   Mary Rose Liverani, Books for our time, *Overland*, 110, 1988, 70.

68   C.K. Stead, Careyland, *Scripsi*, 5, 2, 1989, 5–6.

69   Lorna Sage, Backwards into destiny, *The Times Literary Supplement*, 1–7.4.1988, 363.

70   Matthew Da Silva, Peter Carey's *Oscar and Lucinda*, *Outrider* 6, 2, 1989, 146–59.

71   A.P. Riemer, Brutish and nasty, *The Sydney Morning Herald*, 3.8.1991, 43.

72   Peter Pierce, A stumble, no more, *The Bulletin*, 13.8.1991, 112.

73   Richard Glover, Peter Carey's Sydney Babylon, *The Sydney Morning Herald*, 27.7.1991, 35.

74   Elizabeth Jurman (ed.), Today's people: literary matters, *The Sydney Morning Herald*, 30.1.92, no page number.

75   Lamb, *Peter Carey*, 52–4.

76   Jurman, Today's people.

77   Graeme Turner, Nationalising the author: the celebrity of Peter Carey, *Australian Literary Studies*, 16, 2, 1993, 136.

78   Helen Daniel, The tax inspector and the gremlins, *The Age Saturday Extra*, 27.7.1991, 9.

79   L. Clancy, Brilliant episodes, *Australian Society*, 10, 8, 38–9.

80   Veronica Brady, Births and deaths, *Overland*, 125, 1991, 82.

81   Robert Dixon, The logic of the excluded middle, *Literature in North Queensland*, 18, 2, 1991, 133–41; Robert Dixon, Closing the can of worms: enactments of justice in *Bleak House*, *The Mystery of a Hansom Cab*, and *The Tax Inspector*, *Westerly*, 37, 4, 1992, 37–45.

82   Angela Carter, Only a surface paradise, *The Guardian*, 29.8.1991, 22.

83   Eden Liddelow, New model Carey, *Scripsi*, 7, 2, October 1991, 93–100, 96, 98–9.

84   Turner, Nationalising the author, 136.

85   Philip Hensher, Heaven and Disneyland, *The Guardian*, 11.10.1994, G2, 8.

86   Peter Kemp, Flamboyant fabrication, *The Sunday Times*, 4.9.1994, section 7, 13.

87   Galen Strawson, A little yearning is a dangerous thing, *The Independent on Sunday*, 4.9.1994, 34.

88   Geraldine Brennan, Crossing the high wires, *The Observer Review*, 4.9.1994, 16.

89   April Bernard, Un-Efican activities, *New York Review of Books*, 42, 11, 22.6.1995, 46, 48.

90   Andrew Riemer, The antipodes of tiny Tristan, *The Sydney Morning Herald*, 20.8.1994, no page number.

Bibliography

Useful bibliographies can be found in the books by Hassall and Lamb listed below. Other useful reference points are the AUSTLIT database published by the Royal Melbourne Institute of Technology available on CD ROM, and the annual bibliographies in the *Journal of Commonwealth Literature* and *Australian Literary Studies*.

Works by Peter Carey

FICTION

The Fat Man in History, St Lucia: University of Queensland Press, 1974.

War Crimes, St Lucia: University of Queensland Press, 1979.

The Fat Man in History, London: Faber and Faber, 1980; New York: Random House, 1980 – stories selected from the UQP volumes; reprinted as *Exotic Pleasures* London: Pan, 1981, and thereafter as *The Fat Man in History*.

Bliss, St Lucia: University of Queensland Press; London: Faber, 1981.

Illywhacker, London: Faber and Faber, 1985; New York: Harper & Row, 1985; St Lucia: University of Queensland Press, 1985.

Bliss, The Screenplay, St Lucia: University of Queensland Press, 1986; as *Bliss, The Film*, London: Faber and Faber, 1986.

Oscar and Lucinda, St Lucia: University of Queensland Press, 1988; London: Faber and Faber, 1988; New York: Harper & Row, 1988 (with additional chapter 74); London: Faber, 1995.

The Tax Inspector, St Lucia: University of Queensland Press, 1991; London: Faber and Faber, 1991; New York: Alfred A. Knopf, 1991.

The Unusual Life of Tristan Smith, St Lucia: University of Queensland Press, 1994; London: Faber and Faber, 1994; New York: Alfred A. Knopf, 1994.

Collected Stories, St Lucia: University of Queensland Press, 1994; London: Faber and Faber, 1995.

The Big Bazoohley, London: Faber and Faber, 1995.

Jack Maggs, St Lucia: University of Queensland Press, 1997; London: Faber and Faber, 1997; New York: Alfred A. Knopf, 1997.

True History of the Kelly Gang, Brisbane: University of Queensland Press, 2000; London: Faber and Faber, 2001; New York: Alfred A. Knopf, 2001.

NON-FICTION

Peter Carey in author's statements, *Australian Literary* Studies, 10, 1981, 191–3.

Peter Carey accepts NBC award, *NBC Newsletter*, 13, 2, 1986, 2–3.

Some thoughts on Australian publishing, *The National Times*, 3–11 April 1986, no page number.

Our love affair with losers, *Melbourne Herald*, 15 September 1987, 11.

Sydney side up, *The Sunday Times Magazine*, 17 January 1988, 40–6.

A letter to our son, *Granta*, 24, 1988, 119–35.

Am I safe?, *Vogue Australia*, August 1988, 177, 197.

The thin man makes history: biting the imperial hand, *Australian Author*, 21, 3, 1989, 17.

Local authors likely to suffer under PSA plan, *The Sydney Morning Herald*, 30 October 1989, 13.

Against open slather for book imports, *Age*, 1 November 1989, 13.

Carey on copyright, *Australian Bookseller and Publisher*, 69, 1000, December 1989-January 1990, 14–16.

From an alien to his second son, *HQ Magazine*, Autumn 1993, 96–9.

Home, *The Independent on Sunday*, 21 August 1994, 26–7.

A small memorial, *The New Yorker*, September 1995, 54–63.

30 Days in Sydney: A Wildly Distorted Account, London, New York: Bloomsbury, 2001.

Comment: letter to Robert McCrum about the World Trade Center attack, www.observer.co.uk/comment/story/0,6903,556597,00.html.

SCREENPLAYS

Bliss: The Screenplay. With Ray Lawrence. St Lucia: University of Queensland Press, 1985. (*Bliss,* dir. Ray Lawrence, Window III Productions and New South Wales Film Corporation, 1985).

Until the End of the World. With Wim Wenders, 1991. (*Until the End of the World*, dir. Wim Wenders, Road Movies, Argos Films and Village Roadshow Pictures, 1991).

UNCOLLECTED WORKS

Contacts. In *Under Twenty-five: An Anthology*, eds Anne O'Donovan, Jayne Sanderson and Shane Porteous, Brisbane: Jacaranda Press, 1966, 34–6.

The cosmic pragmatist. *Nation Review*, 8–14 September 1977, 14–15.

MANUSCRIPTS

The National Library of Australia. NLA MS 7566 comprises six boxes of unpublished works and require Peter Carey's permission to consult them. They include correspondence, and drafts of interviews, stories, and unpublished novels. MS 5062 comprises the script for the rock-musical *Illusion* and is available on open access. MS 7017 comprises correspondence to Dr Brian Kiernan and includes a letter by Carey as well as others relating to him.

The Fryer Library, University of Queensland. UQFL 164 comprises a wide range of Carey's work and requires Carey's permission to consult them. They include drafts of published and unpublished works, scripts, articles and background documents.

Interviews and profiles

Australian Broadcasting Corporation: radio interviews with Peter Carey. The following fifteen tapes were consulted for this book – the details give RADA accession number, tape number, date and interviewer's name:

10834; 85/10/798–4; 8.7.1985, Jane Singleton
19110; 80/10/1043–5; 8.10.1979; Jan Garrett
21737; 86/10/414–3; 14.10.1981; Jan Garrett
21753; 86/10/462–2; 28.8.1985; John Baxter
21861; 82/10/619–2; 14.10.1981; Jan Garrett [same as 21737]
27125; 88/10/1238–10; 11.4.1988; Edward Blishen
28923; 88/10/1864–2; 22.10.1979; Robin Ravlich
29725; 88/10/2140–3; 26.10.1988; Andrew Olle
29726; 88/10/2140–4; 26.10.1988; Andrew Olle
30099; 88/7/1957–8; 26.10.1988; John Highfield
30303; 89/10/20–11; 26.10.1988; Chris Clark
30405; 88/10/1644–12; 28.9.1988; Paul Murphy
34974; 89/10/1559–2; 26.7.1989; Andrew Olle
35454; 89/10/1038–9; 26.7.1989; Andrew Sholl
47502; 91/10/1249–1; 25.10.1991; Robert Dessaix

Ahearne, Kate. Kate Ahearne in conversation with Peter Carey, *Australian Book Review*, 99, 1988, 14–5.

Ahearne, Kate, Stephen Williams and Kevin Brophy. Peter Carey, *Going Down Swinging*, 1, 1980, 43–55.

Aiton, Doug. From Bacchus Marsh to the bright lights, *Sunday Age*, 4 August 1991, 3.

Attwood, Alan. Is this man mad? The marvellous mind of Peter Carey, *Time*, 22 February 1988, 54–7.

Attwood, Alan. What the Dickens?, *Sydney Morning Herald* Good Weekend section, 2 August 1997, 24.

Baker, Candida. Peter Carey in *Yacker, Australian Writers Talk About Their Work*, Sydney: Picador, 1986, 54–77.

Baker, Candida. Open book, *The Age Magazine: Good Weekend*, 13 January 1990, 42–6.

Baker, Candida. Carefree Carey, *The Age*, 27 July 1991, 3, 6.

Baker, John F. Peter Carey, *Publisher's Weekly*, 238, 54, 1991, 37–8.

Brass, Ken. The author who hadn't read a book before he turned eighteen, *Australian Women's Weekly*, 24 December 1980, 20.

Birns, Nick. 'The power to create oneself': an interview with Peter Carey, *Writing on the Edge* 6, 1, Fall 1994, 88–96.

Castle, Claudia. The *Honi Soit* interview: your A-Z guide to Peter Carey, *Honi Soit*, 7 June 1982, 8–9.

Coe, Jonathan. The inspector of Oz, *The Guardian*, 5 September 1991, 26.

Dare, Tim. He bit, chewed, and found bliss, *The Sydney Morning Herald*, 27 May 1982, 3.

Dutton, Geoffrey. Carey and the cringe, *The Weekend Australian*, 20–1 February 1988, 7.

Fuller, Peter. Carey gives the lie to some old lies, *The Canberra Times*, 21 August 1985, 27.

Garrett, Jan. *ABC Books and Writing*, 8 October 1979.

Glover, Richard. The tallest story of them all, *The Sydney Morning Herald*, 29 June 1985, 39.

Glover, Richard. Peter Carey: from advertising to tall stories, *The Age Saturday Extra*, 6 July 1985, 3.

Glover, Richard. Peter Carey's Sydney Babylon, *The Sydney Morning Herald*, 27 July 1991, 35.

Green, Stephanie. An Australian author takes US by storm, *The Canberra Times*, 23 February 1992, 23.

Harvey, Oliver. Carey makes a novel switch. *Courier-Mail*, 16 October 1982, 28.

Hawley, Janet. How an ad man found bliss, *The Age*, 26 September 1981, 26.

Heyward, Michael. Australia's literary ambassador, *The Age*, 25 July 1992, 8.

Hock, Peter. Australia does not give a stuff, *Billy Blue Magazine*, 101, Autumn 1988, 20–1.

Huck, Peter. Making of a literary lion, *The Sydney Morning Herald*, 29 October 1988, 82.

Ifeka, Helena. Peter Carey, *Hermes*, 1992, 15–23.

Ikin, Van. Answers to seventeen questions: an interview with Peter Carey, *Science Fiction: A Review of Speculative Fiction* (Sydney), 1, 1, 1977, 30–9.

Jach, Antoni. An interview with Peter Carey, *Mattoid*, 31, 2, 1988, 24–36.

Jardine, Cassandra. Apocalypse free ... with every fifth packet. *New Fiction* (London), 26, 1980, 4–5.

Kellaway, Kate. Every man is a theatre, *The Observer Review*, 11 September 1994, 18.

Kemp, Peter. Putting the land of his mind on the literary map, *The Sunday Times*, 20 March 1988, G8.

Kemp, Peter. Packed lunches: writer's talks, ICA audio casette, 1994.

Koval, Ramona. The unexamined life, *Meanjin*, 56, 3–4, 1997, 667–82.

Lawson, Mark. Sniffing the air at home and away, *The Independent on Sunday*, 25 August 1991, 18.

Lawson, Valerie. Peter Carey, advertising doesn't hurt him a scrap, *The Sydney Morning Herald*, 5 September 1981, 47.

Maddocks, John. Bizarre realities, an interview with Peter Carey, *Southerly*, 41, 1, 1981, 27–41.

Manning, Greg. Peter Carey's latest gamble, *Book Magazine*, 1988, 2, 1, 3–6.

McCrum, Robert. 'Reawakened Ned', *The Observer* Books section, 7 January 2001, 19.

Meyer, Lisa. An interview with Peter Carey, *Chicago Review*, 43, 2, 1997, 76–89.

Morton-Evans, Michael. Carey reaches a blissful peak in his literary career, *The Australian*, 26 July 1984, 8.

Munro, Craig. Building the fabulist extensions, *Makar*, 12, 1, June 1976, 3–12 – extract in *Australian Literary Studies*, 8, 1977, 182–7.

Neilsen, Philip. Excerpt from interview: Tell me what colour you think the sky is, *Australian Literary Studies*, 10, 2, 1981, 191–3.

Neilsen, Philip. Waiting for the barbarians: an interview with Peter Carey, *Literature in North Queensland*, 15, 3, 1987, 66–73.

Nicklin, Leonore. The writer is an ad-man, *The Sydney Morning Herald*, 13 February 1975, 7.

Oakley, Barry. I'm the one who used to work with Peter Carey, *The Australian*, 27 October 1988, 13.

Oakley, Barry. Gothic splendour: Peter Carey returns to a junkyard landscape of old, *The Weekend Australian*, 27–8 July 1991, 1.

O'Donohue, Barry. Write and person, *Arts National*, 3, 2, December 1985, 106–7.

Rolfe, Patricia. An impatient, rapacious reader, *The Bulletin*, 28 July 1992, 90–1.

Sayers, Stuart. In pursuit of logic, *The Age*, 28 September 1974, 16.

Sayers, Stuart. A particular bent for the bizarre, *The Age*, 27 October 1979, 26.

Sayers, Stuart. The glittering literary prizes, *The Age*, 4 March 1986, 11.

Sexton, David. *The Literary Review*, June 1985, 38–41.

Sibree, Bron. Novel difficult to live with, difficult to write: Carey, *The Canberra Times*, 27 July 1991, C7.

Simpson, Lindsay. Private lives: Peter Carey and Alison Summers, *The Age: Good Weekend Magazine*, 27 August 1988, 8–9.

Sorensen, Rosemary. Reputations made and unmade. Rosemary Sorensen talks to Evan Green, Alex Miller and Peter Carey. *Australian Book Review*, 134, 1991, 10–11.

Summers, Alison. Candid Carey, *The National Times*, 1–7 November 1985, 32–3.

Summers, Alison. The thin man in history, *The Bulletin*, 15 November 1988, 156–8.

Tausky, Thomas E. 'Getting the corner right': an interview with Peter Carey, *Australian and New Zealand Studies in Canada*, 4, 1990, 27–38.

Toomey, Philippa. Peter Carey's refreshment, *The Times*, 27 October 1980, 6; reprinted as Fictional future from bits, pieces, *The Canberra Times*, 9 November 1980, 8.

Turcotte, Gerry, ed. *Writers in Action*, The Writer's Choice Evenings, Sydney: Currency Press, 1990, 3–23.

Watchel, Eleanor. We really can make ourselves up: an interview with Peter Carey, *Australian and New Zealand Studies in Canada*, 9, 103–5.

Williamson, Kirsten. The contradictory character of Peter Carey, *Harper's Bazaar*, Summer 1989, 38.

Willbanks, Ray. Peter Carey in *Speaking Volumes, Australian Writers and their Work*, Ringwood: Penguin, 1991, 43–57.

Willbanks, Ray. Peter Carey on *The Tax Inspector* and *The Unusual Life of Tristan Smith*, *Antipodes*, 11, 1, June 1997, 11–16.

Woolf, Sue and Kate Grenville. Peter Carey: *Oscar and Lucinda* in *Making Stories, How Ten Australian Novels Were Written*, St Leonards, NSW: Allen and Unwin, 1993, 33–58.

Wroe, Nicholas 2001. 'Fiction's Greatest Outlaw', *The Guardian* Review, 6 January, 6–7.

Wyndham, Susan. Peter Carey: an unusual life, *The Australian Magazine*, 20–1 August 1994, 41–8.

Yallop, Richard. Carey, the master of human chemistry, *The Age*, 29 October 1988, 16.

Video material

Armstrong, Gillian. *Oscar and Lucinda*, 20th Century Fox video, 1997, screenplay by Laura Jones, London: Faber, 1998.

Lawrence, Ray. *Bliss*, 1985, New World Video, NWV 1051, VHS.

Ross, Peter. Peter Carey, ABC/TV, Channel 2, Brisbane, 1 March 1987.

Penglase, Joanna (co-writer) and Don Featherstone (co-writer and director). The most beautiful lies: a film about Peter Carey, BBC1 *Omnibus*, 1986–7.

Walters, Margaret. Peter Carey, ICA video: *Guardian* conversations, 1988.

Wenders, Wim. *Until the End of the World*, screenplay by Peter Carey and Wim Wenders, 1991.

Websites

Interview with Peter Carey online at: www.randomhouse.com/boldtype/0399/carey/interview.html.

New York Times Author review: www.nytimes.com/books/01/01/07/specials/carey.html.

Interview with Carey: www.bbc.co.uk/arts/booker/carey_transcript.shtml

World Service programme [with very interesting online interview]: www.bbc.co.uk/worldservice/arts/highlights/010803_carey.shtml.

University of Queensland Press author site: www.peter-carey.com.

University of Flinders website: http://ehlt.flinders.edu.au/english/PeterCarey/PeterCarey.html.

Criticism

BOOKS ON CAREY

Hassall, Anthony J. *Dancing on Hot Macadam: Peter Carey's Fiction*, St Lucia: University of Queensland Press, 1994.

Huggan, Graham. *Peter Carey*, Melbourne: Oxford University Press, 1996.

Krassnitzer, Hermine. *Aspects of Narration in Peter Carey's Novels: Deconstructing Colonialism* (Salzburg University Studies), Lewiston/Queenston/Lampeter: Edwin Mellen Press, 1995.

Lamb, Karen. *Peter Carey, The Genesis of Fame*, Sydney: Angus & Robertson, 1992.

GENERAL ARTICLES AND ESSAYS ON CAREY

Adam, Ian. Breaking the chain, anti-Saussurean resistance in Birney, Carey and C.S. Pierce, *World Literature Written in English*, 29, 2, 1989, 11–22; also in Ian Adam and Helen Tiffin, eds, *Past the Last Post: Theorizing Post-Colonialism and Postmodernism*, Hemel Hempstead: Harvester Wheatsheaf, 1991, 79–93.

Ashcroft, Bill. Against the tide of time: Peter Carey's interpolation into history, in John C. Hawley, ed., *Writing the Nation: Self and Country in the Post-Colonial Imagination*, Amsterdam: Rodopi, 1996, 194–213.

Bennett, Sandy. Carey, Jolley and Freeman – three authors from print to celluloid, *Encore*, 22 July 1988, 20.

Bisutti, Francesca. The factory of invention, Peter Carey's real fictions, in G. Bellini, C. Gorlier and S. Zoppi, eds, *Saggi e ricerche sulle culture extraeuropee*, Rome: Bulzoni, 1986, 61–8.

Blaber, Ronald and Marvin Gilman. Illywhacker, in *Roguery: The Picaresque Tradition in Australian, Canadian and Indian Fiction*, Springwood, NSW: Butterfly Books, 1990, 55–60.

Bliss, Carolyn. The revisionary lover: misprision of the past in Peter Carey, *Australian and New Zealand Studies in Canada*, 6, 1991, 45–54.

Bliss, Carolyn. Time and timelessness in Peter Carey's fiction – the best of both worlds, *Antipodes*, 9, 2, 1995, 97–105.

Daniel, Helen. Lies for sale: Peter Carey, in Daniel, *Liars, Australian New Novelists*, Ringwood, Victoria: Penguin, 1988, 145–84.

Daniel, Helen. Peter Carey: the rivalries of the fictions, in Robert Ross, ed., *International Literature in English: Essays on the Major Writers*, New York: Garland, 1991, 405–15.

Dovey, Teresa. An infinite onion: narrative structure in Peter Carey's fiction, *Australian Literary Studies*, 11, 2, 1983, 195–204.

Drewe, Robert. Comment, *The Bulletin*, 5 June 1976.

Fletcher, M.D. Post-colonial Peter Carey, *Span* (Journal of the South Pacific Association for Commonwealth Literature and Language Studies), 32, April 1991, 12–23.

Fletcher, M.D. The theme of entrapment in Peter Carey's fiction, in David Kerr, ed., *Australian Literature Today*, New Delhi: Indian Society for Commonwealth Studies, 1993, 74–9.

Gelder, Kenneth. History, politics and the (post)modern: receiving Australian fiction, *Meanjin*, 47, 3, 1988, 551–9.

Gelder, Kenneth. Sex in Australian fiction, 1970–87, *Meanjin*, 47, 1, 1987, 125–34.

Herman, Luc. Canonizing Australia: the case of Peter Carey, in C. C. Barfoot, ed., *Shades of Empire in Colonial and Post-Colonial Literatures*, Amsterdam: Rodopi, 1993, 109–15.

Huggan, Graham. Is the (Günther) Grass greener on the other side? Oskar and Lucinde in the New World, *World Literature Written in English*, 30, 1 Spring 1990, 1–10.

Ikin, Van, Peter Carey, in L. Henderson, ed., *Contemporary Novelists*, Chicago: St James Press, 1991, 5th edition, 176–7.

Jose, Nicholas. Possibilities of love in Australian fiction, *Island Magazine*, 4, 20, 1984, 30–3.

Kane, P. Postcolonial, postmodern: Australian literature and Peter Carey, *World Literature Today*, 67, 3, 1993, 519–22.

Krauth, Nigel. Peter Carey: a portrait of electricity, *Australian Book Review*, 133, 1991, 18–19.

Larsson, Christer. 'Years Later': temporality and closure in Peter Carey's novels, *Australian Literary Studies*, 19, 2, 1999, 176–85.

Mellors, John. Moral imperatives: the fiction of Peter Carey, *London Magazine*, 31, 7–8, 1991, 89–94.

Muecke, Stephen. Wide open spaces, horizontal readings of Australian literature, *New Literature Review*, 16, 1988, 1–18.

Ommundsen, Wenche. Narrative navel-gazing, or, how to recognise a metafiction when you see one, *Southern Review*, 22, 3,1989, 264–74.

Ross, Robert. 'It cannot not be there': Borges and Australia's Peter Carey, in Edna Aizenberg, ed., *Borges and his Successors, The Borgesian Impact on Literature and the Arts*, Columbia, Miss.: University of Missouri Press, 1990, 44–58.

Sharrad, Paul. Responding to the challenge: Peter Carey and the reinvention of Australia, *Span* (Journal of the South Pacific Association for Commonwealth Literature and Language Studies), 25, 1987, 37–46.

Sheckels, Theodore F. Filming Peter Carey: from the adequate to the distorted, *Antipodes*, 13, 2, December 1999, 91–4.

Stewart, Annette M. Recent Australian fiction, *World Literature Written in English*, 22, 1983, 212–23.

Thwaites, Tony. More tramps at home: seeing Australia first, *Meanjin*, 46, 3, 1987, 400–9.

Todd, Richard. Narrative trickery and performative historiography: fictional representation of national identity in Graham Swift, Peter Carey, and Mordecai Richler, in Lois Parkinson Zamora and Wendy B. Faris, eds, *Magical Realism: History, Community*, Durham: Duke University Press, 1995, 307–28.

Turner, George. Science fiction, parafiction and Peter Carey, *Science Fiction: A Review of Speculative Literature*, 10, 1, 1988, 14–21.

Turner, Graeme. American dreaming: the fictions of Peter Carey, *Australian Literary Studies*, 12, 4, 986, 431–41.

Turner, Graeme. Nationalising the author: the celebrity of Peter Carey, *Australian Literary Studies*, 16, 2, 1993, 131–9.

REVIEWS, ARTICLES AND ESSAYS ON THE SHORT STORIES

REVIEWS

The Fat Man in History, St Lucia: University of Queensland Press, 1974.
>   Green, W. *Westerly*, 19, 4, 1975, 73–6.
>   Harrison-Ford, C. New Australian fiction, *Stand*, 16, 3, 1975, 43–4.
>   Kiernan, Brian. *Meanjin*, 34, 1975, 35–9.
>   McConchie, Rod. The trendy and the true, *Overland*, 60, 1975, 83–5.
>   Rose, Douglas. Curious and fantastic, *Courier-Mail*, 19 October 1974, 17.
>   Stewart, Douglas. Promising first fruits, *The Sydney Morning Herald*, 19 October 1974, 13.
>   Sutherland, John. Division street, *The Times Literary Supplement*, 9 April 1976, 445.

War Crimes, St Lucia: University of Queensland Press, 1979.
>   Clancy, Laurie. A year of varietals, *Overland*, 84, 1981, 26–30.
>   Dutton, Geoffrey. A 'crime' that is utter creativity, *The Bulletin*, 4 December 1979, 66–7.
>   Fabre, M. *CRNLE Reviews Journal*, 1, 1980, 72–6.
>   Pierce, Peter. Future nightmare, *The National Times*, 10 November, 1979, 46.
>   Webby, Elizabeth. *Meanjin*, 39, 1980, 131–2.

The Fat Man in History, London: Faber, 1980. Stories selected from the UQP volumes *The Fat Man in History* and *War Crimes*.
>   Ackroyd, Peter. Galactic races, *The Sunday Times*, 19 October 1980, no page number.
>   Epps, Garrett. *Washington Post*, 11 September 1980, D13.
>   Lewis, Peter. From underground, *The Times Literary Supplement*, 31 October 1980, 1240.
>   Mellors, J. Secret dreams, *London Magazine*, 20, 8–9, 1980, 116–17.
>   Thompson, Paul. Murky spaces, *New Statesman*, 24 October 1980, 26.
>   Tomey, Phillippa. Peter Carey's refreshment, *The Times*, 27 October 1980, 6.

Exotic Pleasures, London: Pan 1981. Retitled paperback edition of above.
>   Kermode, Frank. Knowing, *London Review of Books*, 3, 22–3, 1981, 17.

Collected Stories, London: Faber and Faber 1995.
>   Quinn, Anthony. Soft options on apocalypse, *The Guardian*, 18 August 1995, G2, 6.

Sage, Lorna. Artist from a distant planet, *The Times Literary Supplement*, 4820, 18 August 1995, 19.

Roberts, Michèle. Brillo tales for kids, *The Independent on Sunday*, 20 August 1995, 31.

ARTICLES AND ESSAYS

Ahearne, Kate. Peter Carey and short fiction in Australia, *Going Down Swinging* (Melbourne), 1, 1980, 7–17.

Bennett, Bruce. Australian experiments in short fiction, *World Literature Written in English*, 15, 1976, 359–66.

Callahan, David. Whose history in the fat man's? Peter Carey's *The Fat Man in History*, *Span* (Journal of the South Pacific Association for Commonwealth Literature and Language Studies), 40, 1995, 34–53.

Clunies Ross, Bruce A. Laszlo's testament; or, structuring the past and sketching the present in contemporary short fiction, mainly Australian, *Kunapipi*, 1, 2, 1979, 110–23.

Ikin, Van. Peter Carey: the stories, *Science Fiction: A Review of Speculative Literature* (Sydney), 1, 1, 1977, 19–29.

Manning, Greg. Reading lesson: 'The Fat Man in History', teaching and deconstructive practice, *Span*, 21, 1985, 38–55.

Ryan-Fazilleau, Suzan. One-upmanship in Peter Carey's short stories, *Journal of the Short Story in English*, 16, 1991, 51–63.

Sayers, Stuart. A particular bent for the bizarre, *Age*, 27 October 1979, 26.

Tate, Trudi. Unravelling the feminine, Peter Carey's 'Peeling', *Meanjin*, 46, 3, 1987, 394–99.

REVIEWS, ARTICLES AND ESSAYS ON *BLISS*

St Lucia: University of Queensland Press; London: Faber, 1981

REVIEWS

Barnes, Rory. Salvation on Bog Onion Road, *National Times*, 11–17 October 1981, 42.

Burns, Graham. Romantic pursuits, *Australian Book Review*, 41, 1982, 27–9.

Cooke, Judy. Paradise, *New Statesman*, 20 November 1981, 22.

Durrant, Digby. Colonial capers, *London Magazine*, 21, 11, 1982, 97–8.

Gelder, Ken. Bliss and punishment, *CRNLE Reviews Journal*, 1, 1983, 46–8.

Kermode, Frank. Knowing, *London Review of Books*, 3, 22–3, 1981, 17.

King, Francis. Suburban inferno, *Spectator*, 12 December 1981, 21.

Neville, Jill. Carey leaps crannies in a single bound, *The Sydney Morning Herald*, 10 October 1981, 44.

Roberts, Mark. Peter Carey's first novel, *Going Down Swinging*, 5, 1982, 69–72.

Ryle, John. Magic and poison, *The Times Literary Supplement*, 20 November 1981, 1350.

Stewart, Annette. Recent Australian fiction, *World Literature Written in English*, 22, 2, Autumn 1983, 212–23.

Tranter, John. Hell without logic loses credibility, *The Age*, 3 October 1981, 27.

ARTICLES

Anderson, Don. Introduction, *Bliss, The Screenplay*, London: Faber, 1985.

Hassall, A.J. Telling lies and stories, Peter Carey's *Bliss*, *Modern Fiction Studies*, 35, 4, 1989, 637–53.

Hecq, Dominique. Myth-taken paths and exits in Peter Carey's *Bliss*, *Commonwealth Essays and Studies*, 18, 2, Spring 1996, 99–103.

Riemnatale, A. Harry Joy's children: the art of storytelling in Peter Carey's *Bliss*, *Australian Literary Studies*, 16, 3, 1994, 341–7.

REVIEWS, ARTICLES AND ESSAYS ON *ILLYWHACKER*

London: Faber and Faber; New York: Harper & Row; St Lucia, Queensland: University of Queensland Press, 1985

REVIEWS

Clancy, Laurie. Some beautiful lies: our history mythologised, *Australian Book Review*, 73, 1985, 14–15.

Duwell, Martin. The lie of the land, *Overland*, 101, 1985, 92–4.

Goldsworthy, Peter. The novella in *Illywhacker*, *Island Magazine*, 24, 1985, 56–7.

Hanrahan, John. A dealer in dreams, visions, images and lies, *Age Saturday Extra*, 6 July 1985, 14.

Hislop, Andrew. Whoppers and warnings, *The Times Literary Supplement*, 3 May 1985, 492.

Ikin, Van. Mixed blessings, Phoenix Review, 1, 1986–7, 125–7.

Jacobson, Howard. Dirty very old man, *New York Times Book Review*, 17 November 1985, 15.

Lewis Peter. Ratbags and others, *London Magazine*, 25, 1–2, 1985, 148–52.

Lewis, R. *New Statesman*, 19 April 1985, 32–4.

Mellors, John. Unhappy woman, *Listener*, 25 April 1985, 27.

Mitchell, Adrian. Weaving a tangled web of lovely lies, *The Weekend Australian Magazine*, 6–7 July 1985, 15.

Nicholson, J. *Times*, 18 April 1985, 20.

Sexton, David. *The Literary Review*, 11 November 1985, 4.

Spice, N. Phattbookia stupenda, *London Review of Books*, 7 July 1985, 20–1.

Stewart, Annette. Peter Carey's *Illywhacker*, *Quadrant*, 29, 12, 1985, 86–7.

Webby, Elizabeth. A great short story trapped in a fat novel, *The Sydney Morning Herald*, 13 July 1985, 47.

ARTICLES

Adam, Ian. *Illywhacker* and *The Prowler*: settler society response to ideas of history, *Australian and New Zealand Studies in Canada*, 12, December 1994, 1–10.

Antor, Heinz. Australian lies and the mapping of the new world: Peter Carey's *Illywhacker* (1985) as a postmodern postcolonial novel, *Anglistik*, 9, 1, 1998, 155–78.

Daniel, Helen. 'The liar's stump' or 'A salesman's sense of history': Peter Carey's *Illywhacker*, *Southerly*, 47, 2, 1986, 157–67.

Edwards, Brian. Deceptive constructions: the art of building in Peter Carey's *Illywhacker*, *Australian and New Zealand Studies in Canada*, 4, 1990, 39–56.

Ryan, Sue. Metafiction in *Illywhacker*: Peter Carey's renovated picaresque novel, *Commonwealth Essays and Studies*, 14, 1, 1991, 33–40.

Schmidt-Haberkamp, Barbara. Wider den Pauschaltourismus der Literatur: Peter Carey's australisches Panoptikum *Illywhacker*, *Arbeiten aus Anglistik und Americkanistik*, 17, 1, 1992, 71–82.

REVIEWS, ARTICLES AND ESSAYS ON *OSCAR AND LUCINDA*

London: Faber and Faber; St Lucia, Queensland: University of Queensland Press, 1988

REVIEWS

Anderson, Don. Peter Carey does a wonderful thing, *The Sydney Morning Herald*, 20 February 1988, 71.

Bainbridge, Beryl. Oscar and Lucinda, *New York Times Book Review*, 29 May 1988, 1, 19.

Dyer, Geoff. The long, long love affair, *New Statesman*, 1 April 1988, 28.

Edmond, Rod. From the Victorian to the post-colonial novel, *Australian Studies*, 3, 1989, 88–95.

Harris, Margaret. Eminent Victorians?, *Southerly*, 49, 1, 1989, 109–13.

Jacobson, Howard. A wobbly odyssey, *The Weekend Australian Magazine*, 20–1 February 1988, 13.

Ommundsen, Wenche. Historical fabrications and home truths, *Mattoid*, 30, 1, 1988, 73–6.

Porter, Peter. Puritan gambles, *The Daily Telegraph*, 26 October 1988, 18.

Riddell, Elizabeth. Desire, gambling and glass, *Australian Book Review*, 98, 1988, 14–15.

Sage, Lorna. Backwards into destiny, *The Times Literary Supplement*, 1–7 April 1988, 363.

Stead, C.K. Careyland, *Scripsi*, 5, 2, 1989, 3–8.

Stewart, Annette. The Booker prize, *Quadrant*, 32, 12, 1988, 66–7.

ARTICLES

Brown, Ruth. English heritage and Australian culture: the church and literature of England in *Oscar and Lucinda, Australian Literary Studies*, 17, 2, October 1995, 135–40.

Da Silva, Matthew. Peter Carey's Oscar and Lucinda, *Outrider*, 6, 2, 1989, 148–59.

During, Simon. Literary subjectivity, *Ariel*, 31, 1–2, 2000, 33–50.

Callahan, David. Peter Carey's *Oscar and Lucinda* and the subversion of subversion, *Australian Studies*, 4, 1990, 20–6.

Hassall, Anthony J. The Weatherboard Cathedral: images of the church in Peter Carey's *Oscar and Lucinda*, in *Essays in Honour of Keith Val Sinclair: An Australian Collection of Modern Language Studies*, Townsville: James Cook University, 1991, 193–200.

Ommundsen, Wenche. Narrative navel-gazing, or, how to recognise a metafiction when you see one, *Southern Review*, 22, 3, 1989, 264–74.

Peterson, Kirsten Holst. Gambling on reality, a reading of *Oscar and Lucinda*, in Giovanna Capone, Bruce Clunies Ross and Werner Senn, eds, *European Perspectives, Contemporary Essays on Australian Literature, Australian Literary Studies* Special Issue, 15, 2, St Lucia: University of Queensland Press, 1991, 107–16.

REVIEWS, ARTICLES AND ESSAYS ON *THE TAX INSPECTOR*

London: Faber and Faber, 1991

REVIEWS

Amidon, Stephen, A whole lot of trouble, *The Times Literary Supplement*, 30 August 1991, 21.

Brady, Veronica. Birth, death and taxes, *Overland*, 125, 1991, 80–83.

Carter, Angela. Only a surface paradise, *The Guardian*, 29 August 1991, 22.

Clancy, Laurie. Brilliant episodes, *Australian Society*, 10, 8, 38–9.

Coe, Jonathan. Australian circles, *London Review of Books*, 13, 17, 1991, 12.

Craig, Jen. The real thing, *Southerly*, 52, 1, 1992, 152–6.

Dixon, Robert. The logic of the excluded middle, *Literature in North Queensland*, 18, 2, 1991, 133–41.

Floyd, Chris. *Span*, 33, May 1992, 177–81.

Graeber, L. *New York Times Book Review*, 1993, 32.

Giese, Diana. Diving deep into the dreams of damaged lives, *The Weekend Australian*, 27–8 July 1991, Review, 4.

Hawker, Philippa. Carey's contemporary angels have the potential for destruction, *Australian Book Review*, 133, 991, 15–17.

Kemp, Peter. Toxic shocks, *The Sunday Times*, 1 September 1991, 6.

Liddelow, Eden. New model Carey, *Scripsi*, 7, 2, October 1991, 93–100.

Prose, F. *The New York Times Book Review*, 1992, 1.

Riemer, A.P. Brutish and nasty, *Sydney Morning Herald*, 3 August 1991, 43.

Towns, R. *New York Review of Books*, 39, 12, 1992, 356.

White, Edmund. Recognising Jack, *The Times Literary Supplement*, 30 August 1991, 21.

ARTICLES

Bode, Barbara. Angels and devils – child sexual abuse in Peter Carey's *The Tax Inspector*, *Antipodes*, 9, 2, December 1995, 107–10.

Dixon, Robert. Closing the can of worms: enactments of justice in *Bleak House*, *The Mystery of a Hansom Cab*, and *The Tax Inspector*, *Westerly*, 37, 4, 1992, 37–45.

REVIEWS, ARTICLES AND ESSAYS ON *THE UNUSUAL LIFE OF TRISTAN SMITH*

London: Faber and Faber, 1994

REVIEWS

Bernard, April. Un-Efican activities, *New York Review of Books*, 42, 11, 22 June 1995, 44–8.

Brennan, Geraldine. Crossing the high wires, *The Observer Review*, 4 September 1994, 15.

Frankel, Susannah. Preview, *Time Out*, 7–14 September 1994, 47.

Hensher, Philip. Heaven and Disneyland, *The Guardian*, 11 October 1994.

Kemp, Peter. Flamboyant fabrication, *The Sunday Times*, 4 September 1994, 7, 13.

Korn, E. *The Times Literary Supplement*, 4770, 1994, 10.

Riemer, Andrew. The antipodes of tiny Tristan, *The Sydney Morning Herald*, 20 August 1994, no page number.

Shields, C. *The New York Times Book Review*, 1995, 7.

Strawson, Galen. A little yearning is a dangerous thing, *The Independent on Sunday*, 4 September 1994, 34.

ARTICLES

Bradley, James. Bread and sirkuses: empire and culture in Peter Carey's *The Unusual Life of Tristran Smith* and *Jack Maggs*, *Meanjin*, 56, 3–4, 659–61.

Dawson, Carrie. 'Who was that masked mouse?' Imposture in Peter Carey's *The Unusual Life of Tristan Smith*, *Southern Review*, 30, 2, 1997, 202–11.

Pierce, Peter. Captivity, captivation: aspects of Peter Carey's fiction, in Martin Duwell, ed., *'And What Books Do You Read?' New Studies in Australian Literature*, Queenland: University of Queensland Press, 1996, 140–50.

ARTICLES , ESSAYS AND REVIEWS ON *THE BIG BAZOOHLEY*

Hassall, Anthony J. Winners and losers – Peter Carey's *The Big Bazoohley*, *Antipodes*, 10, 2, 1996, 117–20.

REVIEWS, ARTICLES AND ESSAYS ON *JACK MAGGS*

REVIEWS

Desmond Christy. Inner conviction, *The Guardian* Review, 11 June 1998, 8.

Jose, Nicholas. Carey's labyrinth, *Australian Book Review*, August 1997, 14–15.

Lee, Hermione. Great extrapolations, *The Observer* Review, 28 September 1997, 15.

Porter, Peter. Transporting us, *The Guardian*, 18 September 1997, 16

ARTICLES AND ESSAYS

Bradley, James. Bread and sirkuses: empire and culture in Peter Carey's *The Unusual Life of Tristran Smith* and *Jack Maggs*, *Meanjin*, 56, 3–4, 659–61.

Ní Fhlathúin, Máire. The location of childhood: 'Great Expectations' in post-colonial London, *Kunapipi*, 21, 2, 1999, 86–92.

Hassall, Anthony J. A tale of two countries: *Jack Maggs* and Peter Carey's fiction, *Australian Literary Studies*, 18, 2, 1997, 128–35.

Meinig, Sigrun. An Australian convict in the great English city: Peter Carey's *Jack Maggs*, *Southerly*, 6, 3, 2000, 59; also in Fran de

Groen and Ken Stewart, eds, *Australian Writing and the City*, Proceedings of ASAL conference 1999.

Thieme, John. *Postcolonial Con-texts: Writing Back to the Canon*, London: Continuum, 2001, 102–26.

REVIEWS, ARTICLES AND ESSAYS ON *TRUE HISTORY OF THE KELLY GANG*

REVIEWS

Fraser, Morag. 'Deft Narrative Devices' (review of *True History of the Kelly Gang*) http://home.vicnet.net.au/~abr/Nov00/mf.html.

Kemp, Peter. 'Why Ned was born to run', *The Sunday Times*, Culture section, 7 January 2001, 35–6.

John Kinsella's On Peter Carey's *True History of the Kelly Gang*, online at www.johnkinsella.org/reviews/carey.html

Quinn, Anthony 2001. 'Robin Hood of the outback' (review of *True History of the Kelly Gang*), *New York Times* online at www.nytimes.com/books/01/01/07/reviews/010107.07quinnt.html

Riemer, Andrew 2000. 'Ironclad irony' (review of *True History of the Kelly Gang*), *Sydney Morning Herald*, 17 November.

Rogers, Jane. '*True History of the Kelly Gang*', *The Observer*, Books section, 7 January 2001, 19.

Phil Shannon, 'Ideological gunfighters' for the poor, online at: www.greenleft.org.au/back/2001/447/447p25.htm.

ARTICLES

Huggan, Graham. Cultural memory in postcolonial fiction: the uses and abuses of Ned Kelly, *Australian Literary Studies*, 20, 3, May 2002, 142–54.

General works

BOOKS

Burns, D.R. *The Directions of Australian Fiction 1920–74*, Melbourne: Cassell, 1975.

Clancy, Laurie. *A Reader's Guide to Australian Fiction*, Melbourne: OUP, 1992.

Fiske, John, Bob Hodge and Graeme Turner. *Myths of Oz: Australian Popular Culture*, Sydney: Allen and Unwin, 1987.

Gelder, Ken and Salzman, Paul. *The New Diversity: Australian Fiction*

1970–88, Melbourne: McPhee Gribble, 1989.

Hergenhan, Laurie. *The Penguin New Literary History of Australia*, Ringwood, Victoria: Penguin Australia, 1988.

Hodge, R. and Vijay Mishra. *The Dark Side of the Dream: Australian Literature and the Postcolonial Mind*, North Sydney: Allen & Unwin, 1991.

Ikin, Van, ed. *The Glass Reptile Breakout and Other Australian Speculative Stories*, Nedlands, WA: Centre for Studies in Australian Literature, University of Western Australia, 1990.

Kiernan, Brian. *The Most Beautiful Lies*, Sydney: Angus & Robertson, 1977.

O'Donovan, Anne *et al.*, eds. *Under Twenty-Five, An Anthology*, Brisbane: Jacaranda, 1966.

Shapcott, Tom. *The Literature Board, A Brief History*, Brisbane: University of Queensland Press, 1988.

Turner, Graeme. *National Fictions, Literature, Film and the Construction of Australian Narrative*, Sydney: Allen & Unwin, 1986.

Wilde, William H., Joy Hooton, and Barry Andrews. *The Oxford Companion to Australian Literature*, Melbourne: Oxford University Press, 1986.

ARTICLES

Anderson, Don. I'm going to America in my mind: the American presence in Australian writing 1960–1990, in Margaret Harris and Elizabeth Webby, eds, *Reconnoitres: Essays in Australian Literature in honour of G.A. Wilkes*, Sydney: Sydney University Press, 1992, 176–88.

Bail, Murray. Imagining Australia, *The Times Literary Supplement*, 27 November 1987, 1318, 1330.

Docker, John. Antipodean literature: a world upside down?, *Overland*, 103, 1986.

During, Simon. Postmodern or postcolonial?, *Landfall*, 155, 1985, 366–80.

Harrison-Ford, Carl. How good is the boom in Australian fiction?, *The Australian Author*, 7, 2, April 1975, 4–10.

Ikin, Van, ed. *Australian Science Fiction: An Anthology*, St Lucia: University of Queensland Press, 1982.

Kiernan, Brian. The new wave of short story writers, *National Times*, 2–7 August 1976, 36–7.

Lohrey, Amanda. The dead hand of orthodoxy, *Island Magazine*, 27, 1986, 19–21.

Moorhouse, Frank. What happened to the short story?, *Australian Literary Studies*, 8, 2, 1977, 179–82.

Olsen, Lance. Towards a theory of postmodern humour, or, Christa

McAuliffe and the banana peel, circus of the mind in motion, *Postmodernism and Comic Vision*, Wayne State University Press, 1990, 15–36.

Turner, George. Parentheses: concerning matters of judgement, *Meanjin*, 48, 1, 1989, 195–204.

Webby, Elizabeth. The long march of short fiction: a seventies retrospective, *Meanjin*, 39, 1, 1980, 127–33.

Wilding, Michael. The tabloid short story, in M. Wilding, ed., *The Tabloid Short Story*, Sydney: Wild and Woolley, 1978, 295–316.

Index

Note: page numbers in *italic* refer to main entries